W O K E

DOWN THE RABBIT HOLE

Remember, remember
The fifth of November
The Gunpowder treason and plot;
I know of no reason
Why the Gunpowder treason
Should ever be forgot!!!

Guy Fawkes Night Poem

Automated techniques used to analyse text and data in
digital form for the purpose of generating information,
under Sections 15a, 15b and 15c of the Copyright Act
(text and data mining), are prohibited.

Publisher: BoD · Books on Demand, Östermalmstorg 1,
114 42 Stockholm, bod@bod.se
Printing: Libri Plureos GmbH, Friedensallee 273,
22763 Hamburg, Germany

ISBN:978-91-8080-140-9

On a cold, rainy November night, a soldier called Guy Fawkes finds himself in a big old cellar in central London. The year is 1605. There, at the Palace of Westminster, he is posted to guard several barrels of dynamite. What Fawkes and no-one else in the old parliament building is aware of is that soon several kilos of explosives would detonate, sweeping away years of political oppression.[1] His patient waiting is the result of the secret meeting held about a year earlier. The opening words of the meeting are: "Shall we always, gentlemen, talk and never do anything?" and are spoken by one of the thirteen resistance fighters who, because of this meeting, would go down in history. They initially agree to dig a tunnel under the streets of London all the way to the Houses of Parliament, but by a happy coincidence, and against all odds, they manage to rent a room in the basement vault, directly under Parliament. 36 barrels of gunpowder are transported over the next few months into the basement, a few at a time and in various ingenious ways. The thirteen people involved manage to do it so unnoticed, that their crusade against the British government seems to be backed by a higher power.

Later, after the coup is uncovered, the British government, fearing rebellion, fabricates its own version of events. This was not the last time that government and those in power would revise the public's understanding of events, which will be carried throughout this book, like a long red thread.[2]

---

1   Oxford dictionary,
    https://www.oxforddnb.com/display/10.1093/ref:odnb/9780198614128.001.0001/
    odnb-9780198614128-e-92749

2   James Sharpe, Remember Remember, A cultural history of Guy Fawkes, Harvard University Press, Massachusetts, 2005

Preface

*No-one is more hopelessly enslaved than those who
falsely believe they are free*[3]

Johann Wolfgang Goethe

The common man of the 21st century, lives in the belief
that everything that happened in history is available
for public knowledge. This political Odyssey is written
to dispel this delusion and open up a wider perspective, as the book's author goes back to the very origins
of where it began.

The aim is not only to question and criticise
prevailing political layers. For a long time, people in
the West have been shaped by a hidden political agenda,
the structures of which need to be publicised, analyzed
and brought to the surface. Totalitarianism is usually
attributed to the Soviet regime, China or North Korea.
This book will reveal how such totalitarianism is also
widespread in the West; not an open totalitarianism,
ruling through dictatorships, but a covert one. This is
why this book must confront the Marxist/socialist ideology that has ruled West and other parts of the world
for over a hundred years, as well as the new WOKE generation coloured by Marxism. This raises important
questions about gender dysphoria and sex operations on
young people, Marxist feminism, anti-racism and identity politics. At the same time, the aim is to question
the reputation of right-wing politics and to cleanse
conservative politics of its involuntary association
with Nazism, racism and fascism.

Among other things, the reader will learn how over-

3   Die Wahlverwandtschaften - Hamburger Ausgabe, Volume 6, dtv, Munich 1982,
    p. 397 (II,5)

consumption and big business corporations, through socialist policies and specialised public relations techniques, have been holding a spell on humanity for over
a century. The book aims to enable the reader to simply
wash the image of society and history as it has been
taught through the educational system, and the authors
want the new conclusions drawn to be closer to the
authentic truth.

Authors and other individuals have indeed touched
on these pieces in the past; in this book we try to
make a summarising overview, a narrative anthology, a
kind of ABC-book for all those who fight for truth and
freedom - old and new - and reveal cognitive illusions
and patterns behind corrupt political systems. The book
concludes with proposals for reforming outdated
political structures, enabling a new people-friendly
development. The book endeavours to reveal how political power games have limited human development, but
does not outline all the options that can replace the
old, outdated, corrupt political system, and leaves it
partially open, with the hope that through human potential, new political paths can be found.

What are the state of things - really?

In the middle of the journey of our life I came to myself within a dark wood where the straight way was lost[4]

Dante Alighieri

Let's imagine in a thought experiment that all government officials and politicians are trustworthy and do their work honestly, honestly and openly. No agenda is kept secret from the people – ever; all political decisions are completely transparent, even in war and military operations. The western world is a perfect democracy where people have a say in shaping society – at every stage. People can affect political decisions through democratic referendums and be involved in making new decisions through democratic votes. All big businesses and large corporations have honest intentions, and only want the best for people thus offering products that consumers themselves want to buy. Newspapers, media and journalists clearly report all world events in a neutral, factual and unbiased way – they never – ever – hide the truth.

Throughout all the centuries of human history, there have been rulers - the priesthood or pope, a government or a parliament, a king or emperor; also associated officials who exercised power on behalf of others. One can say that the power has been held by *the elite,* whose shape and name has varied from century to century. But one thing that has remained constant is the unequal relationship between the power apparatus and the rest of the population. If you think that this inequality has diminished with the passage of history,

4   Dante Alighieri, Inferno Canto I:1-60 The Dark Wood and the Hill

and that kings were only cruel and domineering in the past, you are mistaken.

However, throughout the thousands of years that power has been in the hands of the elite, there have also been different types of resistance movements. One of the very first protest movements was the 'Protestants', who gave Protestantism its name. Another movement was the Peasants' Revolt, which gave rise to the right to vote for an entire peasant class. Or the Chartism movement in England in 1838-1848, whose *sufferings* led to the concept of '*suffrage*'. These protest or resistance movements have declined significantly in the 21st century.

If you look at how democracy in the West has been conducted in recent years, you can ask the question – what decisions have I, personally, as an individual made, when it comes to my surroundings, the large society, or "my" small neighbourhood? How does the democratic society we live in function, where "everyone" should be able to be asked about the governance of society and vote? And how powerful are politicians really? This book will try to answer these important questions.

All decision-making processes pushed through by those in power are based on the premise that the decisions are "necessary" or that they must be taken – "progress cannot be stopped". Perhaps an expert or consultant is hired to confirm a proposal. It may be that politicians encounter protests where people oppose this proposal – usually the protest is left unanswered and thus does not influence decision-making. Then, of course, there are people who are not so interested in what politicians do – as long as "everything works".

What position of power does this put the 'ordinary' citizen in? Do they even have time to reflect on their position in society, time to "opt out" of the consumer society, or do they have to work several days a week, several hours a day, only to be swamped by gadgets, technology and clothes, with their attention always diverted elsewhere? We have this idea, especially in the West, that we live in a democracy. And we have an idea that we as individuals can choose how power is exercised. So we are not particularly worried. Instead, we can spend the time that is left, on entertainment, sport and consumption.

And how much power does the consumer society really have over us? To answer the question, you only need to observe your fellow human beings for a short while, perhaps on the subway or in the street, and if you try to estimate the price tag for all the clothes each person is wearing, you can easily reach several hundred dollars.

Furthermore, imagine that the same person has several sets of similar clothes at home and a wardrobe worth 3 to 5 thousand dollars. If you look out into the crowd and add up these figures, you start to get a staggering idea of the massive amounts of money flowing from consumers into the big corporations, and it doesn't stop with clothes. There is a huge stream of consumption going on daily, that most people are not aware of. Clothes have to be replaced a few of times a year, and the same goes for household goods, phones, technology, appliances, furniture. Has it always been like this? Mobile phones lasted for decades in the early 1990s, without breaking. The same durability was found in the hi-fi gadgets of the 1980s. When Apple produced an iPhone that broke down after a few years, became "outdated" and needed to be "updated", the high-tech company created a new trend. Suddenly, people needed to replace their mobile phones after just a few years. This pattern grew strong, so strong that no one would question it anymore.

Has mankind always been so dependent on gadgets and

stuff, one might ask? And were gadgets and clothes made in the past, in the same way as they are now - clothes that only last a year, gadgets that break - for the benefit of big business and just in time for the next trend? The same 'throwaway culture' has also moved into politics: progressivism is partly based on politicians pushing through an idea that changes as soon as the next idea comes along. The sustainable thinking that is so much talked about is missing here as well.

The Father of PR-relations

Thou speak'st like him's untutor'd to repeat: Who makes the fairest show means most deceit. But bring they what they will and what they can, What need we fear?[5]

William Shakespeare – Merchant of Venice

It all started at the beginning of the last century – with a man called Edward Bernays who, despite the enormous impact he left on the world, is relatively unknown. Linking people's subconscious desires to products they *don't* need, Bernays simultaniously created an entirely new revolutionary political method – by satisfying people's inner selves with products and consumption, you make them *more compliant*. These theories were conceived a century ago and are still alive in society today.

At the beginning of the 20th century, Sigmund Freud discovered that people's emotions are located in the unconscious and his ideas were epoch-making. Examining the human psyche and civilisation from a psychological perspective had previously been unthinkable. Freud linked emotions such as aggression and sexuality to external behaviour and gave rise to other major ground-breaking theories. His nephew Edward Bernays, an educated journalist, works as a marketing consultant for successful entertainers in Vienna but the First World War forces him to move to America. During the war, all major political powers use war propaganda to influence the population and the US government hires Bernays as a propaganda consultant. Because of his dedication, he is quickly recognised as a force to count on.

At the end of the war, he is invited to the Paris

5   William Shakespeare Merchant of Venice Pericles, Act I, Scene 4

Conference, aged just 26. He is stunned by the hero's welcome given to President Woodrow Wilson and the way people worshiped him. An idea is born - is it possible to create similar 'mass persuasion' in times of peace?

After the war, Bernays finds the word 'propaganda' too cumbersome and changes the name to 'Public Relations'. Unbeknownst to him, he invents the term that will be used for an entire era to come. His theory is that if you can use propaganda in war - you can use it in peace. Back home, he finds a peacetime America and wants to understand how the masses think. He contacts his uncle, Sigmund Freud, and receives a copy of 'Psychoanalysis' in exchange for a packet of Havana cigars. Edward realises that in order to influence individuals, you have to work with people's irrational emotions. In other words, you can control people's choices. This is groundbreaking. Before Bernays' theory had taken hold, advertising and information had been intended to describe the actual product and invoke its quality characteristics. Now it was realised that it should appeal to buyers' emotions instead - to make them spend more money.

> Deception may give us what we want for the
> present, but it will always take it away in
> the end.[6] - Rachel Hawthorne

Bernays gets a number of jobs and assignments from major companies. One of the assignments is from the tobacco company "Lucky Strike", which wants to get women to start smoking. In this context, the first PR campaign is born. Bernays organises a "happening" and persuades a group of women to smoke during a festival parade. At the same time, Bernays tells the press that a group of suffragettes he calls the "Torches of Freedom" are planning a revolution through smoking, comparing them to the statue of the American Statue of Lib-

---

6   Rachel Hawthorne "Dark of the Moon" novel - August 25, 2009

erty and her torch. In this way, feminists are persuaded to support smoking and the news spreads like wildfire in the New York Times and other newspapers around the world. Bernays' campaign implies that smoking makes a woman stronger and more independent. He realises that people can be persuaded if you connect the product to their inner desires and feelings. Women are not freed by the ctual smoking, but feel freer because of Bernays' manipulation of emotions. Cigarette sales increased significantly. And it was not the last time that Bernays would involve politics in a PR campaign.

Businesses would no longer sell products to buyers' intellect and reason, but to their emotions. The most important thing is not how good the car actually is - but how well the buyer would feel about owning it. Consumers would not just buy a product, they would become emotionally and personally involved in it. In the past, before the war, people had only shopped because they *needed to* - now they shopped because they wanted to. Shoppers began to believe that the products they bought helped them develop their personality and identity. As a result, after the First World War, companies' production had increased significantly and sales figures were high. All sales were previously based on the principle of need and products were marketed in their functionality. Sustainability was *important*. Advertising was all about how good a product was. Now, companies started to rework their ideas by any means possible.

> Paul Mazur of Lehman Brothers, who worked with Bernays, commented: "We must shift America from a *needs* to a *desires* culture.[7]

---

7   What's Wrong with Democracy at the Moment, and Why It Matters for Research and Education
    https://journals.sagepub.com/doi/pdf/10.2304/power.2012.4.3.257

Consumers simply had to be 'trained' to ask for and want new things - before the old was consumed. People's wants must overshadow their needs. Before the war, there were no consumers, only workers and owners, and all products were created for them. They saved money and ate what they needed and bought what they needed. Businesses hired Bernays to change this and during the 1920s, banks and businessmen opened more shops and large department store chains where Bernays' ideas were developed.

> It based modern Western civilisation on the dangerous trend to worship man and his material needs. Everything beyond physical well-being and accumulation of material goods, all other human requirements and characteristics of a subtler and higher nature, were left outside the area of attention of state and social systems, as if human life did not have any superior sense.[8]

Bernays believes that good profits for big business are good for people and the economy. But he doesn't believe this connection can be rationally explained to people - he doesn't trust their ability to understand it. That's why he calls his theories 'the engineering of consent' - the art of getting people to agree to things they hadn't originally intended. Bernays' ideas are disseminated by psychologists and an institute is opened to research techniques for influencing consumers. "Motivational Research" is about advertising influence and buying influence and sales. It seeks to 'uncover' consumers' inner secret feelings and get inside their psyche, to unravel their unconscious motivation. The reasons for consumption are many - sexual, psychological, social, status-giving and self-fulfilling - things that people consider intimate and private. At the In-

8   Alexander Solzhenitsyn, "A World Split Apart", 8 June 1978, Harvard
    University

stitute, studies are conducted to understand purchasing behaviour. People are observed and their reactions when using a product are recorded. Statistics and surveys are used to find out which target groups buys the least of a product. The adverts are then created, based on the data.

The authority that psychologists and doctors had built up is also being used to promote products such as medicine. The adverts are then published as "scientifically independent research", even though the campaign is sponsored by the same company - the one behind the medicine.

The changes brought about by Bernays' ideas do not go unnoticed by everyone. In 1927, an American journalist wrote that a change for the worse had taken place in democratic society, and its name was 'consumerism'. The status of the citizen in relation to his country is no longer just 'citizen' but now also 'consumer'. This is only one of several articles that criticised this new form of society. Today, there are fewer open debates and a culture of silence has emerged.

> Yet Bernays was criticised by journalists in the 1920s, who saw propaganda as corrosive to their ability to seek truth (St. John 2009). Editor and Publisher called Bernays a "young Machiavelli".[9]

In his private life, Mr Bernays is anything but popular; he has a peculiar appearance and is not interested in holding conversations. He never experiences people in their individuality but always thinks of them in thousands. Nevertheless, he is approached again by the government in 1924. President Calvin Cooligde is not known as a popular president in the media and is con-

---

9   Feminist Media Studies. Publication details, including inst ruct ions for
    authors and subscription information: "It's up to the women" by Jane
    Marcellus, Olasky 1987, p. 91

stantly portrayed as 'boring' by journalists. Cooligde wants to increase his popularity and expand his electorate. Bernays is hired for the job and persuades 34 Hollywood film stars to visit the White House. The results are outstanding and after this, more and more politicians resort to election campaigning.

With the help of Bernays' efforts, Freudian psychology becomes popular and all politicians and socialites are undergoing psychotherapy. And as psychoanalysis takes hold in America, a new elite begins to form among politicians and big businessmen on Wall Street. Business owners and politicians establish a partnership in a way that never existed before. Bernays himself is labelled 'The Father of PR relations'. His ideas conquered the UK, Europe and the Nordic countries - for many years to come. Advertising and public relations changed the way people see themselves forever - a phenomenon that carries over into modern society. Bernyas himself is aware of its impact:

> Propaganda is everywhere and it changes the way we see the world. [10]

In the contemporary society, advertising and commercials have proliferated and are everywhere - on trains, street signs, mobile phones and television. Advertising affects the psyche on a subconscious level - people suddenly start to recognise certain brands. Advertisers use loaded value words and an advertising slogan can look like this: "what *really* matters". Advertising affects the senses through the eyes with text or images, and through the ears with music or words. It is not something you can escape unless you are blind or deaf. It is therefore not a voluntary influence.

---

10 Edward L Bernays, "Propaganda", page 12, 1928

> Modern mass culture, aimed at the 'consu-
> mer', the civilisation of prosthetics, is
> crippling people's souls, setting up barri-
> ers between man and the crucial questions
> of his existence, his consciousness of him-
> self as a spiritual being.[11] - Andrei Tar-
> kovsky

The key ingredient in all advertising and propaganda is
not that the information is true, but that the advert
is repeated - over and over again. The wires in our
nervous system are connected when we hear information
often. Eventually, learning takes place - you recognise
a new brand and can connect your deepest, most intimate
feelings to it. Different company brands stick in your
mind when the advert has been shown hundreds or thousands of times. Bernays already knew this in the 1920s:

> We are ruled by people whose names we have
> never heard. They influence our opinions, our
> tastes and our thoughts. [12]

Nerves work the same way in all physical brains; if
you hear something 50 times, it leaves a mark. Advertising can be summarised as a *cognitive illusion*
hidden in plain sight. Another important PR-tech-
nique involves the manipulation of language; for
example, a certain noun activates imagery in our
minds, almost immediately. The same applies to sym-
bolism. Different symbols influence emotions in different directions. Many people believe that this is
true for all other people, but that they themselves
are not affected, because most people want to believe that they can think independently.

The Coca Cola advert is an example. Businesses want
consumers' thoughts and feelings to work in such a way

11   Andrei Tarkovsky, "Sculpting in Time", 1985
12   Edward L Bernays, "Propaganda", page 14, 1928

that they already think of Coca Cola when they plan what to drink. And ideally consumers should drink the same thing every day. The advert shows people involved in social activities while drinking soft drinks - over and over again. When you see Coca Cola, you automatically think of social situations and experience warm feelings. And once you start drinking Coca Cola, you keep drinking it - it becomes a habit. In this way, Coca Cola sells 1.9 billion cans - per day, generating huge financial capital.[13]

In a thought experiment, you can try to remove the product and instead do the things you need to do from the advert - for example, meet friends, drive a car far away, and so on - without buying the product. Another thought experiment to get away from the artificial feelings is to imagine that you have 20 mobile phones. Or 50 cans of Coca Cola.

> The things you really need are few and easy
> to come buy; but the things you can imagine
> you need are infinite and you will never be
> satisfied.[14]

Happiness is one of the self-realisation goals, which is considered worth pursuing. Other goals that people strive for are: family, friends, freedom, and an organised life. Advertisers know what people want and therefore know what they want to sell. In one advert, the name of the product is written together with the text "... *in the company of good friends*". This gives the impression that you cannot be happy without this product and blurs the line between what individuals want and the manipulation of artificially induced emotions and an artificial need for the product.[15] Ancient Greece warned that consumption does not lead to

13   https://www.wallstreetzen.com/stocks/us/nyse/ko/statistics
14   Epicurus (born 341 BC in Samos, died 270 BC in Athens)
15   Documentary: Alain de Botton Philosophy: A Guide To Happiness - Epicurus
     on Happiness, Channel Four, 2000

happiness. In Greek markets, there were signs saying that shopping would not make you happy.[16] The philosopher Epicurus himself lived simply with simple means, and there were whole communities in ancient Greece that lived according to Epicurus' motto - for centuries.

16   Diogenes Laertus, philosopher of ancient Greece.

The best kept secrets are those hidden in plain sight

In a time of deceit, telling the truth is a revolutionary act[17]

George Orwell

The above chapter describes *cognitive illusions* in public relations related to consumption. But how does it work with political propaganda? Is it more neutrally presented or do cognitive illusions also exist on TV and in the news, hidden in plain sight, and if so, how accurate is the information we get from the social media? To find out, we need to go back to some examples in history - where journalists and politicians have failed to present the real, true story - time after time.

> *1932. The Tuskeege Experiment:* In Alabama in 1932, *the United States Public Health Service* begins a study on the effects of untreated syphilis - on humans. The study is conducted on approximately 600 African-American men and women - without consent, full knowledge or personal authorisation. The description of the experiment for the subjects reads as such: "only to take samples and examine the general state of health". 40 years later, in 1972, the New York Times writes about the study for the first time. It was revealed that a large number of the subjects had been living with untreated syphilis and suf-

17   George Orwell "1984", 1948

fering for several years - without receiving the medication required for the disease - and without realising it. A large proportion of these patients are dead; many have unknowingly spread the disease to relatives, especially their children. This leads to changes in medical consent laws, and survivors receive compensation - but it's too late: the vast majority have died before this happens. The so-called *Tuskeege experiment* contributes to the deterioration of the relationship between the African-American population and the US government.

1935. Medical experiments and concentration camps. Throughout the Second World War the countless *medical experiments* that took place, from forced sterilisation and lobotomy to the Germans' experiments in Auschwitz - most of which ended in death - are initially not acknowlegded by the goverments. Even the German concentration camps are kept in secret until the very end and are only revealed during the liberation in 1945; the Gulag and the other prison camps in the Soviet Union remain unknown until long after the end of the Second World War. During the 1930s and early 1940s, Western newspapers instead wrote about the exceptional progress of the Germans and the new Socialist human.

1940. The Vipeholm experiment with sugar. 1,000 people with various medical diagnoses meaning a constant dependance on the care and supervision of health professionals are subjected by the same staff to a government-funded research project in which they are force-fed large amounts of sugar every day until their teeth rot. The experiment is kept secret and the research results are used as a basis for the new Swedish dental care reform. The experiments continued for several decades and were only really recognised in the 2000s.

1944. Operation Paperclip. The Nazis develop a rocket of the highest calibre in terms of speed and power - the workers responsible for its manufacture are concentration camp prisoners, living in slave-like conditions. The inventor of the rocket is Wernher von Brown. He is quickly put on the most wanted list, but never becomes prosecuted for the war crimes he commits. Von Brown is captured by the Americans and recruited along with thousands of Germans to American research institutes. It is his ideas to develop Apollo and take America to the moon. His name is recognised in the Space Camp Hall of Fame as recent as 2007. Other 'recruits' include Nazi doctors - with experience of torturous experiments on humans - who also go free, with the possibility of a career in the US.

1975. BT chemistry in Teckomatorp. In 1973, children in the small town of Teckomatorp in Sweden suffer respiratory problems. Eight women miscarry at the same time and a 17-year-old dies from stepping in toxic mud. A factory that manufactures pesticides becomes the suspected source of the spread. Strong toxins such as phenoxyacids and dinoseb are involved as the area's plants start to die. The chemical factory pays a small sum to the farmers - in return for a promise not to continue the process. The water smells of chemicals but "BT Kemi" as the company is called denies everything. Neighbours notice noises from the factory at night and hear rumours of barrels being dug into the ground. In Vietnam in 1975, the United States sprayed Vietnamese forests and fields with "Agent Orange", the same agent rumored to be used in Teckomatorp, causing a large proportion of Vietnamese children to be born deformed. The factory workers come to the factory's defence, claiming they have no rashes, but the municipality forces BT Kemi to dig up the soil, only to put an end to the speculation. Several hundred barrels are found in the ground, ripped open from the inside. The barrels contain highly toxic substances. At the same time, there is a factory accident in Italy in 1976 and a cloud of dioxide poisons hundreds of people and thousands of animals have to be slaughtered. This forces BT Kemi to test the water in Teckomatorp as well, but the factory's own sampling shows no traces of poison. The area is drained again and a frightening discovery is made. This time, several thousand barrels are found, from which a yellowish sludge flows - Dinoseb. The factory is eventually closed for good, but the managers are acquitted of all charges. During the 1980s, an attempt is made to decontaminate all the toxins, but the samples contain positive results - for the next 40 years. A major decontamination programme begins in 2008, but in 2020 more traces of the toxins are found.[18] The circumstances are not publicised and the residents still lives in Teckomatorp - despite the high risk. "Since the

18 Documentary: Swedish Events - BT Kemi (2012)

company went bankrupt, Swedish taxpayers had to pay for the first clean-up, which cost SEK 50 million, a sum that has increased tenfold to date."[19]

1984. The Bofors Affair. Ingvar Bratt, a former employee of Bofors, reveals that the company sold 300 anti-aircraft missiles to the Middle East while the latter was at war. For this he receives several peace prizes. It is later revealed that Sweden has also planned to sell weapons to India. The company "Bofors", the middleman, is accused of bribing Indian politicians with 80 million Swedish kronor.[20] The price tag for the deal itself is $285 million. Since the prime minister Palme, who later gets shot, is personally involved in the deal, he and the Socialist government are considered to be one of the initiators. Later, international sources write that Wallenberg, a swedish oligarc with his company SAAB is the one behind the deal.[21]

1990 - Smoking causes cancer. Research shows an early link between tobacco and cancer, but Philip Morris and others refuse to recognise it well into the 1990s. Cigarettes sold to adults and minors are not considered unhealthy and are advertised everywhere - to boost sales. No state government opposes this, until the cancer risk is finally proved and information that smoking is harmful is publicised instead.

19   https://www.expressen.se/kvallsposten/teckomatorp-lider-fortfarande-av-giftstampeln/
20   "Bofors deal in Indian court again"
     https://sverigesradio.se/artikel/147010
21   Wikipedia: https://en.wikipedia.org/wiki/Bofors_scandal

1992. The Estonia's last cargo. The Swedish Defence Forces and Swedish Customs enter into a secret agreement whereby the cruise ship Estonia, in addition to being a holiday cruise boat for up to 1,000 passengers a day, can be used to import military equipment from Russia. She runs aground and it is suspected that this has something to do with the secret cargo. The details of the cargo, found on the Estonia's last voyage before she sinks with 852 of her 989 passengers, are still classified. A new investigation was launched by the Accident Investigation Commission in 2020 when new, previously unknown "holes" were discovered in the ship's hull.[22]

2000. Julian Assange, the Australian journalist who uncovers evidence of the great powers' myriad secret wartime abuses in Africa and the Middle East in some 500,000 files, publishes it all publicly. Assange, who sees himself as a freedom fighter, is then immediately imprisoned over an alleged rape, charges that come just as his fight against the US government is at its most successful. Human rights abuses in the handling of his case are not something politicians want to acknowledge. Assange, who tells how badly he is treated in detention, has finally been released in 2024. If Assange was punished for telling the truth, the question arises whether thousands of other journalists should also be punished. According to Assange, this means the end of neutral journalism: "The US government... in terms of its attack on Wikileaks... have tried to construct a theory, which if permitted will mean the end of national security journalism, not just in

22 Wikipedia: https://sv.wikipedia.org/wiki/Estoniakatastrofen

United States but also about the United States."[23] Instead of punishing those responsible for war crimes, the messenger is punished. According to the UN Commission, Mr Assange had long served his sentence and should be financially compensated for the human rights violations committed against him. The US portrays him as a "hacker" and "digital pirate" even though he is an ordinary journalist.

2008, Obama and the seven wars: Barack Obama, being the first Afro-American president gave a lot of hope to the entire world, when elected for the first time in 2008. The Nobel comission awarded him the Peace Prize. During his time as the head of US government, Obama gave orders to start and uphold no less then seven wars against less powerful contries around the world, with millions dead as a result. Afghanistan, Pakistan, Libya, Yemen and Somalia are some of them. The Nobel Prize was never retrieved.

2010, Edward Snowden, a defected CIA agent, leaks classified documents about how the West monitors people through the internet and Google. Snowden is followed by other 'whistleblowers', who claim that people are constantly monitored by big companies and government agencies, who collect data and personal information. Little is done about the situation and most citizens in the Western countries do not protest, so the surveillance continues.[24]

Imagining much of the above material being classified for years before it became public knowledge - one might wonder *how much remains undiscovered* - which is a stag-

23 Julian Assange - Interview on Youtube
24 Wikipedia: https://sv.wikipedia.org/wiki/Edward_Snowden

gering thought. How many classified documents exist in archives around the world? As a guide, the Kennedy assassination alone has around 10,000 classified documents.

When events come to light, these events are labelled "political scandals", in the hope that would be perceived by the general public as "temporary" and "transitory"; not as an constant, underlying pattern, that occurs frequently and has a "continuous" character. The above events, and several others, contribute to the conclusion that the public is not always aware to what really happens behind the curtains. In the past, the above political scandals would rightly have been called conspiracies. Instead, in modern usage, the words "conspiracy theory" have become negatively charged and at the same time a misuse of scientific terminology - a theory must always be scientifically substantiated.

> History would be an excellent thing, if
> only it were true[25] . - Leo Tolstoy

Although the historical timeline is full of similar events, it is not in the modern discourse to question those in power for such 'political scandals'. This approach has emerged, partly because more and more laws have been passed to prevent people from criticising the elite - and thus preventing them from achieving real change. Any questioning is now labelled as 'whistleblowing', a terminology that contributes to the absence of the whistleblower's moral contribution and the risk that this involves. This is despite the fact that citizens in the Western world are supposed to live in a democracy and are backed by many laws and rights. The Freedom of Speach, which makes us believe that we are free individuals living in a democratic society - at least on a theoretical level, is one of them. In a

25 https://www.academia.edu/5328199/
   Tolstoys_Puppet_Show_On_the_Use_and_Abuse_of_Literature_for_Life

free, open and democratic society, government-hidden information, such as classified documents, would not be needed.

People who try to question and dig for the truth are referred to as "conspiracy theorists". Their desire to uncover truth and knowledge about hidden events, which in the 1970s was considered "ordinary" journalism and in the 1990s basic "investigative" reporting, is no longer a given. Whistleblowers have taken over journalism's task of digging past lies and, above all, reclaiming people's authority and right to know the objective truth.

There are a large number of secret documents to which the public does not have access, both in the West and in other countries. These are the documents that Snowden and Assange have published at great risk, documents that instead need to be classified as important information. Instead they are being referred to as "mad" which is a part of what in this book further will be called as "conseptual confusion".

The media and conceptual confusion - where did the words go?

The devil can cite Scripture for his purpose. An evil soul producing holy witness is like a villain with a smiling cheek, A goodly apple rotten at the heart. Oh, what a goodly outside falsehood hath![26]

William Shakespeare - Merchant of Venice

In George Orwell's 1984, there is a famous example where the concept of 'war' is transformed into the concept of 'peace' and the concept of 'peace' means 'war' instead. Orwell called this new play on words 'New Speak', which he used to illustrate totalitarian society. Orwell wrote the novel in 1948 (but switched the last two numbers around) and modelled the content on the communist Soviet regime.

To deconstruct concepts is to reformulate their meaning and fill words with new meaning. Words that for hundreds of years have stood for basic human needs and given meaning to human values have recently withered and become weakened - their meaning and significance are no longer the same.

   "Liberty", "equality", "fraternity". These are big concepts, as is the word "revolution". When the meaning of the words fades away, it also becomes more difficult to relate to the meaning in a practical sense - the historical legacy is eroded because of this. Freedom used to have a completely different meaning and meant a struggle for human development, for human rights, even a struggle for life. Unfortunately, this meaning has been eroded, but not only in the media and political

26 William Shakespeare, The Merchant of Venice

debate. The words continue to be eroded daily in the advertising that surrounds us everywhere. You are 'free' from gluten. Or "free" to choose your car. The real meaning of the word, to be truly free, thus disappears - for the simple reason that companies want to increase their sales and get more consumers on their hook. The same goes for the word 'revolution', which in previous times meant a life-and-death struggle and political emancipation and is now used in new concepts created by PR consultants, such as 'fashion revolution' or 'food revolution'.

The 18th-century struggle for independence and social justice, where people overthrew royalty, has been replaced by a quest for convenience and happiness. Behind the concepts of 'freedom' and 'revolution' was also the basis of human action and the power that lies therein, the want to change and improve society. This meaning too has been eroded and the will to act has been replaced by the will to consume.

For more examples: the terms 'Equality' and 'Equity' are constantly confused with each other. Equality is a word that in modern times has been profiled to refer to specific political situations, at the expense of the word 'equity', which has led to the word 'justice' being used less. 'Justice', and being treated fairly, is something that all people have been striving for - regardless of age, gender and origin - for thousands of years. Many struggles have been fought in the name of justice, which in turn have led to significant changes in human society.

The above is not necessarily an obvious change; no-one is aware of this erosion or informs us in advance what the meaning of a particular word will be in the future. On the contrary, it is an invisible language that haunts us in society. This invisible linguistic discourse can be found in advertising, in the media and in the way we are addressed by authorities and in social messages. The erosion is happening - before our blind eyes.

Advertising posters are full of exhortations, often in a tone of pressure or encouragement. In order to sell their products or draw our attention to them, they use a language that is overbearing and imposes itself on us, the spectators; they 'know' what we want and need. At the same time, strong concepts are used to reach our innermost being in order to influence us in one direction or another. The fact that people are constantly addressed children-like by the media - perhaps to avoid a sense of responsibility? The responsibility that includes, among other things, acting on human rights, democracy and freedom of expression? The right to participate in social change?

The word 'conspiracy theory' has become increasingly common in everyday language. But its meaning has shifted radically. In addition to its actual meaning, it has been used as a negative term - when a new idea, a political position or other opinions go outside the boundaries, set by what is normal in the current moment - this 'loaded' word is used. As a result, new currents of ideas and organic cultural and political views are suppressed and remain unaccepted. Future political ideas and humanistic directions that have not yet become established can thus be stifled and politics continues to tread the same path, with the same kind of corrupt power structures. The word 'conspiracy', which actually means an 'accusation' - that someone has conspired to commit a criminal or immoral act, has instead become, in a projection, turned against the 'accuser' and associated with terms like 'madness' and 'frivolous' or 'amateurish'. When the word conspiracy was used in its true sense, the word corruption was also used to describe politicians misuse of power. Now, however, the word corruption has been eroded and lost its meaning - in favour of corrupt rulers.

The same techniques, invented by Bernays in the happy 1920s, surround us in today's society. Just as then, advertising uses loaded concepts on the one hand and deconstructs concepts that are not 'desirable' on the other. These "marketing techniques" are used constantly before our eyes and are part of higher education programmes in fields such as public relations and marketing in higher education institutions and also exist in politics.

Politicians' speeches, which used to focus on openly stating their party's ideological intentions and reinforcing the spirit of the people, are now, in the spirit of Bernays, appealing to people's emotions - what do voters really want to hear? Statistical surveys are actively conducted, asking questions about voters' interests, and then used in election campaigns. This is now done with the support of the media. The state now has more influence over the media than ever before. So how do these civil servants work to maintain an image of the state and the government as a "safe" governing body that the Swedish people can trust?

Media coverage and media spin

Media outlets, such as newspapers, TV and news websites, whose previous role was to serve their readers with neutral world information and investigative journalism, which earned the media the nickname of the 'third estate' in the past, have taken on a different role.

Journalists have had great power. They belong to a profession that was once considered to be in a powerful position, working as important mediators of the world around them. At the same time, they have been accused of turning a blind eye to developments, asking the same questions and being similar in their views and opinions. It is said that there is a culture of silence and censorship in the media. But if people think alike and have similar values, there is a risk that neutrality will be overlooked, as not all information will be covered and real diversity will be lost. Questioning prevailing norms is blamed and shamed, and if you write what is sensitive, you are portrayed as extreme. What ordinary people talk about, today's journalists refuse to touch.

> Such as it is, however, the press has become the greatest power within the Western countries, more powerful than the legislative power, the executive, and the judiciary. And one would then like to ask: By what law has it been elected and to whom is it responsible? In the communist East a journalist is frankly appointed as a state official. But who has granted Western journalists their power, for how long a time, and with what prerogatives?[27]

> Enormous freedom exists for the press, but not for the readership because newspaper[s] mostly develop stress and emphasis to those opinions which do not too openly contradict their own and the general trend.[28]

An important part of the job is the political neutrality that journalists, whatever the weather, must maintain. They should not take sides on *whether* to scrutinise - instead, they should always scrutinise and ask the toughest questions. Their job, as the name 'Public Service' suggests, is *to serve* the public by providing factual information, i.e. objective truth. In today's society, whistleblowers have taken over this role. For

---

27 Alexander Solzhenitsyn, "A World Split Apart", 8 June 1978, Harvard University
28 Alexander Solzhenitsyn, "A World Split Apart", 8 June 1978, Harvard University

a few years after the IB affair was revealed in the 1970s, there were no more revelations. Whether this was because the journalists in question were sent to prison, and the rest of the journalistic community in Sweden became afraid of consequences and a worse reputation, or because the intelligence organisation in turn strengthened its security, is not entirely clear. Moving forward in time, one can see that the origin of the IB affair is still denied. Instead, independent actors and bureaucratic decisions are blamed.

When events of a serious nature come to light in society, journalists should be the first to question them, not the last to report them. Otherwise, they contribute to creating a divided society with greater distance between those in power and the population. When people know what society is really like - they can influence it; if they are blind to events, they cannot find a solution. Therefore, civilians need to know society - as it really is.

> Nothing can now be believed which is seen in a newspaper. Truth itself becomes suspicious by being put into that polluted vehicle. The real extent of this state of misinformation is known only to those who are in situations to confront facts within their knowledge with the lies of the day.[29] - Thomas Jefferson

What used to be jokingly referred to as 'media bias' and 'media spin' is now replaced by a blind and unquestioning faith in the media. Readers no longer question the veracity of content. The common view is that what is written in a serious newspaper is probably true. If you read that there has been a stock market crash, there has been a stock market crash; if it says there has been a war, there has been a war. Most people are very comfortable with the picture of reality

29 Thomas Jefferson

presented in the media. And what has not been shown is not considered real, like the famous saying "out of sight, out of mind".

Today, people read the media as they used to read the Gospel - they take what is written as unassailable truth. Any questioning of this 'self-evident truth' is considered inconvenient, frivolous and labelled 'conspiracy theory'. Instead, one is expected to believe all the political propaganda served up in the newspapers. This submissive attitude is not something that the state has forced on the Swedish population, as it tried to force citizens into blind obedience in the Soviet Union; it is something they have chosen for themselves. Or at least they think they have.

In the early 20th century, a new kind of reformist politics takes hold, which also influences journalism, combining psychology and politics to make people more amenable to state influence. After society is reformed into a consumer society, politicians also begin to show interest in Bernays' view of man. Times are getting tougher and after several popular uprisings in the US and Europe, caused by mass unemployment, higher authorities now want to find new methods to curb the angry mob. Together with trained psychologists who have drawn their inspiration and theoretical knowledge from Sigmund Freud, his daughter Anna Freud but above all his nephew Edward Bernays, who is hired as a consultant to President Franklin D. Roosevelt[30] - a psychological methodology is beginning to be incorporated into political election campaigns, journalism, childcare and education, leading to a huge social change. The change takes place in the name of democracy and ushers in a whole new way of looking at media and communication technologies as tools.

30 Feminist Media Studies. Publication details, including instructions for
    authors and subscription information: "It's up to the women" by Jane
    Marcellus

> Think of the press as a great keyboard on
> which the government can play.[31] - Joseph
> Goebbels

Political propaganda

In the first half of the 20th century, United Fruits,
which owned plantations throughout Guatemala in Central
America, works with dictators to consolidate its power
over the country's resources - to keep the plantations,
which are a large part of Guatemala's land, in its pos-
session. When a new president, who promises to kick
United Fruits out of the country in favour of the
indigenous people, wins the sympathy of the population,
United Fruits turns to Bernays in desperation to get
rid of the new political candidate.

Bernays starts by changing the candidate's "image"
from a reputable politician, who will save his people,
to a "threat" who takes "risks", just when the Cold War
is on the doorstep. Guatemala's democracy is portrayed
as under threat. As part of the campaign, Bernays sends
down influential journalists from the US to spread the
word that the candidate and the country are under
communist attack. At the same time, he sets up an agency, on the American home front, which repeatedly informs the US media that Russian communists is planning
to attack Guatemala. To create provocation and fear,
the US military drops also disguised bombs in Guatemala, and Bernays, along with the intelligence community
and journalists, makes it look like the Democrats are
"liberating" Guatemala. They are staging the liberation
of a communist regime by "the people", an indigenous
army secretly trained by the CIA. This concept is something completely new. No one had ever gone this far to
secure a position of power. This 'success' lays a new
foundation for the future methods of the CIA and

---

31 Joseph Goebbles, https://time.com/archive/6750957/germany-scared-to-death/

intelligence services, but details of Eisenhower and the CIA secretly training an army in Guatemala are not made public until much later.[32]

According to Dr Daniele Ganser, a Swiss historian and peace researcher, similar cooperation still exists between the media and politicians, but on an even larger scale. Ganser, who has founded a peace institute in his home country, says the media and news content can be trusted when it comes to sports and weather reports. But the problems start, he says, when it comes to more complex issues related to world politics and international power structures.

For example, many reports about the war in Syria, and the reports made about the war in Afghanistan, carry such complexity and Ganser argues that one needs to nuance the questions, instead of "just" reading the articles straight up and down. The questions that can put the complexity in its proper light are - *who* are portrayed as the "good guys" in the war? *Who* are the 'bad guys'? *Who actually* started the war and how? These questions are often answered one-sidedly in the media, with a distorted sense of truth. Nobody checks what the newspapers write more carefully, and many journalists imitate each other's articles. Every now and then, researchers and historians compare and map these events, usually 10-20 years later, and by that time it is too late - those responsible can no longer be held accountable.

Not necessarily that the media would lie about the content - the media report does not cover the whole picture. A war is made up of many complex components and some never reach the public eye. The 'snapshots' that we read about, which are the focus of newspaper coverage, do not cover the whole picture, the whole that is rooted in the military, in intelligence, top politicians, in arms exports and in big business investment.

32 Dr Daniele Ganser: Can we trust the media? https://www.youtube.com/watch?v=4bF-3rulJz0&t=931s

Basically, PR campaigns have been developed that contain something else than products in a shop, namely propaganda for society, politics and war.

So, in a similar way, techniques are used to influence thoughts and feelings towards military action - otherwise all people would be against war, as most people do not want suffering. The part of war that is chosen to be reported, is published in the news in an appropriate way and with a purpose that involves readers' emotions. War and war atrocities can be hidden or emphasised through communication. And this technique is used in media reporting to influence the reader. Bernays was outspoken about this - in his time:

> Each individual comes into contact with the same, exactly the same impressions as millions of other citizens... Everyone receives the same influence... This very rarely leads to independent thinking.[33]

> In theory, every free citizen forms his or her own opinion... In practice, however, it is not possible for everyone to get to grips with every complex subject... From opinion formers and the media, we receive the evidence and various perspectives on the subject under discussion.[34]

When it comes to complex topics like the war in Afghanistan or Brexit, you have opinion leaders who go out into the media and share their views and expertise. These opinion leaders, who are often rooted in politics, use their space in the news to reach and influence the population. One example is a PR campaign in which politician Colin Powell appeared with a glass can, said to contain biochemical weapons. He waves the can around and says that Saddam Hussein has plenty of

---

33 Edward L Bernays, "Propaganda", page 18, 1928
34 Ibid

such weapons and that is why the USA must go to war. Biochemical weapons, and bacteria in particular, evoke feelings of fear and discomfort. The combination of the image and Mr Powell's speech thus creates an emotion in the viewer. This emotion becomes a legitimate reason for allowing the military action to continue and the viewer is thus convinced. If this convincing report had not been broadcast, there might have been more protests against the war.

Another example is Tony Blair who, in a major PR campaign, told British viewers that the opposing side had chemical and biological weapons and missiles that could hit their target within 45 minutes. If Mr Blair had instead said that the missiles could hit their target within 45 years, there would not have been the same sense of urgency, the need to go to war. Blair is also Prime Minister and therefore the truth of the statement "must" be great. In the 1960s, *the Stanley Milgram Experiment*, a government experiment on information and influence, looked at how people obeyed authority and how people became persuadable.[35] They wanted to know - why did so many Germans obey the Nazis during the Second World War? They wanted to show that hierarchies of power and obedience play a crucial role in the military, as in the rest of human society. Society is made up of hierarchical systems where authority affects both the individual and the masses. Titles and expertise are thus an important factor, providing a sense of authority and authenticity. Powell later admitted that his news campaign was bad, so bad that he even named it a stain on his career. However, by that time, 1,000,000 Iraqis were already dead.

The difference between ordinary advertising and war propaganda is that behind the war propaganda, a missile tank and warships have left one country to attack

35   Torsten Thuren,"Theory of Science for Beginners" Associate Professor of
     Journalism and Ph. Lic in history. Active at Stockholm University.

another. In Iraq and the affected countries, there is a war going on with shells and bombs. In the West, there is also a war going on - but with pictures and news reports in the media. One way to convince a population of the justification of an event is to show only part of the event, while omitting what defeats the purpose.

Framing - an ability to influence our opinions

A contemporary PhD student in linguistics, language and cognitive science, Elisabeth Wehling, has published a manual on communication techniques for those in power, including information on how the media "frame" parts of world news. "Framing" is a media tool that takes a piece of information out of context, bases the entire news story on that particular piece - and leaves out the rest of the information. The reader then does not get the full picture of a situation, but only the selected piece, which in itself affects the perspective. In order to analyse what framing is, some examples should be considered below.

In the 1960s, newspapers report that the Russians have nuclear weapons deployed in Cuba. Only a year earlier, in 1959, the Americans deployed missiles in Turkey, which posed a threat to Russia. This is not reported in the media and readers do not get the full picture of the Cuban situation. This cutting out of reality, which is a typical example of "framing" as a propaganda technique - offers an extremely one-sided picture. Another technique is to publish only part of a timeline, excluding everything that happens before and after. If readers only have one part of an event, they cannot fully choose their opinions, such as: who are the "good guys" in this war, or the "bad guys"? Nevertheless, framing is portrayed as a positive method by the media. Here is how one major newspaper describes the framing technique:

> "Framing" - an ability and skill in using certain words and language and images to influence our opinions. A means of politics and advertising. Critics call this 'brainwashing'.[36]

Here one can clearly see how the article tries to deconstruct the concept of framing, which would otherwise seem like a manipulative tool, into a concept with positive characteristics. The words "ability" and "skill" are positively charged concepts that most people can relate to, making the framing technique sound positive and good. "Influence" - another positively charged word used in the article, instead of words that could sound more negative like "deceive" or "manipulate". In addition, bringing up the "critics" de-dramatises the concept, as if it has "already been" criticised, while making it seem like a matter of "criticism", rather than healthy questioning. Last but not least, there is the word "brainwashing", which is an older, less used word that also means "manipulation". "Brainwashing" is a negatively charged word, which is in the same sentence as "criticism", while the positive concepts of "ability", "knowledge" and "influence" belong to the sentence of framing technique. In this way, words, concepts and sentences are loaded, which keep the reader in certain preconceived notions and opinions. The word "brainwashing" is itself manipulated because it actually means to wash a brain clean, but has come to mean the opposite.

> What sort of responsibility does a journalist or a newspaper have to his readers, or to his history -- or to history? If they have misled

---

36 Dr Daniele Ganser: Can we trust the media?https://www.youtube.com/watch?v=4bF-3ru1Jz0&t=931s

public opinion or the government by inaccurate information or wrong conclusions, do we know of any cases of public recognition and rectification of such mistakes by the same journalist or the same newspaper?[37]

Ganser says that you should use a lot of your own critical thinking. He also says that you should observe how you feel and think when you read certain articles. Being observant helps to maintain a critical and objective approach to information scrutiny and the use of source criticism. Therefore, says Ganser, it is good to compare between different media sources if possible. This example can be compared to food, if you have a choice, you can choose what you put in your mouth, before you swallow it. When you read a framed or deconstructed article and you don't have a choice, you "swallow" the information without futher action, which happens thousands, millions of times a day, as Bernays also pointed out.

With the printing press and the newspaper, the railroad, the telephone, telegraph, radio and airplanes, ideas can be spread rapidly and even instantaneously over the whole of America.[38]

A reader opens the paper and already the editor's thoughts are in his head. Five streets away, another reader does the same. This is called mass information. Thanks to newspapers and the media, the state has an 'opportunity' to lead the population in more or less the same direction, as Bernays describes in his book, 'Propaganda':

Popaganda controls the psyche of the masses in a similar way to the command of the mil-

37 Alexander Solzhenitsyn, "A World Split Apart", 8 June 1978, Harvard University
38 Edward L Bernays "Propaganda", page 12, 1928

itary to which soldiers physically submit.
The number of the manipulable is great.[39]

Bernays compares propaganda to the training of soldiers, which requires not independent thinking, but blind submission to information. Through constant repetition - listening to authority over and over again, the concept eventually becomes accepted. But, says Ganser, it is easier to understand how soldiers are trained to perceive orders from above, how 50 men perform the same exercise at the same time, than to understand how exactly the same thing happens to our thoughts and feelings. This is because the process of emotions and thoughts are largely an invisible process.

For example, if you sing the vignette for an commercial, a feeling is triggered. Nothing special happens on the outside - but on the inside the feeling has already established itself. There is a process where thoughts and feelings are focussed towards different goals. If you can understand this, you can also stop it. Photo manipulation is also used to create different emotions - of joy, fear or sadness, while making a political or commercial point. It can involve taking pictures to make buildings or explosions look bigger, or photoshopping people out of a picture to get the desired effect. Any idea can be implemented in this way through social engineering. You just need the right strategy.

"Overton Window"[40] is a concept that means the "window" of the accepted ideas and opinions within a society. Within the confines of the "window", live the thoughts and opinions that are accepted in a contemporary society. What was accepted 500 years ago is for example less accepted today. The theory behind the concept can explain the formation of public opinion and how new ideas

39 Edward L Bernays "Propaganda", page 22, 1928
40 Glenn Beck, "The Overton Window" 2010

are born and embraced in a society. The scale for the reception consists of four judgements; from 'popular', to 'acceptable', to 'radical', to 'unthinkable'. A new idea may be received as unthinkable at first, and then gradually accepted as acceptable. The window may become wider or narrower in times of social crisis or during special circumstances. The concept is used by governments when, for example, there is an agenda that they wants to implement without protests or riots; when they wants to make the hitherto 'unthinkable' the new 'normal'. The technique is used when you want a population to get to know an idea and not dismiss it, such as for example - raising the retirement age. To further manoeuvre with the emotions of the recipients, an idea that is more radical than the original idea is initially presented with the aim of getting people to reject the first idea. Then, after a while, a similar, less radical idea is presented - which sounds less radical and is suddenly no longer as unthinkable.

> The smart way to keep people passive and obedient is to strictly limit the spectrum of acceptable opinion, but allow very lively debate within that spectrum(...) That gives people the sense that there's free thinking going on, while all the time the presuppositions of the system are being reinforced by the limits put on the range of the debate.[41]

These strategies have been used on the Western population for decades. What many students in journalism or marketing institutions do not realise is that the same communication or propaganda techniques taught in universities today are those invented by Bernays and further developed - by the greatest war criminals of all time. We live in the ghosts of Stalin, of Goebbels

41 Noam Chomsky "The common good", 1996

- we live in a world where we do not know the building
grounds for the society that surrounds us.

What's hidden in snow, comes out in thaw...

The only thing necessary for the triumph of evil is for good men to do nothing[42]

Edmund Burke

In contemporary historical narratives, the political direction of Germany during the Second World War is often portrayed as 'right-wing' - but is this true? At the dawn of the Second World War, three types of socialism could be discerned in the world - Bolshevik Socialism (Communists) in Russia, Welfare Socialism (Democrats) in the United States and Sweden (Social Democrats), and National Socialism (Nazis and Fascists) in Germany and Italy.[43] What is not clear in today's political discourse is that all these movements had their roots in socialism and the left. There was a desire to unite workers internationally, across national borders, but this did not materialise, due to the huge economic losses caused by the First World War, and unification took instead place within the nations. National socialism, which was moving in two different directions, one in Germany and the other in Italy, was opposing to individualism and capitalism and instead focused on uniting the people.

These socialist movements had certain basic ideological principles in common, including the desire for all institutions, industries and enterprises to be state-owned and conform to state regulations. The political alignment of the time can be observed in the parties' election manifestos: the National Socialist

---

42 Edmund Burke. Letter to William Smith [January 9, 1795]
    https://quoteinvestigator.com/2010/12/04/good-men-do/

43 The Best Enemies Money Can Buy: An Interview with Prof Antony C. Sutton,
    https://www.youtube.com/watch?v=zTDvLmEBESY

(Nazi) party manifesto of the 1930s - called for state healthcare, state newspapers and state banks. The National Socialists also promised guaranteed jobs, abolition of all income that was not 'earned', state ownership of all companies and funds, profit sharing in all major industries, abolition of child labour, abolition of church power to be replaced by state power. If you compare this to the party programme of a contemporary socialist party, you will find several common points.

The same was true of the Fascist party programme - which promised an 8-hour working day, the right to vote for women, the abolition of the privileges of the nobility, a minimum wage, labour reforms, the distribution of the nobility's lands, state schools to educate proletarians, and the taking of church assets for the state.[44] The Fascists, led by Mussolini, had a political orientation very similar to socialism, probably because Mussolini had grown up with a father who had read Karl Marx's 'Capital' to him as a child. Named after a revolutionary in Mexico, he began his political career as a socialist leader and was greatly admired by both Trotsky and Lenin. Inspired by socialist progressivism, Mussolini always said "Avanti", which is not dissimilar to today's socialist slogans - Democratic President Barack Obama, for example, said "Foreward" as a slogan. When Mussolini was expelled from the Socialist Party for supporting World War I, he said: "Whatever happens, you will not lose me, 12 years of my life in the party should be a guarantee of my socialist faith. Socialism is in my blood!"[45] Mussolini remained a socialist even as a member of the Fascist Party. What is not talked about in the public discourse nowdays is that Mussolini's policies were part of the new left socialist

---

44 Jonah Goldberg "Liberal fascism: the secret history of the American left, from Mussolini to the politics of change", 2009
45 Speech at the Italian Socialist Party's meeting in Milan at the People's Theatre on Nov. 25, 1914, quoted in Revolutionary Fascism by Erik Norling, Lisbon, Finis Mundi Press (2011) p. 88.

structure that was emerging after the First World War, not a *contradiction* to it; today, Mussolini's policies are considered the opposite of left socialism. Why is that?

A new kind of co-operation

Economic co-operation also begins between the socialist countries. After the First World War, businessmen began to take an interest in investing in various industries and political campaigns around the world. All three socialist movements were financed in different ways, according to historian Anthony Sutton, by large corporate groups that had grown in size after industrialisation - including through Wall Street - even though the socialist wave movements also had in common their opposition to capitalism and the privatisation of companies and institutions[46]. The leader of the National Socialists, Hitler, went so far as to think that Jews and capitalism were one and the same. He wanted to get rid of both them and their capital and the Nazis believed that:

> We are socialists and mortal enemies of capitalism, with its exploitation of the economically weak, its unequal wage system and its immoral way of judging people on the basis of their monetary capital.[47]

Funding for industries and socialist election campaigns came from corporate groups - via the state. Cooperation between big business and politicians began creating state monopolies - making it harder for small businesses. Before the outbreak of World War II, socialist politicians in the United States cooperated in various ways with the fascists in Italy, the communists in Rus-

46 Antony Sutton, "Wall Street and the Rise of Hitler" 1976
47 Gregor Strasser "Thoughts about the Tasks of the Future", by Gregor Strasser - (1926 June 15)

52

sia and the National Socialists in Germany. What they have in common is that they want to get rid of capitalism and the aristocracy, while the state begins to support big business and its monopolies.[48]

What is not being talked about today is that most of the world is, in the beginning, taking inspiration from Italy, Germany and Russia and celebrating the progressive values that these countries are said to have. Journalists around the world are impressed by the success of the communists and Nazis and are spreading their praise in hundreds of articles. Not only the media, but also some of the world's largest companies are impressed and interested in the new party in Germany and want to invest in the progressive spirit of the new era. As a result, Adolf Hitler and other leaders have their entire political careers sponsored during the 1920s and 30s. Heinrich Himmler, head of the SS, is given his own fund that can be linked to corporate tycoons such as ITT, General Electric and Standard Oil. Henry Ford, the American car magnate and industrialist and creator of the Ford car brand, with many connections in American politics - is one of them. In 1938, Ford is awarded the Grand Cross of the German Eagle[49] for his economic achievements in building the new Germany. The medal is awarded by none other than the National Socialists.

---

48 Antony Sutton, "Wall Street and the Rise of Hitler" 1976
49 https://rarehistoricalphotos.com/henry-ford-grand-cross-1938/

An important part of the story that has not been publicised is that the fateful election that Hitler eventually wins is based on election campaigns that are largely financed - from outside. The money comes from an account sponsored by several large international companies based in America. These include names like Ford, General Electric, Ozram and Standard Oil, the latter owned by Mr Rockefeller. General Electric, which is responsible for building up electricity in the United States, even sets up a large electricity branch in Germany, right before the Second World War.

In addition to financial sponsorship, Germany also gets some of its munitions from these big companies, including *tetra-ethyl* for petrol, which is developed in ethyl laboratories in the US and then shipped to Germany. The oil is obtained through a process entrusted to them by Standard Oil, which also gives them access to other technological and chemical processes. These factories owned by US corporations, are not bombed by the Allies after the end of World War II, when the Germans lose the war. British and American banks also lend large amounts of capital to the National Socialists. Many millions of dollars are lent just as they come to power. In this way, both military and medical research in Germany are sponsored.

Ten years after Virginia passed its sterilisation act, Joseph DeJarnette, superintendent of Virginia's Western State Hospital, observed in the Richmond Times-Dispatch, "The Germans are beating us at our own game." America were funding Germany's eugenic institutions as well as providing the framework and guidance for the development of their eugenics research. By 1926, the Rockefeller Foundation had donated some $410,000, almost $4 million in today's money, to hundreds of German researchers.[50]

What is not clear from the history books is that this admiration - and willingness to co-operate - is mutual. Hitler is inspired by the United States and uses American restrictions on immigration and segregation, which are based on race, as a model for Germany's domestic Jewish policy: the new National Socialist legislators, tasked with writing laws on issues including the Jewish question, are inspired by the Ku Klux Klan. They look at how the United States defined the African-American population during slavery and establish the same kind of order in Germany. Hitler himself praises the progressive immigration restrictions, noting that: "By simply excluding certain races from acquiring Naturalisation (citizenship)", the National Socialists' idea of a white supremacist state was approached. He also praises laws against interracial marriage created by the American Democrats. "The Germanic inhabitants of the American continent," he wrote in Mein Kampf, "who have remained pure and unmixed, rose to become the masters of the continent; they will remain masters as long as they do not fall victim to impure blood.[51]

---

50 Black, "Eugenics and the Nazis -- the California Connection" - A Study of
    the United States Influence on German Eugenics, Cameron Williams, East
    Tennessee State University
51 Dinesh D'Souza, "Death of a Nation." page 152, 1918

> Then Hitler remembered what Andrew Jackson
> and his successors did to the American In-
> dians. Jackson's Indian Removal Act had driv-
> en tens of thousands of Indians - the Chicka-
> saw, the Choctaw, the Creek and the Seminole
> - out of their ancestral homes, forcing them
> to relocate further west. When the Cherokee
> resisted, they were forcibly removed, leading
> to the infamous Trail of Tears.[52]

Hitler, on the other hand, disliked Lincoln because, by abolishing slavery, he prevented "the beginning of a new social order based on the principle of slavery and inequality".[53] But both Mussolini and the Nazis were inspired by 'The New Deal', launched by the Democrat Franklin D. Roosevelt, a major reformist campaign in the United States that would remove privatisation and introduce state control of all institutions, businesses and other social services. When it came to big business and the sponsors of the National Socialists, something else was to apply, namely the establishment of a com-pletely new form of co-operation which, among other things, meant that all big business oligarchs would be protected by the state.

> We too, as German National Socialists are
> looking towards America." FDR, (Roosevelt)
> the Nazi publication said, was replacing "the
> uninhabited frenzy of market speculation" of
> the 1920s with a "adoption of National
> Socialist strains of thought in his economic
> and social policies.[54]

Roosevelt himself had an association with the American equivalent of Hitler's terrible racial policies. Wood-row Wilson, the Democratic politician who had re-es-

52 Dinesh D'Souza, "*Death of a Nation*." page 152, 1918
53 Documentary: *Death of a Nation*. Dinesh D´Souza, 2018
54 Documentary: *Death of a Nation*. Dinesh D'Souza, 2018, *Völkischer Beobachter*

tablished the Ku Klux Klan and been responsible for its growth throughout America, had continuous close association with Roosevelt. Roosevelt also co-operated with other high-ranking Klan members who held office in the US Senate. One of these progressives who gained much attention was nurse Margaret Sanger. Her ideas of 'helping humanity to advance' through eugenics and racial biology, inspired Hitler and he expressed gratitude for her suggestions in their letter exchange.

A in the subject "Aron" stands for Ambros

This co-operation continued after the end of the Second World War, but now in secret. Operation Paperclip, one of the secret military operations of the US intelligence service, aimed to get hold of the weapons technology developed by the National Socialists. Before the war, Americans had invested money in military technology in Germany and therefore did not want to let go of what the military industry had produced. Above all, they wanted the engineers behind the projects. When Germany was liberated, the American soldiers found a list of 1,600 scientists who are the brains behind the technology, and both the Soviet Union and the United States wanted them for their own. The spoils are huge - the Germans had invested much of their capital in research. As a result, the US is willing to pardon the Nazi scientists and secretly spare them from the Nuremberg trials. Some 1,600 men, engineers, doctors and scientists who had committed war crimes on the same scale as the accused were smuggled out.

Instead, the Nazi scientists went to the United States to enjoy both capital and professional careers in high office - in key US institutions such as NASA and the US government. One of the criminals is Siegfried Knameyer, a pilot who is considered to be one of Göring's closest men. Göring calls him 'my boy' and Siegfried in turn is called Göring's right-hand man. In recognition of Knameyer's research work for the US government, the US government awards him the highest military medal available. Several of the other scientists also receive awards from NASA.

Another example is Otto Ambros, Hitler's favourite chemist and Nazi scientist, with extensive responsibility for Auschwitz. It is described how he and his colleagues, after work, went to play tennis on a court close to the crematorium. After the war, Otto Ambros pursues a career as a chemist in the United States. The 'A' in the subject 'Aron' stands for Ambros - his surname. Other examples include Dr Blom and Dr Schreiber, who conduct horrific experiments on human beings during the war and after the war conduct research at medical institutes in the United States.

Some of the researchers socialise with President John F Kennedy and others high up in American society. Some go on to work for the CIA and the US Secret Service. Several work on rockets and develop the famous Apollo rocket. Two of the moon's craters are named after Nazi scientists and one of them gets a prize named after him, awarded well into the 21st century.[55]

Paradigm shift

Why are these 'missteps' by politicians and business leaders in the West not more widely publicised? Educational institutions, textbooks and public debate should collectively inform and remind us of these unpublicised segments of history, so that all the events described above are given their rightful place in history books. But this is not the case and there is a reason for this. When the millions of victims of the Second World War were revealed and many of those responsible in Ger-

---

55 Lecture: Annie Jacobsen, Operation Paperclip
    https://www.youtube.com/watch?
    v=DdoIKaCLOIo&pp=ygUjQW5uaWUgSmFjb2JzZW4sIE9wZXJhdGlvbiBQYXBlcmNsaXA%3D

many were held accountable for their war crimes, there was a huge uproar. The whole world began to work together to put things right. At the same time, politicians, the elite and big business owners realise that they have supported Hitler too far. Now they want to wash away the unwanted stain of Nazism. All responsibility – is therefore shifted to the Germans.

Within the socialist movement worldwide, a purification process begins and, in order not to be associated with the terrible crimes of Nazism, Nazism is redefined as "right-wing", despite the obvious lack of logic. The Nazi ideology, previously associated with the working class, the left, the "SS", being called "National Socialism", is suddenly redefined as belonging to the right wing of politics. Now the term Nazism is to be associated with "conservatism" instead of "socialism" in this deliberate confusion of concepts. This does not solve the problem of Nazi ideology, but merely "shifts" it to someone else. In this way, the politicians who supported Hitler and the Wall-Street tycoons who sponsored Nazi Germany do not have to take financial responsibility for anything that happened during the Second World War. Exactly who was responsible for this paradigm shift campaign is not yet known, the documents are probably still classified. Is the paradigm shift a campaign created by the socialist rulers, big business and leaders of the time to stay in power? To avoid being held accountable for their Nazi sympathies, their invested capital and their collaboration with Hitler that later led to the extermination of millions of Jews?

Much of the "narrative" socialist leaders around the world are pushing in their election campaigns today, is about anti-racism and an inclusive view of minorities. A revealed collaboration with Hitler would probably tarnish this perception.[56]

56 Documentary: Hillary's America: The Secret History of the Democratic
    Party, 2016

Vipeholm

Not only in the US, but the Socialist governments around the world took influence from the Nazi regime. The death toll at Swedish Vipeholm, the institution for the so-called insane, was rising around 1945. Shortly before, those responsible state that these patients should no longer be a problem. On 9 June 1944, the Socialist Gustav Möller, head of the Ministry of Social Affairs, proposes that medical experiments should be carried out at Vipeholm. The idea is to induce tooth decay by giving the patients huge amounts of sugar and sweets, which will eat away at their teeth. The subjects are denied dental treatment despite great pain, as depicted in the film *Sockerexperimentet (The Sugar Experiment)* 2023.[57] The results of the experiment then serve as a basic model for the whole of Swedish dentistry. Sweden, is often said to be the leading example of dental care around the world, has never publicly acclaimed this hidden part of history to be the big reason behind its success. Thanks to Vipeholm, the Swedish people learn how to take care of their dental hygiene - with best possible results. The patients who are sacrificed - with great suffering - are never repaid. The "dental experiments" continue until 1955, when the centre is forced to close due to massive public criticism.

Forced sterilisation - a Swedish world record

In 1946, the Socialist government in Sweden broke the world record for forced sterilisation, a practice that had been in use in Europe and the United States for years. The Socialist Rickard Sandler, the same man who was responsible for the commission of inquiry of Swedish concentration camps, reviews the book *Parenting*

---

57   Film: The Sugar Experiment 2023,
     https://sv.wikipedia.org/wiki/Vipeholmsexperimenten

and Racial Culture in the Social Democratic magazine "Tiden" and writes:

> The inferior may live and live as well as possible - but they must not be allowed to corrupt future generations; they must be deprived of the right of parenthood. Thus shall humanity towards the living be united with the equally important humanity towards the unborn.[58]

In 1922, Socialist Alfred Petrén initiates a motion approving the forced sterilisation of, among others, the mentally ill. Among other things, he justifies it by saying that:

> To illustrate this fact, some examples given by the Swedish Poor Relief Association of the racial hazards of the reproduction of the insane may be cited here.[59]

They travel to Hamburg to learn about the latest sterilisation techniques in Nazi Germany and then lay the foundations for a compulsory sterilisation law that gives the right to sterilise both children and adults. Gunnar Myrdal and Alva Myrdal, sociologists, psychologists and educators, criticise the law and think it is - too weak.

In 1941, even those considered antisocial are sterilised. People were sterilised for eugenic reasons. Most were not insane in the modern sense - if you shoplifted, you were considered insane. 63,000 people are sterilised against their will. Even Olof Palme, during his first seven years as Swedish prime minister, bears supreme responsibility for the implementation of this terrible state practice. Until 1976, people continued

58 Tiden / Third year. 1911 no 345 (1908-1940)
    https://runeberg.org/tiden/1911/0351.html
59 Motion 1922:38 First Chamber No 38 https://www.riksdagen.se/sv/dokument-och-lagar/dokument/motion/motioner-i-forsta-hammaren-nr-38_dj2c38/

to be forcibly sterilised. The Swedish Socialist Party prefer to keep a lid on this. This is how former prime minister Stefan Löfven, for example, addresses the history of the labour movement:

> And if there is anyone who has stood up for democracy and the equal value of people throughout history, modern history, it is the labour movement (Socialist party), there is no denying it, it is we who stand up for this.[60]

Right or left?

Were the Conservative politicians on the side of the Nazis, or is it a myth, created by the same socialist government that has been in power for over 100 years?

For more then 100 years, the Socialists have been in power in Sweden as the largest party. For just as long, they have managed to keep the full picture of their history out of school textbooks and public debate. Since the heyday of industrialisation, a collective spirit that fits left-wing politics like a glove has flourished in Sweden.

> In industrial society, a sense of collective good developed. Because of the unique form of the mills, a sense of community emerged; workers were organised into teams and did not have the luxury of working individually. Ultimately, trade union pressure created a strong hold that the Swedish labour movement continued to have on the population.[61]

60 Minutes 2015/16:96 Thursday 21 April § 1 Notification of subsidiarity tests 42 Prime Minister STEFAN LÖFVEN (S) https://www.riksdagen.se/sv/dokument-och-lagar/dokument/protokoll/protokoll-20151696-torsdagen-den-21-april_H30996/html/
61 Roland Huntford, "Blind Sweden" (The New Totalitarians), 1971

This spirit has meant that people have kept their backs to each other; many of the documents relating to the events of the Second World War are still classified. Those involved have never been held to account: instead, as in the rest of the world, there has been an attempt at a paradigm shift, simply deconstructing the origins of Nazism through fabrication, so that it became part of the Right for many years to come.

This manoeuvre, as in the rest of Europe and the United States, lacks both logic and justification. There exists ample evidence that the Swedish Right Party, later the Moderates, and the Conservatives were opposed to both Nazism and Hitler during this period. For example, they broke with pro-German organisations such as the Swedish National Youth League - as early as 1934. [62]

The leader of the Right Party, Arvid Lindman, firmly distanced himself from Nazism and took the information about what was happening in Germany seriously. The Right Party were also involved in developing the new democracy that would come after the turn of the century. The political endeavour of the Right and conservatism of Sweden were peaceful social development and monarchy - not war.[63] Nazism and Fascism were not 'national', they believed, and not Swedish. It was against the monarchy, it was critical of Christianity, which was strongly rooted in conservatism. "We should not import foreign dictatorship ideas." was the position and slogan of the Moderates or the old Right Party during this time.

The Right and anti-Nazism is thus a theme that research has "forgotten". Based on its values, the Right mobilised itself for an anti-Nazi stance. In doing so, it blocked Nazi recruitment within conservative groups and even played an important role in opposing Nazi

62 Torbjörn Nilsson "Ideologies 2019 - The Moderates' ideas".
63 Leif Lewin, & Torbjörn Nilsson, "Historical Axess 2019 - Democracy 100
    years"

takeovers.[64] Despite this, the Nazi or National Socialist ideology was, by means of conceptual confusion and PR manipulation, displaced to the right side of politics.

In the early 20th century, the Right opposed classical parliamentarism, where the winner takes all and forms a government while the loser is excluded; according to right-wing politics, everyone should be included, especially if you want 'real' democracy. They want to satisfy not only the majority but also the rest of the political spectrum. The right-wing party introduces universal male suffrage, but when it is introduced in 1909, both Hjalmar Branting (Socialist) and Karl Staff (Liberal Party) vote - no! The old Right thus had constitutional ideals of co-operation instead of party fighting, which inspired the young democracy.

The co-operative politics of 19th century conservatism is thus part of the model for today's democratic model in Sweden. The Right's policy included taking responsibility for society and not just pursuing the selfish interests of their own party. Among other things, they ensured that the King was not deposed. In 1918, the monarchy was thus saved because it was considered that the King was a symbol of the calm development of society. The King was also persuaded to support the new reform. The right-wing supporters accepted democracy and the aim was to ensure that social development was calm and lawful. They were worried that things would turn out like in Russia after the Marxist takeover, and did not want a revolt and therefore agreed to implement democracy and improve society for all classes. Despite their efforts, they ended up outside the government - for many years.[65] And they have not tried to clear their policies or actions from the Nazi label, or from the accusations levelled against them - by far not enough.

64 Torbjörn Nilsson "Ideologies 2019 - The Moderates' ideas"
65 Leif Lewin, & Torbjörn Nilsson, "Historical Axess 2019 - Democracy 100 years"

64

Outstanding social democratic leadership

When the battle for Europe and the Second World War was finally over, no one in the Swedish Socialist Party wanted to recognise the collusion with Nazism. It was revealed, this time with evidence, that the Germans had committed a host of war crimes and the opposing side showed no mercy.

> Hitler Germany's top figures, Göring, Ribbentrop, Hess and the other war criminals, were tracked down, imprisoned and tried at Nuremberg. Eleven were sentenced to death by hanging.[66]

In Sweden, neither the Swedish Nazis nor the Nazi sympathisers were punished; nor did any of those responsible, had even the slightest consequences. Instead, a theory was presented out to the world that Sweden - throughout the Second World War - was neutral, which was also written in history books that were presented in Swedish schools. All the names of streets and squares, belonging to Swedish Nazi sympathisers; all the statues and honours erected in the name of Nazi sympathisers - were never removed, as the names of Nazi war criminals had been removed in Germany. Not a single street in Germany is now called "Göring-Straße" or "Adolf-Hitler-Platz". In fact, unlike in Germany, Sweden continues to honour these Nazi sympathisers, men and women, in various ways, for example with scholarships and prizes. There is no 'Himmler scholarship' in Germany, that would rightly seem appalling and grotesque.

---

66 "The war years and the birth of the people's home" - Aftonbladet's editor-in-chief *Rolf Alsing* describes the Swedish 1940s

In Sweden there are following awards, dedicated to Swedish Nazi sympathisers, which have remained in place, on the Socialist Partys website:

- Gunnar Myrdal (Socialist) receives the Nobel Prize, which has not been revoked

- Alva Myrdal (Socialist) - a statue on Djurgården, and a street named after her.

- The Alva and Gunnar Myrdal Foundation and Alva Myrdal, who believed that there should be a ..."weaning of highly unfit individuals (...) through a "rather ruthless sterilisation procedure."[67] has its own research centre at Uppsala University named after it. The Alva and Gunnar Foundation even became tax-exempt in 1982.

- Per Albin (Socialist prime minister)has his own museum and bust in his home town of Kulladal, and two roads named after him - one in Kulladal and one in Stockholm. He, who was responsible for thousands of forced sterilisations, also has a foundation. His motto was: "Sweden for the Swedes - the Swedes for Sweden!"[68]

- Hjalmar Branting (Socialist) had a monument built in honour of his achievements, as well as a foundation with grants and scholarships.

- Hinke Bergegren (Socialist) is recognised at Kalmar County Museum. He said: "For my part, I consider petty murder to be just fine... We shall instil the poison called hatred so that we become ripe for any kind of violence".[69]

---

67   Alva and Gunnar Myrdal "Crisis in the Population Question", 1934
68   https://arbetet.se/2024/02/21/sd-kan-aldrig-aterskapa-per-albin-hanssons-folkhem/
69   Second Congress at the turn of the century 17-20 May 1891

- Bengt Lidforss' (Socialist) bust can be found in the Biology Building at Lund University, as well as a statue of an eagle erected in his honour. Lindforss once said: "mixing with other races would be cause for cultural decline in Sweden".[70]

- Alma Hedin (Socialist) is the founder of Blomsterfonden, which still owns property and runs several elderly care homes in central Stockholm. It has been said of her: "She became a great friend of the new rulers and sympathised with Hitler's regime."[71]

All of these old Nazi sympathisers are still admired and honoured today. If the Socialists had the anti-Nazi orientation they claim to support, they would have long ago purged the above tendencies and taken responsibility for what happened at the expense of millions of victims. Instead they never criticize the actions of old party members; the old Nazi sympathisers are instead presented as role models for their good leadership. The following foundations are listed on the Social Democrats' website: the Hjalmar Branting Memorial Foundation and the Per Albin Hansson Memorial Foundation:

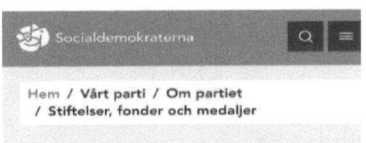

Stiftelser, fonder och medaljer

Här hittar du information om stiftelser inom socialdemokratin.

Stiftelsen till Ernst Wigforss minne, Stiftelsen till Hjalmar Brantings minne, och Stiftelsen till Per Albin Hanssons minne.

Stiftelserna har inrättats med syfte att hylla framstående socialdemokratiska ledarinsatser. Genom stiftelsernas verksamhet är tanken att minnet av ledargestalternas gärningar ska leva vidare och påminna om deras insatser för arbetarrörelsen och svenskt samhälle.

> The foundations have been set up to honour outstanding socialistic leadership. Through the foundations' activities, the idea is to keep alive the memory of the deeds of the

70 Bengt Lidforss, "Drafts and Silhouettes", 1922
71 Bibi Jonsson "Brown pens. Nazi motifs in Swedish women's literature", 2012

leaders and remind people of their contributions to the labour movement and Swedish society.[72]

Notice how they admire and emphasise the "deeds of
these leaders" and "their contributions (...) to Swedish society". What deeds are they referring to exactly? The Nazi statements? Preventing Jewish refugees
from crossing the Swedish border? Complacency towards
the Nazis' shipping of Norwegian political refugees?
Forced sterilisation?

There, on the website, is also Tage Erlander's Medal
of Honour, which costs SEK 1500 to buy and engrave. The
Branting Medal, which costs only SEK 250, is also a
badge of honour, which shows that you admire the Socialist government as you used to admire the men of the
church.

Isolation, ignorance and hierarchical tastes
made Swedes easy to control, and the identity
between church and state favoured politicians. Although the religious background has
now become very weak, the church's legacy of
political subservience and intellectual ser-
vitude lives on. If the various reorganised
regimes in Sweden, from the liberals of the
19th century to the social democrats of the
1960s, have been able to implement rapid and
often uncomfortable changes virtually without
resistance, it is because conformity has been
made a cardinal virtue and dissent a mortal
sin.

72   From the Social Democrat website "Foundations, funds and medals"

The only people who do not lie are the dead

Patricia: You think people will buy this?

Dascombe: Well, why not? This is the BTN. Our job is to report the news, not fabricate it. That's the government's job.

- V for Vendetta 2005

According to the commonly held view in the West, the people of a nation, through democracy, are free to influence political developments. This is not true. For most of the 20th century, the political structure across the world has been hijacked by the ideas created by Karl Marx and Friedrich Engels. Thus, for more than 150 years, most Western politics has been characterised by the philosophy of Marx and Engels. This philosophy culminated in the Soviet Revolution in the beginning of the 20th century; no other philosophy has exterminated so many people while being so revered and the Western culture are still allowed to idolise those responsible. We are talking about an extermination of some 100 million victims, with the question of guilt and responsibility is still not fully resolved. What the dark past of the communists conceals about the crimes committed has not been sufficiently prioritised in public discourse, thus allowing a fairer and more realistic image of communism to develope. This chapter is intended to paint a more nuanced picture of the crimes of the communists but also of their cooperation with the socialist regime in the West, which modern socialist parties try to deny. Socialism, known in its early days as 'scientific communism', developed parallely and, despite its less prominent totalitarian agenda, shared many of the basic features of communism, like a sibling.

> Having experienced applied socialism in a country where the alternative has been realised, I certainly will not speak for it.[73]

> The well-known Soviet mathematician Shafarevich, a member of the Soviet Academy of Science, has written a brilliant book under the title *Socialism*; it is a profound analysis showing that socialism of any type and shade leads to a total destruction of the human spirit and to a leveling of mankind into death.[74]

WAR of classes

The culmination began with the Russian Revolution, which in 1917 lead to the expulsion or execution of all opponents of communism. At first, the revolution is a class struggle, but violence quickly escalates. In 1917, Lenin calls this 'The War of Classes'. According to Bolshevik theory, harmony in a society can only arise when certain groups or classes of people are 'eliminated'. During the Russian Revolution, about 10% of the population is therefore killed. Anyone who is intellectual, rich, noble, educated and part of the cultural establishment is executed in favour of the new social structure.[75] Those who oppose Marxist or Communist ideas are shot and more than 10 million die.[76] The aristocracy and all those in power are deposed, inclu-

---

73 Alexander Solzhenitsyn, "A World Split Apart", 8 June 1978, Harvard University
74 Alexander Solzhenitsyn, "A World Split Apart", 8 June 1978, Harvard University
75 Vladimir Bukovsky (1942-2019, writer, dissident, activist and critic of the Soviet Union, The Soviet story, 2008
76 Norman Davies, Cambridge University, The Soviet story, 2008

ding educated managers and engineers. Without manpower, the factories, which after all have provided jobs for millions of people for dozens of years, are forced to close. A large proportion of the workers can no longer support themselves, the class for whom the country is supposedly being reformed, and a massive famine begins - Russian workers starve to death. Exports fall dramatically because the Bolsheviks themselves are unable to operate the factories.[77] The new Communist regime encounters its first major failure and, as with all its defeats, denies everything.

> I have spent all my life under a Communist regime and I will tell you that a society without any objective legal scale is a terrible one indeed.[78]

Many of the cultural greats - artists, writers and composers - flee the country; Chagall, Bunin, Stravinsky, Prokofieff and Diagileff go to France and Rachmaninoff goes to California. There is a purge in cultural life to create space for communist propaganda. There is also a migration of scientists whose research crosses the 'boundaries' of the scientific line demanded by the new government. This phenomenon has affected many communist dictatorships. Many of the Soviet scientists flee to the United States, whose government, during the revolution, closely followed the events in Russia. But their role in the revolution was to be more than just that of observers.

Who picks up the tab?

Prof A. Sutton, California State University, and Stanford University, in his major research paper "Western Technology and Soviet Economic Development", argues

---

77 Anthony C Sutton, "Triology Of Western Technology And Soviet Economic Development 1917 To 1930, 1930 To 1945, 1945 To 1965", 1968
78 Alexander Solzhenitsyn, "A World Split Apart", 8 June 1978, Harvard University

that the West did play a major and decisive role in the birth of the Communist Soviet Union. A large number of countries and institutions supported the Bolshevik advance - the US government, the major European powers, and the big Wall Street firms.[79]

According to Sutton, both Lenin and Trotsky were previously in exile in the United States, Canada and England, due to previous failed revolutionary attempts against the Russian state. Trotsky and the Russian Communists are now in need of help and financial support. President Woodrow Wilson and the British Secret Service provide Trotsky with both passports and capital. On his way back, he brings with him as much as $10,000 in gold, although his own salary does not exceed $600 a year. Reportedly, this gold and later other capital comes from businessmen and investors in Europe and Wall Street. Lenin, who is in exile in Switzerland and Germany, is also encouraged and praised for his revolutionary actions. He too is funded by both Europe and the US. The revolutionaries are initially only 10,000 strong and in dire need of capital. At the same time, in Europe and the United States, the political structure is becoming entrenched in a comprehensive socialist reform. One of the goals is an autocratic socialist world government.[80] In the same spirit, the Bolsheviks are being assisted, as they want to reform the entire Russian Empire. Several of the sponsors who are at the top of Wall Street circles have just published books on the utopian socialist society, such as the founder of the razor company Gillette who is writing the book "The Human Drift"[81] , at a time when corporate corporations were still openly engaging in political power plays.

79 The Best Enemies Money Can Buy: An Interview with Prof Antony C. Sutton
    (early 1980s)
80 Wall Street and the Bolshevik Revolution - Antony Sutton,
    https://www.youtube.com/watch?v=kEVOIO4TbZs
81 King C Gillette, "The Human Drift" 1894

Several of the Wall Street financiers hold political positions in communist parties around Europe and the US, or have relatives who do. The dream is to start a socialist international or globalist empire and financing a revolution is part of this empire. These facts are mostly beyond public knowledge. They are an indication of the role played by the big business elite in the history of the 20th century, the account of which is missing from the historical discourse.[82]

A major reason for the financial contributions is that the communist reform itself was not innovative; instead, the new communist regime would need to export a new technology. Here, big business leaders saw an investment opportunity. The behaviour of the Russian Bolsheviks, who used their new capital to exterminate the Russian intelligentsia, academia and engineers, automatically made the new Soviet dependent on the outside world. After an extensive struggle against starvation, they ask the outside world for help. Some 200-300 American companies come to the rescue and begin to rebuild the new Soviet Union in various ways. The aim is to open up factories and build new industries. This would include adopting the latest Western technology and industrial processes.[83]

In 1917, at the outbreak of the revolution, there is a great fall in Russian economy; before that, the Russian Empire is booming with splendour and urban construction. The economic boom is largely due to the infrastructure built across the country.[84] Before the Bolsheviks took over, Russia was a strong country, including being married into the European royal houses. Technocrats and bureaucrats own industries that in turn crea-

---

82 The Best Enemies Money Can Buy: An Interview with Prof Antony C. Sutton (early 1980s)
83 The Best Enemies Money Can Buy: An Interview with Prof Antony C. Sutton (early 1980s)
84 KASB Webinar on Investing in emerging markets - lessons from Russia with Hasan Malik

te millions of jobs. Culture thrives. Russia is rich in natural resources and has good investment opportunities and geopolitical co-operation.[85]

The new deteriorating economy under the revolutionaries' auspices creates conditions for the Western players. Citibank and Midland Bank (UK) open their Russian offices in 1917 and, thanks to the investors, industry and the economy pick up again. France, England and Germany are the main players and, according to Sutton, the United States is also included.[86]

> "I feel more certain then ever that Russia itself will come out in the end stronger than ever. I still consider all foreign investments here advisable and safe and I sincerely hope that the United States will now be willing to help Russia more in every way" 1917, Federal state reserve director.[87]

Why did the Western players invest in the communist Soviet Union and sponsor its military actions instead of extending a helping hand to the falling Russian empire? How did this case benefit the investors?

Today it is argued that Bolsheviks and Communists were opposed to banking and capitalists, but they themselves were waging a financial war and financial restructuring. Lenin understood economics and admired the international financial architecture. They used finance as one of their revolutionary tools.[88] The powers that were in the West recognised this and were establishing cooperation that payed off. Russian financial investments gave the economic powers access to the global market to a greater extent than before. Wall Street

85 "Bankers & Bolsheviks": an interview with Hassan Malik
86 KASB Webinar on Investing in emerging markets - lessons from Russia with Hasan Malik
87 KASB Webinar on Investing in emerging markets - lessons from Russia with Hasan Malik
88 KASB Webinar on Investing in emerging markets - lessons from Russia with Hasan Malik

would now have control over a global market, a Socialist market.[89] Global financial policy changed and so did the flow of capital. The old privately owned banks faced competition from the jointly owned new "global" banks.[90] Marx's ideas were, after all, about global cooperation.

> In short, the Communists everywhere support every revolutionary movement against the existing social and political order of things. The Communists (...) openly declare that their ends can be attained only by the forcible overthrow of all existing social conditions.[91]

> Of course, in the beginning, this cannot be effected except by means of despotic inroads on the rights of property, and ... further inroads upon the old social order.[92]

Even humanitarian financial aid to the Russian population, sent from the United States, went to the Bolsheviks, who continued by all means to build the Soviet communist state. By 1928, the Soviets were back on their feet, with the help of European and American investors. According to Anthony Sutton, financial support continued for another 60 years or so.[93]

A more detailed example of the oligarchs' involvement is the Red Cross campaign. After extensive correspondence between the Communist revolutionaries and their economic allies, it is discovered that the Communists' advantage has come to Moscow but no further. It is then

89 The Best Enemies Money Can Buy: An Interview with Prof Antony C. Sutton (early 1980s)
90 "Bankers & Bolsheviks": an interview with Hassan Malik
91 Manifesto of the Communist Party. IV "Position of the Communists in Relation to the Various Existing Opposition Parties"
92 Manifesto of the Communist Party. II "Proletarians and Communists"
93 The Best Enemies Money Can Buy: An Interview with Prof Antony C. Sutton (early 1980s)

decided to support the Communist troops once again - in secret, using the Red Cross as a cover. The Red Cross, a charitable organisation, is initially opposed to this mission, but is persuaded, as many of those involved come from the Wall Street establishment. The campaign brings together bankers, businessmen, doctors, lawyers - funded by, among others, William Boyce Thomson, owner of shares in the Chase Manhattan Bank Federal Service System, the bank founded by Rockefeller.

The mission is to be there to assist the Bolshevik revolution - using the Red Cross as a pretext. It brings over $1,000,000 from the US to Russia so that the military coup can go ahead and the Bolsheviks can take over more than just Moscow. Pressure is also put on the US government to send arms to the revolution, which is done in 1918. Trotsky sends letters to the US government appealing for American instructors to train the new Russian army. In this way, they have a common enemy - aristocratic, cultural Russia, which they see as an opponent of international socialism. Similarly, socialist reforms break out elsewhere in the world.

In 1918, the Bolsheviks control only part of Russia, with non-communist troops still holding out in St Petersburg. In addition to substantial financial support, the US government deploys American soldiers to guard the Trans-Siberian railway. The directive is to 'hold' the railway until the Bolsheviks can take over. In 1919, the New York Times writes in a headline: "At last the Bolsheviks have taken the railway". The same article also thanked the American army for its efforts.[94] However, opposition arises within the growing number of communists. Some 70,000 Bolsheviks start calling themselves 'Greens' when they realise that the Communists have sold out to American corporations. The Greens switch sides and instead fight alongside the White Army.[95]

94 The Best Enemies Money Can Buy: An Interview with Prof Antony C. Sutton
    (early 1980s)
95 Antony C. Sutton - The Bolshevik Revolution Speech (1976)

Now the construction of the factories begins. Millions of Russians, who opposed to the Marxist regime are sacrificed in labour camps as the industries grow. Most of the production comes from the big companies and investors. The mining tools and metal processes come from Joy Manufacturing. All the synthetic fabric processing and industrial technology for nuclear weapons likewise comes from outsiders. Trains come from General Electrics. Aircraft engines come from Rolls Royce. Ship hulls are also made in the West. Technology from IBM, Dunlop, Standard Oil, General Electric, Ford, Douglas Aircraft all contribute in one way or another.[96] They don't just export to the Soviet Union. They also sponsor Communist parties around the world. Averell Harriman, Almond Hammer and Julius Hammer - members of Wall Street's top echelon, are all leaders of rising communist parties in the US.[97]

Bolsheviks and National Socialists

What the Wall Street Elite at the time does not realises is that it is sponsoring a revolution resulting in extermination, during which millions of people are disappearing in horrific conditions, which is going on both before and after the Second World War. The survivors were never allowed either to publicly acknowledge the ruthless atrocities or to heal their wounds, thus, much of the Soviet persecution has faded from public memory - unlike the Nazi persecution, where the victims have received more extensive redress, including holding those responsible to account and honouring the victims with monuments, books and an accurate account of history. There is a big difference in the way the outside world has treated the survivors,

96 Ibid
97 Ibid

77

inspite of the similarities between the persecutions in Nazi Germany and the Soviet Union.

The Soviet Union is the first communist nation in the world to not only draw inspiration from Marx, but to fully incorporate Karl Marx's communist theories into the whole of society - and is essentially a social experiment. Yet it is not so different from its European neighbours: one of the Communists' aims is to create a new human, a better ideal, similar to what the National Socialist government intends. The 'new' socialist and communist human being that appears in propaganda images around the world, is not unlike the Nazi human being. The common position is that 'natural' human is inherently inadequate and that there is great potential to make him perfect. The Nazis want healthy, beautiful, blond and happy people. That is the original goal, as Alfred Rosenberg tells us during the Nuremberg trials, and part of their utopian paradise. The project fails in Germany, as does the Soviet new human.

In both cases, millions of innocent people die instead. What many people don't realise is that violence and death was what Marx and Engels envisaged when they laid out the instructions for the socialist revolution.

The indispensable violence

Marx and Engels have had a major impact on the political structure of the 20th century and are recognised as historical authorities in educational institutions around the world. But how do they actually relate to mass murder, war and violence? Writing in 1849 in the Neue Rheinische Zeitung about class war, Engels argues that genocide is inevitable and a necessary evil:

> The next world war will result in the disappearance from the face of the earth not only of reactionary (those who hinder a revolu-

tion, f.a) classes and dynasties, but also of entire reactionary peoples. And that, too, is a step forward.[98]

Engels argued that this extermination of certain groups of the population is a step forward. Marx further writes that the inevitable violence needed to ensure a revolution would be made more effective by "revolutionary terror":

> There is only one way in which the murderous death agonies of the old society and the bloody birth of the new society can be shortened, simplified and concentrated, and that way is revolutionary terror.[99]

Not only do Marx and Engels accept genocide as a viable option, but they believe that cultures that are not advanced enough to carry out a revolution should be destroyed for this very reason. Backward societies, or as Engels called them, "popular waste products", "völkerabfelle" and populations that were, according to him, "two steps behind in development", "could not", according to Engels, carry out a revolution - because of their "inability".

> These remnants of a nation, ruthlessly trampled underfoot by the course of history, (...) these remnants of nations, will always be and remain the fanatical bearers of counter-revolution until they are completely exterminated or denationalised, just as their very existence is a protest against a great historical revolution.[100]

98 Friedrich Engels, "The Magyar Struggle," first published in Neue Rheinische Zeitung No. 194, January 13, 1849.
99 Karl Marx, "The Victory of the Counter-Revolution in Vienna," Neue Rheinische Zeitung No. 136, November 1848.
100 Friedrich Engels, "The Hungarian Question" (Neue Rheinische Zeitung) 1848/49

Marx and Engels are not the only ones to call for violence. Lenin said in 1917: "The state is an instrument for coercion ... We want to organise violence in the name of the interests of the workers."[101] Heavily influenced by the ideology of Marx and Engels, Lenin writes that revolutionaries have the right to exercise "organised violence" in the name of the workers. Violence is even, according to the communist politician Dzerzhinsky in 1918 - "indispensable".[102]

> The public and the press misunderstand the character and tasks of our Commission. We stand for organised terror - this should be frankly stated - being absolutely indispensable in current revolutionary conditions.[103]

This violence becomes an integral part of the Soviet regime's methods and continues to be practised during the years of famine in Russia and the 'Holodomor', the mass extermination in Ukraine. The strategy is the same. Between 1937 and 1941, over 10,000,000 people are murdered in Russia.[104] Contrary to the human rights of the UN Charter, adopted in 1948, Communist leaders had the perspective that organised violence was an effective tool long after the end of the Second World War. The philosopher and senior Soviet politician Leon Trotsky wrote as late as 1940:

> Under all conditions, well-organised violence seems (...) the shortest distance between two points.[105]

---

101 Vladimir I. Lenin, quoted in George Leggett, *The Cheka: Lenin's Political Police*, Oxford University Press, 1987

102 Documentary: George Watson, Professor at Cambridge University, The Soviet story, 2008

103 Felix Dzerzhinsky, press interview in early June 1918, quoted in Leggett, *The Cheka*

104 Documentary: Natalia Lebedeva. Historian, "The Soviet Story", 2008

105 Leon Trotsky, "Stalin - *An Appraisal of the Man and his Influence*", unfinished manuscript published in 1941

A mutual admiration society

Apart from organised violence, there were several points on which the National Socialists considered themselves equal to their communist comrades. Goebbels himself said in a newspaper interview that Lenin was the idol of the National Socialists and that only Hitler was greater than him, and that the differences between Nazism and Communism - are small. [106]

> National Socialism derives from the pure idea that characterises it; national resolution from bourgeois tradition; vital, creative socialism from the teaching of Marxism.[107]

> What has been overlooked throughout history is that the Nazis were also inspired by Marx and Engels. Hitler says that his Nazism was based on the ideology of Karl Marx as a doctrine and that he learnt a lot from Marx.[108]

Traces of these similarities can be seen in Nazi election posters and campaigns. The hammer and sickle are used in propaganda images, symbolising the Nazi ideology.

> The hammer will once more become the symbol of the German worker and the sickle the sign of the German peasant.[109]

At the outset, the Communists and Nazis are not rivals but see themselves as allies. In the Soviet Union, they consider themselves to be striving for international socialism, while in Germany they consider themselves to be striving for national socialism.

Just like Victorian England, the Germans want to

106 New York Times in November 1924
107 Hanns Johst interview with in *Frankforter Volksblatt* January 27, 1934,
108 Documentary: "The Soviet Story", 2008, George Watson, Professor at Cambridge University
109 Adolf Hitler, May Day speech in Berlin, May 1, 1934

bring their national socialism to the world, as a form of imperialism. Hitler wants to make Germany what he calls: "Mistress of the earth".

> "Had the German people possessed that hard-like unity which served other nations so well", says Hitler in his book, "The German Reich would today be the mistress of the Earth".[110]

The mindset is reminiscent of the philosophy and claims of the ancient Chinese emperors - the same emperors who sat on the imperialist throne of China for a millennium during the 'Middle Kingdom'.

What is not always clear from history books is that Hitler was thus a leftist, a socialist at the root of his ideology, and was also supported by the left. One of those who supported Hitler wholeheartedly was the writer Bernard Shaw. He wrote that the left was well aware that Hitler would kill, and supported Hitler - because he dared to use violence. As a leftist, Shaw supported Mussolini, Hitler and Stalin:

> This remark may puzzle readers who are aware of Shaw's fervent enthusiasm for Soviet Communism. Actually there is no contradiction, no deliberate paradox in Shaw's attitude. He admired Hitler and Stalin, just as he had admired Mussolini, because these men were trying to get something done and because they had all got rid of the "pseudo-democratic" party system - that "unparalleled engine for preventing anything being done." For G.B.S. dictatorship was "the only way in which government can accomplish anything."[111]

110 Congressional Record: Proceedings and Debates of the second session of thisvety-fifth Congress of The United State of America, Volume 82 part 1, November 13, to December 7, 1937 - United States. Congress
111 H. M. Geduld, "Bernard Shaw and Adolf Hitler," pp 11-20. 1961

Shaw was inspired by the National Socialists' views on how some people were considered 'useless' and could not contribute to society. Bernard Shaw even called for the invention of a gas that killed painlessly.[112] - 10 years later, Zyklon B, the 'humane gas', is invented.

We will save our brothers

A former Soviet agent revealed that the Gestapo visited Russia in the 1930s to study concentration camps and their organisation. In Russia, they had already existed - for 20 years.

A few years later, in 1938, Germany and the Soviet Union organise a secret meeting in Krakow to discuss the 'Jewish question'. The minutes of the meeting are signed by both the National Socialist and Communist sides. The document states that all Semitic people, shamans, clairvoyants, dwarfs, anyone with physical defects, crooked, poor, would be eliminated by the KGB and Gestapo. A large part of the Jewish population tries to flee Germany to Russia but Stalin sends them back at the border. At the same time, persecution of Jews also increases in the Soviet Union. The Russians 'deliver' many Jews and other 'undesirables' to the Germans. Leon Trotsky, who now warns the world about Stalin's anti-Semitism and the co-operation between the KGB and the Gestapo, is murdered shortly afterwards.

The general belief that claims history in the West is that all the war crimes of the Second World War were committed by the Nazi Germans and that the Soviet Union has little or no culpability in what happened. The atrocities that took place in the Soviet Union have been more or less covered up and the Bolshevik war criminals have been let off the hook. Soviet officers who had shot 20,000 unarmed people were considered to

112 Bernard Shaw, The Listener 7 Feb 1934

have performed a great deed and, instead of punishment, they received high pensions, carreers and medals.

(*The following section is taken from two lectures, see reference below*)[113]

The pact document did not only contain directives for the mass murder of "undesirable elements" in society. The secret pact, written on a piece of A4 paper, declares that Germany and Russia are dividing Poland, Finland, and all the Baltic states between Moscow and Berlin. Internally, the division is called a "terrorist reorganisation", even though it involves several military interventions of the most terrible kind. Despite the fact that 40 million people are affected by this single A4 piece of paper, Stalin and Hitler choose to keep the pact - secret.

Russia, a country rich in natural resources, promises in the document to assist Germany with natural resources in exchange for finished products, such as weapons and the latest military technology. Additional documents, consisting of drawings of manufacturing processes, finished weapons, descriptions of raw materials and resources - categorise and even *decide* the war. Without the very specific exchange of assets between the Soviet Union and the National Socialists, the war would be impossible to launch. Hitler and Stalin plan all their military objectives based on the opportunities the Pact gives them.[114]

The landmark agreement between the Soviet Union and Germany is thus the reason why World War II started at all. Without this agreement, events would probably have

113 1. Discussion by Roger Moorhouse and Norman Davies on the 75th anniversary of the Soviet attack on Poland, accompanying "The Devils' Alliance" book launch. 17 Sep 2014 at the Embassy of the Republic of Poland in London. 17 Sep 2014 at the Embassy of the Republic of Poland in London.

2. Roger Moorhouse - Hitler and Stalin: the Forgotten Relationship Between the Two Superpowers of WWII, 2 January 2020. Muzeum II Wojny Światowej w Gdańsku (Museum of the Second World War in Gdansk)

114 Ibid

been very different. Both in the West and in the Soviet Union, these events and their significance are excluded from the historical narrative. The Pact and its enormous impact on the Second World War do not appear in history books, except possibly in small notices, despite attempts in the West to publicise large parts of the document as early as 1946, under the name "A Secret Protocol". The Soviet reaction was to claim that the protocol was a forgery. They denied that the Soviets had anything to do with the war in 1939-41 and claimed that the Soviet Union was completely neutral during this time.

The fact that the war did not start until 1941 is still widely believed - both in the Soviet Union and in the United States. This is despite all the victims of the first years. In the United States, the war is still claimed to have started in 1941 - at Pearl Harbor. Anything before that is seen as mere 'preparation' for war - despite the massive war crimes committed during those two years.[115] In the Soviet Union, anything said against the USSR's public version of history is labelled anti-Soviet propaganda and the Gulag is presented as 'popular labour in a growing industry'. The pact lasts a full 22 months, in favour of both the Communists and National Socialists.[116]

War breaks out a week after the document is signed, and in 1939 the two powers attack Poland - Stalin famously saying 'we will save our brothers'. Instead, one and a half million Poles are deported to Siberia, and as many to the concentration camps built by the Germans. The Red Army and the SS are thus fighting on the same side. The Communists invade parts of the Balkans and Arabia - through deportation, execution and perse-

---

115 Discussion by Roger Moorhouse and Norman Davies on the 75th anniversary of the Soviet attack on Poland, accompanying "The Devils' Alliance" book launch. 17 Sep 2014 at the Embassy of the Republic of Poland in London. 17 Sep 2014 at the Embassy of the Republic of Poland in London.
116 Ibid

cution. In the Western narrative, the Nazis are accused of committing the worst war crimes - not the Communists.

In reality, in the 1940s, the Communist parties in the United States, England and France take the news very hard when the pact - becomes public knowledge for a short period of time. Party members are unable to cope with the guilt and, in some places, a suicide wave breaks out. The announcement of the pact is such a major event in world history that it is remembered as 'the axis of the earth rotating'. As Stalin put it: "Together with Germany we are unstoppable".[117] Yet the Pact is now completely forgotten in the West.

Drawing attention to this hidden part of history does not in any way exonerate Hitler. There is a black and white thinking in the modern Western debate that needs to be worked out; just because you criticize one side does not mean you are in favour of the other. Both the National Socialists and the Soviet Union were wrong and were the most terrible European regimes of the 20th century.[118]

A reduced number of pupils

In Ukraine, an independent republic at the time, protests against Marxism and the Soviet takeover emerge. To quell the uprisings, the Soviet Union stops sending food and other supplies to Ukraine in 1932-33, cutting off all food supply chains to and from abroad. No one is allowed to enter or leave the country. All food production and cultivation stops. This is the beginning of one of the most horrific man-made disasters in human history.

At the beginning, people eat from the saved resources they have left. Then the Soviet army also confiscates

117 Ibid
118 ibid

the stored food.[119] Ukraine's population begins to die of hunger. Fewer children return to school after the holidays and the number of pupils in the first and second grades is continuously decreasing, as can be seen from the figures in the teachers' documentation and attendance records that remain from this time. The reason is that pupils are dying of starvation. Instead of providing help, the Soviet government sanction soldiers and other volunteers, who are assigned to help carry corpses to mass graves. The pay is one piece of bread per corpse. When foreign actors try to send food to the starving people, this is also stopped and the Moscow leadership claims that there is no famine and that the rumours are - bourgeoisie propaganda. Only in 1989, at the fall of communism, does the Russian government admit that 3.5 million people died of starvation in Ukraine during the pre-war period, what would later be called the Holodomor. The real figures are about 10,000,000:[120]

> Professor of Kyiv Shevchenko University Volodymyr Serhiychuk is a Chair of the International Association of Holodomor Researchers competed an impressive work on studying of archives and evidences of the period 1920 - 1940. In his presentation he persuasively demonstrates that generally-accepted number of Holodomor victims is significantly underestimates the true picture. His study is showing that the number of Ukrainians who died in Holodomor has to be at least doubled up to the value of 7 million on Ukrainian

119 Norman Davies, Cambridge University. Professor at the Jagiellonian University, professor emeritus at University College London, a visiting professor at the Collège d'Europe, and an honorary fellow at St Antony's College, Oxford.
120 Volodymyr Ivanovych Serhiychuk: Doctor of Historical Sciences, Professor, Head of the Department of Ukrainian History at Taras Shevchenko National University of Kyiv, Head of the Educational and Professional Programme of Advanced Studies of Foreign Languages for the Bachelor's Degree "World Ukrainians in Civilisational Progress". http://serhijchuk.unicyb.kiev.ua/

territory and 3.5 more million outside
Ukraine.[121]

The left begins to oppose Nazism in the early 1940s,
believing that by this time Hitler has destroyed
socialism beyond all recognition. Gassing people based
on their nationality is not forgivable. However, people
protest less and are more forgiving when the selection
is based on class.

In the Soviet Union, people are executed, left to
starve, and everything is officially blamed on the
class war and the class of the victims. But unofficial-
ly, class plays a minor role. If the enemy or opponent
doesn't surrender - regardless of class - they must be
executed. There were special sections in prisons where,
under the Communist regime, prisoners were shot -
without trial. Up to 100 could be shot every night.
Only 50 years later, families and relatives learnt
where the victims' mass graves were located. All geo-
graphical regions of Russia have mass graves, showing
the scale of the mass murder and the number of victims
- figures that can otherwise be difficult to understand
and accept.

Millions of Ukrainian children become homeless
because of missing parents and start begging on the
streets. Stalin decides that children can be shot from
the age of 12 upwards, on the grounds that otherwise
they will not look good in front of tourists.[122] The
Ukrainian gold and valuables are confiscated, no one
knows where it goes - there is no evidence left of
this. These possessions are taken from the victims in
the same horrific way that gold and valuables were confiscated in Nazi Germany.

On the other hand, there is documentation showing
where the Ukrainian population's food went - the food

121 Documentary: "The Soviet story", 2008, Professor Volodymyr Serhiychuk's
    Holodomor Research (YouTube)
122 Documentary film: "The Soviet Story", 2008

that had been planted by themselves. All the food, grain and seeds confiscated – is exported to the West. In 1930, Ukraine's exports suddenly go up – to as much as 2000% and stay that way for three years. News of Ukraine's terrible plight reaches the Western newspapers, which report on what is happening, but to no help. Aid is not getting through and the famine continues.

A staggering 7,000,000 Ukrainian men, women and children are exterminated in just one year, in 1933. It is the most efficient extermination humanity has ever witnessed. The event is known as *the Holodomor,* Голодомор, and the term '*holodom moryty*' means 'to inflict death by hunger'. The Ukrainian verb 'moryty', морити means 'to poison, to drive to exhaustion or to torment'. The grammatically perfective form of moryty is zamoryty, "to kill or drive to death".[123] The deceased victims of the Holodomor and their descendants have received no compensation, apology or redress from the Communist regime, despite the fact that the Holodomor was as bad or worse then Holocaust in Europe. The lack of redress is so widespread, that the Holodomor is not even recognised as a word in the Word writing program, while the word Holocaust is in the digital vocabulary.

After the end of the Second World War, it will be a long time before the truth about the terrible war crimes in Ukraine comes out. In 1945, the Allies win the Second World War and after the end of the war, Stalin does not destroy the camps, where the cruel conditions drive many prisoners to their deaths, as happens with the concentration camps around Europe. Instead, the Communists continue to use the camps for a long time. And the reign of terror does not stop, neither in Russia nor in the Baltic countries. They

---

123 https://sv.wikipedia.org/wiki/Holodomor

confiscate flats and houses from Baltic citizens and move them from their homes to concentration camps in Siberia. Instead, 'communist war heroes' are moved into their flats, which are used as 'holiday apartments'. Similarly, communism continues to claim its victims in the 1950s, 60s, 70s and 80s. Even in the 21st century, soldiers who served the communists are considered heroes and respectable veterans. Most have received high pensions and have been honoured. Their fate has never been investigated, despite the countless documents, documentaries and books that have been published and released on the subject. Europe has long been dependent on Russian natural resources such as gas and oil and petrol. Is this a reason to why the war crimes of the Communists never have been questioned?

The invisible ones

In 1970, a massive revelation occurs when writer Aleksandr Solzhenitsyn informs the West for the first time about the Soviet Union's practices in detail.[124] His heroism is celebrated and he is honoured in a speech at a prestigious Western university in 1978:

> The powerful directness of his (Solzhenitsyn's) work which so clearly reflects his own experiences illuminates for us the perils we court if we do not take heed and cherish the rights and privileges we enjoy.[125]

But the road there is long and dangerous. Solzhenitsyn is an ex-convict, a survivor of the Gulag in Siberia. After serving his sentence, he is assigned by the communist regime to carry out a project for the government that will give him access to letters and documentation from Gulag survivors. He decides to

124 Discussion by Roger Moorhouse and Norman Davies
125 Alexander Solzhenitsyn, "A World Split Apart", 8 June 1978, Harvard University

compile it into a book, even though he knows how risky it is to save testimonies. In 1965, two other writers are arrested on suspicion of depicting the events at the Gulag. The KGB suspects that their story will be sent to the West and deports them to Siberia. All trace of them is then lost. It's a very dangerous project and Solzhenitsyn goes to great lengths to hide the various chapters in different places. But he is helped by a group of people who become close to him. They eventually start calling themselves 'the invisibles' and are a handful of quite ordinary citizens: a photographer, a bookbinder, relatives of the survivors, an interpreter. The prisoners' accounts are written down in various notebooks and Solzhenitsyn prepares a secret hiding place at a friends house in the countryside to finish the book.

This friend and the other 'invisibles' risk their lives for the project. If the KGB catches them, the punishment is very severe. Solzhenitsyn and the others make a habit of changing buses and trams every time they go on errands related to the book, to avoid being followed. All the parts of the book are scattered in different places. When the book is finally finished, all the chapters are gathered for the first time at the bookbinder's - only for a few hours. In total, three volumes with four copies of each, one of the "invisibles" finally manages to get out. The bookbinder and his wife stand by the window, praying that nothing will happen to her as she walks out into the street below. "I am eternally grateful to them. Without them I could not have done this. One man alone cannot fight against such a system." Solzhenitsyn later says of his friends' tremendous efforts. At the same time, it is a book he feels he owes to the victims to write.[126]

And if I'm writing this book it is solely from a sense of obligation because to many

126 Documentary: Secret story: The Gulag Archipelago, 2008

91

stories and recollections have accumulated in my hands and I cannot allow them to perish. I don't expect to see it in print anywhere with my own eyes and I have little hope that those who managed to drag their bones out of the Archipelago will ever reed it.[127]

A photographer helps to take a picture of the finished manuscript on a microfilm. In 1968, a political conference is held in Moscow. One of the interpreters, who is translating at the conference, has had previous contact with the 'invisibles' and 'Natalia' approaches him a second time. She asks "Would you have the courage to take the volume?" to which the interpreter replies yes. He then doesn't sleep for four nights, worried about how to secretly smuggle the film out. They decide a secret meeting place. There, the film is handed over by yet another person. On the way in the car, they drive past KGB headquarters while the microfilm is hidden in a jar of caviar. The operation succeeds, but Solzhenitsyn does not dare to release the book for publication right then and there.

In the West, they read other, previously published books written by the author and intend to honour Solzhenitsyn with the Nobel Prize. This proves to be very difficult and the committee fails time and time again. Eventually, with the help of a Swedish journalist, they succeed.[128] Stig Fredrikson secretly sets up several meetings with the author. But after the Nobel Committee's courtship, KGB surveillance of Solzhenitsyn and his friends increases. They are now being bugged.[129] In 1973, Elizabeth Varanjanskaya, who has the latest version of the book in print, is arrested. It is a version that they initially decide to burn. Elizabeth, who cannot bring herself to burn the book, is persecu-

127 ibid
128 ibid
129 ibid

ted for several months. She is 66 years old when she is arrested. The KGB are ruthless and get hold of the copy of the yet unreleased book. She is found hanged soon after, with stab wounds. This hits Solzhenitsyn hard, and in his grief he realises he must publish the book because otherwise the enormous efforts of his friends will have been in vain. A French publisher agrees to translate and publish the book. Only three people at the publishers know what is going to happen. They start by publishing it in Russian and the book is smuggled into Russia where it is read during reading chains. Because of the risk of being arrested and sent to Siberia, it is borrowed for only one night and then passed on to the next reader.[130]

The KGB steps up its attack and begins to arrest and detain the others of the 'invisibles'. Solzhenitsyn is exposed and both the media and the KGB are brought to action. The newspapers calls him as a traitor, describing the crimes he has committed. In a final meeting, he says goodbye to Stig Fredrikson and kisses him in the Russian way, on both cheeks. He is arrested the same day in 1974. They interrogate him but by a happy coincidence he is not killed. The KGB realise that if they kill him, there is a risk that the foreign media will find out, proving that everything he writes is true. Instead, they expel him from the country. However, his wife and children must stay.[131]

> I have done my duty to those who perished. Gives me relief and peace of mind. The facts have been destined for annihilation. They've been trampled on, drowned, burned, reduced to dust. But now they are alive in print and no one can ever erase them.[132]

130 ibid
131 ibid
132 ibid

The world learns the truth about the Gulag concentration camps and the Holodomor, but the matter is hushed up and silenced. None of the Allied countries speak out against Soviet rule or demand reparations for all the victims who perished. Despite the struggle of Solzhenitsyn and his friends and the widespread distribution of the book, the myth of 'good' communism lives on. The hammer and sickle is used as a communist symbol in left-wing politics and statues of Marx and Engels can be seen decorating streets and squares all over the world, despite all the victims. Had it been Hitler and the Nazis, the symbol and the statues would have been long gone, which is concrete proof that the Communists have escaped the consequences of their crimes. Instead, the Communists are admired by the Western left - worldwide.

> The communist regime in the East could stand and grow due to the enthusiastic support from an enormous number of Western intellectuals who felt a kinship and refused to see communism's crimes. And when they no longer could do so, they tried to justify them. In our Eastern countries, communism has suffered a complete ideological defeat; it is zero and less than zero. But Western intellectuals still look at it with interest and with empathy, and this is precisely what makes it so immensely difficult for the West to withstand the East.[133]

In the West, despite all the above, the Soviet Union is considered one of the Allies in the Second World War. In the general debate, people want to believe that Stalin was on the side of the good guys. They are happy

---

133 Alexander Solzhenitsyn, "A World Split Apart", 8 June 1978, Harvard University

to go along with the general opinion that the 'good guys' are the British, the Americans and the Russians, while the 'bad guys' are the Nazis. This moral manoeuvre, which came into effect after the Second World War, still has a strong hold on public education. Instead, the truth is that one ruthless despot fought another - equally ruthless despot. World War II was not a war of the 'bad guys' against the 'good guys', but a war between the 'bad guys' and the equally 'bad guys'. The public's misconception is difficult to change or replace with the more truthful whole. The perception is that there is only one 'bad guy' and that is - Hitler.[134]

Marxism instead of religion

> And the new order socialism will triumph by overwhelming Christianity through institutions.[135]

Antonio Gramci, quoted above, whose ideas was infiltrating many institutions, universities and media in many countries, understands that the best way to carry out a revolution is at the cultural level.[136] In societies all over the world, the 20th century saw a gigantic transformation - religion and spirituality were replaced by submission and worship - of the state and its leaders. Even in socialist Sweden, religion is being replaced by politics:

> In 1969, an official in the Social Democratic Party said that reforms had to be implemented with a speed limit to avoid opposition; kings and chancellors in the 17th and 18th centuries acted on exactly the same

134 Hitler-Stalin Pact: Discussion by Roger Moorhouse and Norman Davies, 17 Sep 2014 at the Embassy of the Republic of Poland in London
135 Antonio Gramci from Uncle Tom II 2022, reprinted in Antonio Gramci, 'Audacia d Fide' in Avanti! Reprint In Sotto la Mole, 1916-1920, p. 148.
136 Uncle Tom II: An American Odyssey,2022, Carol Swain

principle. The Reformation took place in Sweden over the course of a century, at a leisurely and comfortable pace, but always with the same end goal in mind: "A country with one Lord and one King" to quote a Swedish bishop of the time, Nicolaus Olai Bothniensis at the Uppsala meeting in 1593: "Now Sweden is one man and we all have one Lord and one God".[137]

When the communists start blowing up, burning down and destroy churches, the Marxist leaders are instead elevated to saints with a new prophetic content in order to swindle the obedience of the people. Marxism's replacement of God with the state, is part of the process - which was intended by Marx. On large propaganda posters and banners, communist leaders appear as popes or saints. It is as if Nietzsche asks the question and Marx answers it.

> Because what socialism promises is a utopia
> It promises heaven on earth. A peace that the
> world has not yet known and if we hunker down
> and come together all in pursuit of this hea-
> ven on earth, that we can accomplish that.[138]

They worship political leaders in the spirit of communism and socialism; the same worship then passes to film stars and sports stars in the spirit of consumerism - with the same respect and reverence that people did shown God, religion and the sacred for thousands of years. "...They desire to place themselves in the place of God."[139] If one did not know better, one would have thought that Communism had exploited people's faith in the higher, the faith that humanity always had, a sort of place in the human spirit that had

137 Roland Huntford, "Blind Sweden" (The New Totalitarians), 1971
138 Uncle Tom II: An American Odyssey,2022, Chad Jackson
139 Uncle Tom II: An American Odyssey,2022, Virgil Walker

a potential. This same 'potential' was then filled by PR consultants and big business, with the idolisation of the rich and famous, and the need for products - to make people spend more.

> As humanism in its development became more and more materialistic, it made itself increasingly accessible to speculation and manipulation by socialism and then by communism. So that Karl Marx was able to say that "communism is naturalized humanism."[140]

Even the true meaning of the holidays was forgotten, replaced and celebrated in a new way as religion is increasingly replaced by consumerism. In the 1940s, the nature of the holidays changes, merging instead with the windows of shopping centres. Halloween and Christmas are old traditional holidays hijacked by the consumer society, while 'Valentine's Day' is created by corporations to encourage consumers to shop more.

In Germany, Hitler also wanted Christianity to completely vanish from the country, just as it had done in Russia. In schools, everything religious that children took part in was to be replaced by a worship of Hitler. The following children's song, sung in German schools in the 1930s, is a clear example:

> We are the happy Hitler youth
>
> We have no need for Christian virtue
>
> For Adolf is our intercessor and our redeemer
>
> No priest no evil one can keep us from feeling like Hitlers children
>
> No Christ do we follow but Host Vessel!

140 Alexander Solzhenitsyn, "A World Split Apart", 8 June 1978, Harvard University

away from incense and holy vessel
pots.[141]

The National Socialists, on the other hand, used religious elements for the party's own benefit - to increase the people's allegiance and admiration. They
marched through Germany in constant parades, with flags
flying high in the air, each banner covered with a
black Swastika. The Swastika was also used on Soviet
roubles and Red Army clothing, as well as on Communist
state documents from 1917 to 1922, before the Germans
took it over. The Nazi symbol or Swastika comes from
India and originally has a positive meaning. The Swastika, which in many parts of Indian culture represents
hope, peace, happiness, prosperity and success, has
been given a completely different meaning by the West.
The symbol has been exploited for almost a century by
the Nazi political ideology; restoring the symbol to
its correct meaning would only be fair. Indians have
every right to reclaim this sacred symbol, and the
cultural and political elite in the West can no longer
use the Swastika by fortifying it with a Nazi meaning.
Even among the American Indiginous people, this symbol
can be found, also loaded with positive meaning. In
addition, the widely distributed Swastika is found in a
variety of cultures, engraved on historical artefacts
and objects, including Greece in 800 BC, the Minoan
culture in 3000 BC, Italy in 700 BC and Africa in 1400
BC.[142]

The word Swastika comes from Sanskrit: स्वस्तिक, roman-
ised: *svastika*, meaning "conducive to well-being". In
Hinduism, the right-facing symbol, clockwise, 卐 is ca-
led Swastika and symbolises Surya, 'sun', prosperity
and happiness, while the left-facing symbol, counter-
clockwise, 卍 is called Sauvastika and symbolises night

141 https://www.historyonthenet.com/what-did-hitler-believe-in
142 https://en.wikipedia.org/wiki/Swastika

or tantric aspects of Kali.[143] There is an urgent need to liberate this great Indian symbol from Nazi ideology and it should count as a violation of UN human rights not to have done so already - worldwide. Australia has begun a process of restoration by banning Nazis from using the symbol. It is however allowed to be used artistically and in connection with the practice of the Indian religion.

---

143 https://en.wikipedia.org/wiki/Swastika

художник Ю. Юров

"Badges worn by the Kalmyk formations of the Red Army in 1919"

I play to win and if it looks like I've lost its only because its not over yet

And the great dragon was cast out that old serpent called the devil and satan which decieved the whole world

Revelation 12:9

Since ancient times and the beginning of the world, all societies had people in positions of power. Often, these rulers have been fully visible to their people, like kings, priests, emperors and nobles. However, their actions, due to their sometimes less honourable nature, have not always been as visible. This has not prevented the population from forming a relationship with their king, often based on a more or less realistic image.

With the decline of the monarchy, the increase in population and the growth of cities, began a major shift in the relationship between rulers and their subjects. A curtain fell, relegating the leading position to a political sphere in the background, protecting the ruling elite. Now you no longer needed to be crowned before thousands of spectators to have power. Instead of inheritance and blood - capital ruled, allowing the actors to become more and more anonymous.

The 20th century saw unprecedented growth in business and the birth of a global stock market. Entrepreneurs played an increasingly important role in the global economy. New concepts and terms were invented to facilitate the global market. And with it, the biggest companies were growing. The big business corporations and the state authorities started to co-operate more and more, and new laws were invented to promote this co-operation, which resulted in monopolies - and at the same time, the laws would prevent certain types of capital growth that could outcompete the monopoly.

> Defined by the Cambridge Dictionary, the "elite" are "those people or organisations that are considered the best or most powerful compared to others of a similar type."[144]

As their power and capital grew, the elites took on more and more responsibility. They began to form organisations and associations to organise a growing national and international economy. One of these organisations is called the Triateral Commission, an institution set up in 1973 to assist the world's most powerful.

Men we have never heard of

The Commission's representatives are made up of one-third members from the United States, one-third members from Asia and one-third members from Europe. The members, who have always held high-level economic or political positions in their own countries, gather at the Rockefellers Manhattan Bank in the United States, a bank that promotes global interests of the world. The basis of their mission is to develop and organise the international economy, which they themselves both establish and shape.

On its website, the Commission gives a fairly accurate picture of what it stands for:

> The Trilateral Commission is a global membership organisation that for decades has brought together senior policymakers, business leaders, and representatives of media and academe to discuss and propose solutions

144 https://dictionary.cambridge.org/dictionary/english/elite

103

to some of the world's toughest problems. Founded in 1973 by David Rockefeller, the Commission has long been an important venue to incubate ideas and form relationships across sectors and geographies.[145]

The Commission's work is sponsored by the Rockefeller and Ford Foundations, among others. The members, who enjoy the Commission's support, are world-famous and include President Jimmy Carter, Bill Clinton, Al Gore, Henry Kissinger and Carl Bildt. Jimmy Carter won a presidential election, thanks to the Commission's generous sponsorship of his campaign.

The Commission has a long-standing co-operation and partnership with the US government, as well as with other world governments; through financial support or politicians serving on the Commission, it helps shape laws and decisions. Many of its members sit in the US House of Representatives and other bureaucratic institutions based in Washington. George Bush SR was also a member of the Trilateral Commission. He has also expressed the objectives of the Commission in one of his public speeches and believes he speaks for all of humanity:

> What is at stake is more then one small country, it is a big idea a new world order where diverse nations are drawn together in common cause to achieve the universal aspirations of mankind.[146]

The Commission's task is to uphold the 'responsibility' that it has, due to its enormous capital, and to find ways to consolidate this responsibility in the outside world. Among other things, they see it as their task to 'influence' international relations and the global eco-

---

145 Triateral Commission website https://www.trilateral.org/about/

146 Bush SR, State of the union address, 29 Jan 1991

104

nomy. On the website, research reports are published continuously, discussing the current world situation. For a publicly unknown organisation, its members and initiators have a lot of power.

> Yet with changing times and the proliferation of similar groups, the leadership of the organisation - across its three pillars of North America, Europe, and Asia - has critically examined the Commission and instituted changes in order to rejuvenate the Commission and increase its impact. In particular, we have sharpened our mission and returned to our roots as a group of countries sharing common values and a commitment to the rule of law, open economies and societies, and democratic principles. We acknowledge that, today, our societies are grappling with difficult social, economic, technological, and political issues that are causing deep cleavages at home.
>
> These divisions are, to different extents, compromising the ability of individual countries - from the United States to Europe - to play the leadership roles they have long assumed in the international system. For this reason, the Commission has broadened its aperture to look at more internal issues, while at the same time focusing on the ability of the Commission to affect the unfolding of foreign policy and national security strategies.[147]

The media rarely write about this Commission. They are not often featured in news articles or news clips, despite their enormous capacity to shape the world. At the same time, several leaders of the biggest media groups are members of the Commission. The Chicago Sun

147 Triateral Commission https://www.trilateral.org/about/

Times is on board, as is Time Magazine. Mr Rockefeller, the Commission's founder, makes a statement himself during an internal meeting, thanking the newspapers for their discretion.

> We are grateful to the Washington Post, The New York Times, Time Magazine and other great publications whose directors have attended our meetings and respected their promises of discretion for almost forty years. It would have been impossible for us to develop our plan for the world if we had been subjected to the lights of publicity during those years. But, the world is now more sophisticated and prepared to march towards a world government. The supranational sovereignty of an intellectual elite and world bankers is surely preferable to the national auto-determination practised in past centuries.[148]

There is surprisingly little information to be found about the Commission, their mission, and their actual relationship with nations around the world. Although the members of the Tripartite Commission have long been active in world politics, they do not feature in the generally recognised historiography – nor in Universities, history books or school textbooks.

Instead, there is an official version that the public is familiar with, the one they learn in school, about parliament, government and democracy. But schoolchildren don't know about international commissions set up by corporate oligarchs with global interests. According to Professor Anthony Sutton, there is no coincidence behind this phenomenon:

> There is an Establishment history, an official history which dominates history text-

148 David Rockefeller, 1991, "Thanks Media for Covering NWO's arse".
https://rumble.com/v1xn8no-david-rockefeller-1991-thanks-media-for-covering-nwos-ass..html

books, trade publishing, the media and library shelf's. The official line always assumes that events such as wars, revolutions, scandals, assassinations, are more or less random, unconnected events. By definition events can NEVER be the result of a conspiracy, they can never result from premeditated planned group action.[149]

Why is the relationship between the civilian population and those in power uneven? One contributing factor may be that those behind today's ruling power - founded their capital and the modern feudal power structure at a time when the spirit of elitism was more permissible, accepted and perhaps even necessary?

David Rockefeller, one of the founders of the Tripartite Commission,[150] belongs to one of the richest families in the world. He and his family have built their fortune through the Standard Oil company. Through the Commission and in other ways, the Rockefellers are active in a number of political organisations, including the environmental movement. They have been criticised for a 'messiah complex' stemming from their association with the Baptist movement, due to their excessive involvement and continuous interference in a wide range of political, economic and international affairs.

In 1860, John D Rockefeller grows up in a poor family in the USA. His father is a snake oil salesman and embezzler who lives a dissolute life with women and alcohol. He himself grows up not smoking, not drinking, not dancing. Instead, he saves all his wages and invests wisely. His capital grows and he starts a business. As his business grows, he believes that the oil has been given to him - to create a better world. However, he is a ruthless businessman, knocking out many

149 Antony C Sutton, "America's Secret Establishment: An Introduction to the Order of Skull & Bones" ,1986
150 https://www.trilateral.org/about/

other businesses - in order to succeed and grow his own company, Standard Oil. The business grows, as does John's family, and soon it is one of the largest and richest companies in the United States.

During the 1930s, the family's co-operation with the US government begins and Rockefeller helps build the United Nations. An unofficial entity, the Council of Foreign Relations, is set up as a subsidiary body to assist the UN and further develop a global organisation. Rockefeller and other wealthy 'benefactors' and sponsors sit on the 'Council'.

It is a time when Wall Street's most ambitious are increasingly involved in politics. FDR - Roosevelt himself is related to a third of the Senate, his relatives are in high places as railway tycoons, bankers and heads of large corporations.[151] He himself sits on many boards, up to 20, of the largest financial associations and Wall Street firms. Other US presidents and leaders are also involved in corporate and financial affairs.

> We are governed, our minds are moulded, our tastes formed, our ideas suggested, largely by men we have never heard of. This is a logical results of the way our democratic society is organised. Vast numbers of human beings must co-operate in this manner if they are to live together as a smoothly functioning society (...) They govern us by their qualities of natural leadership, their ability to supply needed ideas and by their key position in the social structure. Whatever attitude one chooses to take toward this condition, it remains a fact that in almost every act of out daily life's, whether in the sphere of politics or business, in our social conduct or our ethical thinking, we are dominated by the relatively small number of per-

151 Anthony C Sutton, "Wall Street and FDR: The true story how Franklin D. Roosevelt colluded with Corporate America" 1975

sons - a trifling fraction of our hundred and twenty million - who understand the mental process and social patterns of the masses.[152]

The line between political and economic interests is blurring, with devastating consequences for some parts of the world. Before the Russian Revolution, the Russian Empire was a strong economic power to be reckoned with. With its vast natural resources and established monarchy and nobility, Russia is a strong competitor to European countries and the United States. At the turn of the century, imperial Russia was considered the greatest threat to Woodrow Wilson's United States. It had the latest technology, a growing industry and capital. But with the Russian Revolution, both Russia's industrial society and economy collapse. Woodrow Wilson and the US government choose not to assist the Tsar; instead, they contribute financially to the revolution, creating huge investment opportunities.[153] After the revolution, Russia becomes more economically fragile and the US and Europe gain the upper hand.

The same group of Wall Street tycoons who invested in the Bolshevik revolution are also investing in the construction of National Socialism in Germany. Through this, they want to establish a strong market in Central Europe. IG Farben, a German business empire, sponsored and owned by the American Standard Oil and CHEMNYCO, owns its own banks, coal mines, electrical factories, its own iron and steel industry and many companies. With their profits, they in turn sponsor the Nazis. At the end of the war, IG Farben faces penalties and sanctions for its sponsorship of the Nazis, unlike the American investors who face no consequences - at all. All go free, despite their close involvement in Nazi activities. CHEMNYCO, whose CEO in New York was Rudolph

152 Edward L Bernays "Propaganda", pages 9-10, 1928
153 Anthony C Sutton "Wall Street and the Bolshevik Revolution", 1974

Igner, is the brother of Max Igner, the CEO of the German IG Farben empire. [154]

After the Second World War, David Rockefeller, John Rockefeller's son, and other members of the family are given leadership positions in government and business. Negotiations are held on how to develop the UN and where to locate its headquarters. Mr Rockefeller proposed 'Kykuit', at the 'Rockefeller Estate', a privately owned piece of land where the family clan lives. But the UN said no to this. John D Jr then buys a piece of land in New York and donates it to the UN - which is accepted. The large UN skyscraper is then built there. The chief architect is personally employed by Rockefeller and sets up a number of buildings and institutions right next to the UN building. By this time, in the 1950s, Standard Oil is a huge global company. But even that can be improved and grow further.

In the United States, Rockefeller and Standard Oil are forced to negotiate business matters with each state. Instead, they want to facilitate their own business activities and avoid complicated regulations, while at the same time making it more difficult for their competitors. Standard Oil wants economic and political rules that are aligned and unifying - both within the United States and around the world. The same customised regulatory framework everywhere means more business and less competition.

One of the UN's main concerns at this time is the issue of nuclear weapons, considered a global threat. While reviewing the rules on nuclear weapons and international relations between countries, the Council of Foreign Relations reviews trade agreements and customs agreements for business activities - to bring about an adjustment and change in global economic conditions. Rockefeller establishes a strong link with the World Bank, including former Chase Manhattan Bank em-

154 Anthony C Sutton "Wall Street and the Rise of Hitler" - Antony Sutton, 1976

ployees. Several global movements and institutes are founded that work to break down economic and political barriers. Kykuit invites royalty from other countries when establishing contacts with the outside world.

The power of big business is moving from the local and regional level to the supranational global level, and economic democracy, which means the right to influence laws and decisions at a regional level, is slowly being destroyed and is disappearing more and more. Standard Oil is one of the first big global companies and has therefore been committed to internationalisation and globalisation. They have a strong interest in globalisation. The complicated global regulations, which Standard Oil has helped to create, make it more difficult for smaller local companies to grow. The regulations are complicated and it takes a lot of financial resources to be able to fulfil the requirements in the US, abroad and in Europe.

The same approach that was used with nuclear weapons and trade agreements is later used with other similar crises. The Tripartite Commission's website has research reports available that warn of different kinds of crises. The Commission's headquarters then comes up with various favourable economic solutions. They set an agenda for what the problem is, with the intention of solving it. At the same time, investment companies around the world recognise the agenda and invest accordingly, following the 'new' trends. The Commission is constantly creating these trends. With the help of the United Nations, it builds global economic co-operation while reviewing the political situation.

In the 1950s, an organisation called the American Committee for Uniting Europe is founded. The United States is very interested in creating a united Europe and therefore funds the committee in 1948. From the beginning, the project is seen as an experiment, a test of

111

what it is like to operate globally. Rockefeller is involved as a sponsor of the project, which later develops into the EU model we have today.

An offer they cant refuse

A characteristic of the elite class is that they move between higher positions without much difficulty. One example is Hillary Clinton, who was "First Lady" at first, then changed position to "Senator", and then to "Secretary of State". For the elite, it's all about the right connections in political circles and the right education - which Clinton has. During the 1970s in the US, she meets Marxist Saul Alinsky, whom she looks up to - he becomes a mentor to her, and she becomes radicalised. Alinsky's first tool in the theory of 'Community Organising' is to push from the outside in a revolution. Hillary herself believes in taking over and infiltrating from within.[155]

> And, her senior thesis was about Saul Alinsky. This was someone that she "greatly admired and that affected all of her philosophies subsequently", the former presidential candidate told in a speech.[156]

Saul Alinsky is a political inspiration for Marxists and the radical left, writing books in the 1960s on how the left and Marxism should infiltrate society and how to train party members to gain political ground - through various people manipulation techniques, similar to Bernays. As a young man, he flirted with the American Mafia, which may explain his relentless political tactics.

---

155 Documentary: Hillary's America, Dinesh D'Souza, 2016
156 Ben Carson Said Saul Alinsky Was Hillary Clinton's Hero. Who Was He? By Mahita GajananJuly 20, 2016 4:18 PM EDT https://time.com/4415300/ben-carson-saul-alinsky-hillary-clinton/

Saul Alinsky, mentor to Obama and Hillary, learnt his political lessons from the Al Capone mob in Chicago. Mobster Frank Nitti was impressed with Alinsky because he found Alinsky to be more ruthless and callous than he himself was.[157]

Obama, like Hillary, learnt the art of the shakedown from their political godfather, Saul Alinsky. Obama was teaching other community organisers how to extract money and power from corporations and the rich by (in the words of the Don Corleone) "making them an offer they can't refuse."[158]

Alinsky and Clinton become close and exchange letters. Hillary's academic work is about the Alinsky model, the one he describes in his book, 'Rules for Radicals'. She writes that she misses their conversations and he offers her a job straight out of college.

Alinsky became a mentor of sorts for Clinton and was the subject of her senior thesis at Wellesley College in 1969. Her academic paper was entitled, "'There Is Only the Fight...': An Analysis of the Alinsky Model. Clinton interviewed him for her paper, and the pair swapped letters with one another as well. In some of those letters obtained by the Washington Free Beacon, a then-23-year-old Clinton refers to Alinsky as Saul. She thanks him for his encouraging words and says she misses their "biennial conversations." "Hopefully we can have a good argument sometime in the near future," she concludes. In her 2003 memoir, "Living History," Clinton mentioned being of-

157 Dinesh D'Souza, "Stealing America, what my experience with criminal gangs taught me about Obama, Hillary, and the Democratic party", page 201, 2015
158 D'Souza, Dinesh, "Stealing America: what my experience with criminal gangs taught me about Obama, Hillary, and the Democratic party," page 202, 2015

fered a job by Alinsky after graduation, but turning it down in favour of law school.[159]

Barack Obama also follows the same educational path and becomes one of Alinsky's students. Obama even teaches Alinsky's "Community Organising" and the Marxist techniques that accompany Alinsky's theory, when he works in education. Saul Alinsky himself was a so-called "community organiser" early on. As a young man, he finds a way to rip off chain restaurants for food, and encourages his fellow students to do the same. They set up an organisation specialising in scamming restaurant food, while he receives a scholarship in criminology. He decides to study Capone and gets close to him, following him for several years. He is shown all the Mafia's operations and later writes that he learns a lot from the harsh, manipulative environment. It was there that he found the inspiration for his famous 'Rules for Radicals' book, which Hillary Clinton later wrote her essay on and which is used by left-wing politicians around the world.

> Saul Alinsky is the father of community organising and progressivism that you see manifested across America. He was a Marxist but he was very practical. And he was into tactics.[160]

> Alinsky: People do not get power except when they take it or when they're strong enough so that the other side gives it up.[161]

Together, Clinton and Obama are taking Alinsky's legacy to the US Senate and - to world politics. Alinsky is a

---

159 Who Is Saul Alinsky? Ben Carson Claims He Was Hillary Clinton's 'Role Model' July 20, 2016, 7:00 PM GMT+2 / Updated July 20, 2016 By Erik Ortiz https://www.google.com/amp/s/www.nbcnews.com/news/amp/ncna613341
160 Documentary: Uncle Tom II: An American Odyssey,2022, Carol Swain
161 Documentary: Uncle Tom II: An American Odyssey,2022, Saul Alinsky

name they both benefit from having among their contacts.

Hillary meets Bill Clinton and together they conquer left-wing politics. With their career comes great financial wealth and the Clintons soon become among the richest and most powerful people in the world - an elite. With their financial surplus, they create investments and make profits. Among other things, their organisation 'sells' jobs to higher-ups and their 'Clinton Foundation', a charitable organisation, is accused of taking up to $100,000 in bribes. The price tag for their services is very high. Just a short speech by Bill Clinton costs $500,000 to $750,000[162]. Their group of companies also co-operates with other billionaires to extract uranium in different parts of the world. The uranium is then sold off on an international market. The profits made by the Clintons are not officially disclosed by the media or by their own admission. They prefer to keep their own assets secret.

The "sacred bond"

In 2010, one of the largest earthquakes takes place in Haiti. Disaster strikes and the whole of Haiti is immediately in need. The Clinton Foundation takes over much of the charity and fundraising work for the country, which is carried out during prime time on the main national news channels. The organisation raises millions of dollars from individual donors. The campaigns are visible in the media for several weeks. However, after the campaign ends, protests are heard from Haitian citizens. They claim that only 10% went to the Haitian people in need - the rest went to "administrative" expenses.[163] Which is perhaps not surprising. It's

---

162 https://www.politifact.com/factchecks/2015/apr/26/peter-schweizer/fact-checking-clinton-cash-author-claim-about-bill/
163 How the Clintons robbed and destroyed Haiti By Takudzwa Hillary Chiwanza, African Exponent, Feb. 18, 2020 https://canada-haiti.ca/content/how-

expensive to hire a Clinton. Reportedly, the Clintons have demanded a price tag of $12,000,000 in compensation for appearing with the King of Morocco for his political campaign.[164]

The Clintons themselves live like a true elite with private schools and mansions, far away from Haiti's needy, which is not an unusual behaviour in elite circles. The politicians who make the decisions often have no interest in living with the consequences of those decisions. They themselves live in seclusion and on their own terms with their own security forces and rules.

Nevertheless, a good image is essential. Hillary Clinton is very keen to be portrayed publicly as a philanthropist, anti-racist, feminist and politically committed to the environment. But what about in her private life? Up to 30,000 secret files have been published in which she makes statements about how environmentalists should get a life. She has also spoken out against gay marriage, while officially saying she supports it. Below is an example where Clinton, in the context of a statement, says no to same-sex marriage.[165]

> I believe that marriage is a sacred bond not just a bond but a sacred bond between a man and a woman.[166]

Speaking of the "sacred bond", information has come to light in which Bill Clinton has been accused of several sexual assaults against various women, which he denies. There have also been reports that Bill Clinton has had dealings with the criminal Epstein, which is also denied by both Hillary and Bill.

clintons-robbed-and-destroyed-haiti
164 Wikileaks: Moroccan King Donated $12 Million to Hillary Clinton - Fredrick Ngugi, October 21, 2016 https://face2faceafrica.com/article/wikileaks-moroccan-king-donated-12-million-to-hillary-clinton
165 Hillary Clinton: A 13 Minute Montage of Lies YouTube
166 Sen. Hilary Clinton, 2004 in New York: https://www.youtube.com/watch?v=1sGwGB71KE0

Hillary Clinton's role in this "scandal" has been to "clean up" after Bill Clinton. His victims have been offered money to keep quiet, those who refuse to take bribes and dare to stand up and fight for their rights are denied. All those who have come forward with allegations have been denied by the couple, despite evidence and the victims' detailed accounts in interviews. Hillary Clinton has even run feminist campaigns saying "you have a right to be believed", referring to sexual abuse and rape. Clinton talks a lot about feminism and calls herself a feminist during election campaigns. She is supported by US feminists in her election campaigns and gets their votes. Hillary Clinton, who claims to be against sexual repression, has denied - all the women Bill Clinton has abused and has also testified in court against all of Bill's victims.

However, as the victims are only private individuals, they have less chance of winning against rich magnates from the elite establishment. Those who belong to the elite or the top of the power structure assume a non-personal role, a non-human role, as "state" officials. This "state" is then in conflict with the small "private" person, which in turn creates an uneven process. When state officials make mistakes, they have the means to take back what is theirs - if they lose, they are always 'cleaned up' after, whereas private individuals who are victimised are often psychologically and financially unprotected and the wrongdoing they suffer has consequences - for the rest of their lives.

Feminism is not the only policy area where politicians' campaigns and reality do not match. Hillary Clinton, who has a long political career, has been linked to several people she considers her mentors. These in turn have had a strong connection to the Ku Klux Klan. These include one of her great role models, Margaret Sanger, and her mentor, Senator Robert Byrd. He was a leader in the Ku Klux Klan and has said, among other things:

I shall never fight in the armed forces with a N*gro by my side. Rather I should die a thousand times, and see Old Glory trampled in the dirt never to rise again than to see this beloved land of ours become degraded by race mongrels, a throwback to the blackest speciment from the wilds.[167]

As recently as the 2000s, Byrd says "There are white n*ggas and Ive seen a lot of whita n*ggas in my time"[168], a statement referring to those individuals who have one parent of African-American background and one parent of "white" background. Hillary herself considers her "friend" and "mentor" Robert Byrd to be a man of nobility when she shows her admiration in a speech after his passing:

Today our country has lost a true American original. My friend and mentor Robert C Byrd. Senator Byrd was a man of surpassing eloquence and nobility.[169]

This is not information voters can read about in the "mainstream" media before an election. Nor does it come up, that Bill Clinton is speaking in a forgiving and apologetic way about Senator Byrd and what Clinton calls his "misdemeanours":

They mention that he once had a fleeting association with Ku Klux Klan and what does that mean; I tell you what it means. He was a country boy from West Virginia, he was trying to get elected. And maybe he did something he shouldn't have done.[170]

---

167 *Byrd wrote to Senator Theodore Bilbo of Mississippi in 1944: When affirmative action was White* by Ira Katznelson (New York City: W.W. Norton & Company. p. 80/81. ISBN 0-393-05213-3)

168 https://grabien.com/story.php?id=7761

169 Clinton statement on the passing of Senator Robert C. Byrd - https://2009-2017.state.gov/secretary/20092013clinton/rm/2010/06/143705.htm

170 Obama, Clinton, Biden Honour Sen. Robert Byrd. July 2, 2010

This speech was attended by several Democrats, such as Joe Biden and Barack Obama, who also gave speeches themselves. These Democrats, who have come a long way in their careers, have also worked with politicians who have been involved, in one way or another, with segregation and the Ku Klux Klan movement. On the subject of African-American youth, Hillary Clinton makes the following demeaning statement:

> They're not just gangs of kids anymore, they are gangs of kids called super predators. No conscience no empathy. We can talk about why they ended up that way but first we have to bring them to heel.[171]

Perhaps it was because of this attitude that the Ku Klux Klan movement has made several contributions and donations[172] to Hillary's election campaigns. They believe that she is only making certain political statements to win the election. She is, according to a spokesperson for the Klan, a Democrat, and the Klan - has always been Democratic.

The entire left-wing elite, the American cultural left, Hollywood, the feminists, all the left-wing radicals supported Hillary Clinton against her opponents in an election campaign in the 2000s. She herself called her opponents "Basket of Deplorables" - racists, homophobes and sexists.[173] Her own racist, sexist and homophobic statements have not been brought to the attention of the electorate, nor have her husband's actions.

171 Hillary Clinton, Keene State College in New Hampshire, 28 Jan 1996 - https://www.c-span.org/video/?c4582473/user-clip-hillary-clinton-superpredators-1996

172 KKK Claims $20K In Clinton Donations: https://www.youtube.com/watch?v=Of5zBXQwYtU&pp=ygUXa2trIGRvbmF0aW9uIHRvIGNsaW50b24%3D

173 LGBTQ fundraiser in New York City on Sept. 9, 2016: https://www.youtube.com/watch?v=PCHJVE9trSM&t=55s

> Nobody believes a rumour here in Washington until it's officially denied - Edward Cheyfitz[174]

The media and journalists, whos main task was to uncover the truth, have now become more co-operative with government and politicians. Therefore, it is not surprising that most of the voters do not know what is happening behind the curtain. Moreover, voters are not fully aware that the same regimes that are known to be 'socialist', i.e. 'good', and democratic, are the ones that allow wars and conflicts to continue to take place in the poorer parts of the world. A good example is one of the US presidents who won the Nobel Peace Prize and started seven wars during his term of office, says researcher Daniele Ganser.[175]

> Mr Obama was elected in 2009 partly of his opposition to the Iraq war and was awarded the Nobel Peace Prize after he assumed office. The arguably optimistic decision taken by the Nobel Committee was taken just nine months into his Presidency and came as he was trying to manage the war in Afghanistan. His famous 'A New Beginning' speech in Cairo saw the President declare he was seeking a fresh start "between the United States and Muslims around the world", increasing hopes he would be the antidote to George W. Bush's controversial term.[176]

---

174 This quote has been attributed to several people such as Otto von Bismarck, Cynical Broker, Hy Sheridan, Claud Cockburn, Edward Cheyfitz - https://quoteinvestigator.com/2015/08/07/believe/

175 Lecture: Daniele Ganser, Illegal Wars, https://www.youtube.com/watch?v=vOuGpnORiwk

176 Peace' President? How Obama came to bomb seven countries in six years. US has engaged in conflict in Iraq, Afghanistan, Pakistan, Somalia, Yemen, Libya and now Syria - https://www.independent.co.uk/news/world/middle-east/peace-president-how-obama-came-to-bomb-seven-countries-in-six-years-9753131.html

Despite the hopes pinned on Barack Obama, his term in office was one of the most violent American periods ever. How is it that the first African-American president, who became one of the most popular faces of power, had such a disastrous record on warfare and military attacks?

> Almost six years later, Mr Obama has approved military operations in Iraq, Afghanistan, Pakistan, Somalia, Yemen, Libya and now Syria. The Bureau of Investigative Journalism (BIJ) estimates the Obama administration has launched more than 390 drone strikes in five years across Pakistan, Yemen and Somalia - eight times as many approved during the entire Bush Presidency.[177]

Approved at the highest level

> The hand of Vengeance found the Bed To which the Purple Tyrant fled The iron hand crush'd the tyrant's head And became Tyrant in his stead.
>
> — William Blake[178]

According to Mr Ganser, all wars are illegal under the UN Declaration of Peace adopted in 1945. Yet President George Bush Sr. invaded Kuwait in 1990 - even though it is a war crime under the law. Since it is not stated in the media or in history books that war is illegal and a crime, the idea of the illegal nature of a war does not arise immediately; the nervous system does not connect this to the brain, instead, we can line up 15 different shoe labels. The possibility of stimulating the nervous

---

177 Peace' President? How Obama came to bomb seven countries in six years. US has engaged in conflict in Iraq, Afghanistan, Pakistan, Somalia, Yemen, Libya and now Syria - https://www.independent.co.uk/news/world/middle-east/peace-president-how-obama-came-to-bomb-seven-countries-in-six-years-9753131.html
178 The Grey Monk by William Blake

system, a possibility that has been given to humanity and could have been used in many marvellous ways, has instead been wrongly used for consumption and advertising - and what is not in the newspaper or in the media - is not in the nervous system or the public consciousness either, says Ganser.[179] In this way, people have for some time kept their focus on everything but war and illegal military operations.

After the outbreak of the war in Iraq (2003-2011), Kofi Annan, the Secretary-General of the United Nations, said in September 2004 that the war was illegal:

> Lessons for the US, the UN and other member states: I hope we do not see another Iraq-type operation for a long time - without UN approval and much broader support from the international community. I have indicated it was not in conformity with the UN charter from our point of view, from the charter point of view, it was illegal.[180]

In the speech, Kofi Annan opposes the war and says that war is an illegal act. But this comes a full year after the war had broken out. Otherwise, the chairs of protest, especially in comparison to the Vietnam War, have been empty.

If the only "legitimate" reason for war was to get more oil, people would not want to go to war, according to Daniele Ganser. Nobody wants to die and suffer for oil and why should they? So the government needs a better reason to get the population to accept strategic military action. For example, that "they" are the "bad guys" - while "we" are the "good guys". Once the public has been convinced of the 'evil' side, they forget that

---

179 Lecture: Daniele Ganser, Illegal Wars, https://www.youtube.com/watch?v=vOuGpnORiwk
180 BBC: Iraq war illegal, says Annan (15 September 2004)
http://news.bbc.co.uk/1/hi/world/middle_east/3661134.stm https://archive-yaleglobal.yale.edu/content/war-was-illegal

all military troops going to war are human beings. The troops are always the foot soldiers; those who initiate the war for whatever reason, are never on the battle-field, not like in the old days when kings stood in the front of warcampaigns with a banner in their hand.

And how do you get people to think in terms of 'good and evil'? One example, according to Ganser, is the use of material that easily evokes emotions, such as babies, in war propaganda. How does this work? Just before the Iraq war (Gulf War), the following story is published in the Western media - Hussein attacks Kuwait and in one of Kuwait's hospitals an infant ward is attacked. A young woman, who is claimed to work at the hospital, tells an interview about the invasion. She has tears in her eyes and seems upset. Viewers watching the interview experience strong emotions, perhaps anger or protective instincts. The interview is broadcast on TV and played over and over again. When the audience is finally convinced of the "evil" of the opposing side and emotionally "ready" to accept war on these terms, the US military enters the country and carries out bestial massacres of Iranian soldiers. The example of the interview was a real propaganda campaign and was called "Nayirah Testimony". It later turned out that the testimony was false. The clip was rehearsed and "Nayirah" is none other than the daughter of the Mayor of Kuwait.[181]

Nobody reacted to the bestial murders of the Iranian soldiers at the beginning, partly because many people did not know about it, but also because Saddam Hussein and his troops were portrayed by propaganda as the 'bad guys'.[182] These and similar PR or propaganda campaigns

181 Nayirah testimony https://www.c-span.org/video/?c4686475/user-clip-nayirahs-testimony - https://www.democracynow.org/2018/12/5/how_false_testimony_and_a_massive
182 Lecture: Daniele Ganser, Illegal Wars, https://www.youtube.com/watch?v=vOuGpnORiwk

are thus planned by various bureaucratic bodies at higher levels. According to Mr Ganser, this is a common procedure to prepare the western public for war. Politicians co-operate with military officials high up the career ladder. The intelligence services also work with politicians. Perhaps the best-known intelligence organisation in the United States is the CIA.

In the immediate aftermath of the Second World War, there is a gap left by secret military operations called OSS, which took place only during wartime. A former spy, Allen Dulles, and President Harry Truman set up the substitute organisation, the CIA, the year after the end of the Second World War, together with a group of military agents. Both the government and the intelligence agents want to continue the military activities of the OSS - in the same spirit as before. The CIA website even writes openly about espionage, intelligence and covert military operations:

> Our Agency is built on the creativity and agility of intelligence officers dedicated to safeguarding our Nation. The Office of Strategic Services (OSS), our Agency's forerunner, was created during World War II and was America's first global intelligence organisation. OSS was capable of coordinated espionage, covert action, and counterintelligence-all of which are pieces of today's CIA.
>
> As the war ended, OSS's success proved that strategic intelligence had its place in times of both war and peace. A few years later, President Truman signed the National Security Act of 1947 [July 26]. This established the CIA. Take a closer look at how American intelligence evolved to form the basis of today's Intelligence Community.[183]

183 https://www.cia.gov/legacy/

The post-war powers wanted an intelligence organisation that could influence society and major institutions, including the establishment of guidelines, while planning military interventions against other countries. Through this new organisation, they want to be both the spies - and the decision-makers.

According to the CIA, humans and tribal cultures have been spying on each other since ancient times. CIA Director Allen Dulles and his brother, John Dulles, launch many operations in connection with the Vietnam War. One incident took place at a political convention when Ho Shi Min, the communist leader of Vietnam, had conquered a piece of land from Indonesia. John Dulles, who opposed this power grab - stood up and left the meeting in protest, even though the rest of the convention's participants - Europe's leading powers, had accepted the takeover. It was the first time a Secretary of State had done so. John went and called his brother Allen, who took matters into his own hands and pulled some strings. With immediate effect, a secret military operation was launched to get rid of Ho Chi Minh. Spies were assigned to the mission and networks were built to stop the Vietnamese leader. In the context of this example, it could be argued that the CIA went beyond its rights. Although most military operations have been conducted in a similar way - the decision-making process is closed, within the walls of the organisation; the approach is often ruthless and the public is kept in the dark - despite this, the self-image at CIA headquarters is that of 'sacrificing' to 'help' other nations. Had Allen Dulles not pulled the strings, the US might never have entered the Vietnam War. But according to Dulles and the CIA, top politicians were always consulted and approved before a mission, despite the illegal nature of the operations.[184]

184 Their Secret World War: Stephen Kinzer on The Brothers, John Foster Dulles
   and Allan Dulles. Massachusetts School of Law at Andover

> No time has the CIA engaged in any political
> activity or any intelligent activity that was
> not approved at the highest level [185]

During Dulles' heyday and for many years to come, the
CIA was involved in many military operations. According
to the UN Charter, all wars have been illegal since
1947. The UN also says it is illegal to kill people,
especially if they are accused without trial. This has
not stopped the CIA. Among other things, the CIA has
been involved in numerous assassinations of various
leaders and personalities abroad, whom it has listed as
"terrorists" - without any public trial or evidence.

General Kassim Suleiman, was assassinated as recently as 2020, by US missile drones. For the first time in
history, the US government did not try to deny the
incident but immediately recognised the murder. Newspapers followed in their footsteps - and wrote about the
murder openly.

> Mixed reaction to the news that Maj. Gen.
> Qassim Suleimani died in a targeted strike by
> the United States at Baghdad International
> Airport.[186]

The journalists did not offer a comprehensive picture
of the event so that readers could get a nuanced and
objective view of what happened. They did not describe
the forces behind the assassination. The CIA is part of
a huge secret network, which in turn is linked between
the US military and the Pentagon. The US defence budget
in 2020 was a whopping $730 billion - for the military
forces alone. That's $2 billion - per day. Their op-
ponent country has $20 - per day. This imbalance means
that the US is in a constant state of advantage and

185 Allen Dulles the founder of the CIA. Their Secret World War: Stephen
    Kinzer on The Brothers, John Foster Dulles and Allan Dulles. Massachusetts
    School of Law at Andover
186 https://www.nytimes.com/2020/01/02/world/trump-qassim-suleimani-
    twitter.html

Gina Haspel, the head of the CIA, was able to plan and delegate the assassination of Suleimani without difficulty. Below are more examples of CIA assassinations going back further in time.

- Germany - Alfred Herrhausen 1989

- Cuba Fidel - Castro 1961

- Congo - Patrice Lumumba 1961

- Vietnam - Ngo Dinh Diem 1963

- USA - John F Kennedy 1963

- Chile - René Schneider 1970

- Italy - Aldo Moro 1978

Kennedy, who wins the 1961 presidential election, wants to reduce US involvement in wars during his term. He is known for his strong commitment to peace and for being stubborn. Years before, the CIA carries out an operation to overthrow Ernesto Che Guevara and Fidel Castro. Eisenhower, the president before Kennedy, had developed this plan together with the CIA. After the election, Kennedy is appointed and is informed that there is already a covert operation planned that he, Kennedy will carry it out. Kennedy initially agrees. But not everything goes according to plan. CIA chief Allen Dulles' operation involves painting the US attack plans with Cuban revolutionary flags. This conspiracy, ordered by Dulles, fails, as Castro and his men shoot down the planes and discover that they are actually mislabelled American planes. The CIA pushes for America to follow up with further attacks, partly to cover up the failure, but Kennedy flatly refuses. The Cubans then complain to the UN.[187] The operation fails and is also publicised. At the CIA, there is great chaos and

187 Daniele Ganser "Illegal wars", p. 98, 2016

many high-ranking officials take Kennedy's action as an injustice. They believe Kennedy should have shot Castro - instead he betrays the CIA. Kennedy does not back down and a toxic conflict erupts between Dulles and the CIA on the one hand and John F. Kennedy on the other. Just before the fateful day of the assassination, Kennedy orders the withdrawal of all military bases from Vietnam, to the further chagrin of the CIA, according to the testimony of Robert McNara, Secretary of State under Kennedy. [188]

After further escalation of the conflict, Allen Dulles, the head of the CIA, is fired by Kennedy. Allen in turn announces that Kennedy is a threat to US imperialism and top US circles.[189] 50 days after ordering a reduction of military influence in Vietnam, John F Kennedy is assassinated. The succeeding president, Lyndon B Johnson, immediately throws in more troops, expanding US involvement in the Vietnam War instead.

During his time as head of the CIA, Allen Dulles assembled a 'team' designed to take out foreign actors.[190] Through his actions, Dulles became involved at a level known as the "Deep State", a higher division of the government where crimes are allowed to be committed without punishment. Based on these premises, several attempts were made to assassinate Castro, including with poisoned cigars and poisoned cash. Castro survived like a cat with nine lives. Others did not fare so well. Kennedy was one of the few who had the courage to resist the ruling elite.

> For the greatest enemy of the truth is very
> often not the lie-deliberate, contrived, and
> dishonest-but the myth-persistent, persuasi-

---

188 In Retrospect The tragedy and losses of Vietnam p.444
189 Lecture: Dr Daniele Ganser: Kennedy assassination in Dallas 1963 (Dresden 25.10.2020)
190 David Talbot "Devils Chessboard", 2015

ve, and unrealistic. - President John F. Kennedy Yale University June 11, 1962

A commission called the 'Warren Commission' is appointed in 1964 to investigate John F. Kennedy's assassination and the result is an 880-page official report. The only problem is that the entire commission is made up of Kennedy's archenemies, including Dulles and others from the CIA, who Kennedy fought against before he was assassinated. The commission concludes that the government and the CIA had absolutely no involvement in the assassination of John F. Kennedy. Instead, the CIA focuses on stifling any suspicions, both internally and abroad. Below is an extract from a previously classified document, an advanced order from the CIA announcing the decision that all articles and books that could raise questions about the assassination of John F Kennedy must be criticized and misrepresented in various ways:

> The aim of dispatch is to provide material for countering and discrediting the claims of the conspiracy theorists, so as to inhibit the circulation of such claims in other countries. Background information is supplied in a classified section and in the number of unclassified attachments. (...) To employ propaganda assets to answer and refute the attacks of the critics. Book reviews and feature articles are particularly appropriate for this purpose. (...) Our play should point out, as applicable, that the critics are (I) wedded to theories adopted before the evidence was in, (II) politically interested, (III) financially interested, (IV) hasty and inaccurate in their research, or (V) infatuated with their own theories.[191]

191 CLAYTON P. NURNAD, DESTROY WHEN NO LONGER NEEDED. 1 April 1967 (CIA no. 1035-960)

This message is sent to all US embassies and agents around the world - including China, Germany, Switzerland and Vietnam. Within the US borders, it is easier to dispel suspicions. Former CIA agent Howard Hunt admits in his biography that there were media outlets that co-operated with the CIA between 1949 and 1970, including ABC, NBC, The Associated Press, UPI, Reuters, Newsweek and others, which is basically the majority of the US media.[192] The CIA wants to prevent it from coming out that the murder is a conspiracy, which would mean that there were *multiple* culprits involved. If there was a single killer, the murder ceases to be a conspiracy. But to portray the CIA as an innocent organisation is to wish the population to believe that there only existed conspiracies in Caesar's time.[193] The CIA were certainly not innocent.

> He was perfect for the CIA. He never felt guilt about anything. -St. John Hunt, reflecting on the life of his father, CIA agent E. Howard Hunt

In connection with the assassination, two of JFK's closest mistresses were also murdered - Marilyn Monroe and Mary Pinchot Meyer - the latter the ex-wife of a high-ranking CIA official.[194] In retrospect, it has been suspected that, because of their association with Kennedy, they knew too much about Kennedy's plans and who was behind the assassination. Mary Pinchot Meyer, who was shot on a park walk 'association-style', was murdered just ten days after the Warren Commission report was released. She had been accused by the CIA and her ex-husband of having long talks with Kennedy - about peace.

192 Howard Hunt American SPY My secret history in the CIA Watergate and beyond
193 Lecture: Dr Daniele Ganser: Kennedy assassination in Dallas 1963 (Dresden 25.10.2020)
194 Peter Janney, "Mary's mosaic: the CIA conspiracy to murder John F. Kennedy, Mary Pinchot Meyer, and their vision for world peace", 2016

> RFK's son, Robert Kennedy Jr, said his father
> thought the Warren Commission was "a shoddy
> piece of craftsmanship," when he was publicly
> interviewed by Charlie Rose in January. "The
> evidence at this point I think is very, very
> convincing that it was not a lone gunman,"
> Kennedy Jr. said in the interview.[195]

Robert Kennedy, John's brother who was also running for president, wanted to get to the bottom of JFK's assassination. He was to start cooperating with the FBI in 1968, at the same time as he wanted to clear his brother of rumours of treason, spread by the CIA. Robert F Kennedy was also shot before he could begin the investigation.[196] Since then, very few US presidents have dared to go their own way.

Who are the governing actors?

> Welcome to the world, everybody, I'ma paint
> you black and white. I'ma make you hate each
> other so that everyone will fight. ...

> And I'ma give you borders, they're imaginary
> lines. If you cross them, go to war and win
> when everybody dies.[197]

In China, a human assessment system called the 'Social Credit Score' was invented in the 21st century, whereby everything you do in your personal or professional life is scored in a 'correct' or 'right' way. If the score goes down to zero, you can be cut off from most of your life; from your assets in the bank, from your job, and even your family. In the West, a similar system is

---

195 JFK: Why JFK's assassination has spawned so much speculation, Melissa Erickson | The Bulletin
https://www.norwichbulletin.com/story/special/special-sections/2013/11/08/jfk-why-jfk-s-assassination/41953000007/
196 Lecture: David Talbot Who killed JFK?, https://www.youtube.com/watch?v=KEEsddcHBmE
197 Tom MacDonald, "The System"

being worked on - the ESG score: "Environmental, Social, Governance - score". For private individuals, it has so far only been applied in theory, but for western companies it has become a practical, real-world reality. All banks and major companies now have this scoring system.

In the case of private individuals, everything we write, buy and do is stored in various databases and registers without our actual consent. Companies then use people's private information to develop - together with digital search engine giants - consumer algorithms that entice consumers to spend more and be rewarded for it. The relationship between individual freedom and the right to privacy has shifted radically in the 21st century and the private sphere is being completely erased. The engineers working for the digital companies call the algorithm system "Sky Net"[198]. This way of handling information about the private lives of civilians has even broken the law - but the government has allowed the big digital high-tech companies to pass some new laws adapted to the new technology, to make it easier for them. For example, when the police search an individual's house, they need authorisation from different authorities; searching someone's digital life is, thanks to the new legislation, more or less automated. These technologies give companies great power. Large tech companies have started to use this power more widely, for example, digital media giant Tik Tok suspended its users' accounts with a simple 'message' asking users to contact politicians and protest the suspension of Tik Tok. Once the task was completed, the account was switched back on.

This specific approach, which allows for the recording of data belonging to individuals in various ways, was introduced in the United States in the early 2000s in

198 Terminator II, 1991

the wake of the terrorist attacks. Following the terrorist attacks in New York in September 2001, a series of civil liberties restrictions were implemented throughout the Western world, particularly in the United States. The new laws, known as the 'Patriot Act', included the US anti-terrorism laws, the Guantanamo detention centre, the freezing of bank accounts, and the increased possibilities for wiretapping and monitoring of computer traffic. The politician Ron Paul, who was in the Senate at the time, warned that the state would eventually start using the laws against ordinary citizens.[199] At first, everything was motivated by the need to protect Western civil society from the threat of terrorism.[200] Subsequently, the laws became more and more accepted in other contexts and eventually became the norm.

These decisions were taken centrally and a similar example started to apply in Sweden. The G20 changed the rules for banks, which meant that banks could now freeze depositors' money. Such an approach would not have been possible if cash had still been used. However, all major banks in Sweden have closed their vaults and all money management is done - digitally. Freezing bank accounts has now been legislated in Sweden but has not yet been used in practice. An example of when it has been used is when truck drivers in Canada started a protest called "Freedom Convoy" protesting against Covid restrictions, their assets were frozen and their cars were confiscated to stop the demonstration, as the Canadian government considered the demonstration illegal. Such political totalitarianism is part of the new winds of progressivism, where social control and social incitement are part of the governance of the digitised society by various experts, bureaucrats and government officials - towards specific

199 https://en.wikipedia.org/wiki/Ron_Paul
200 Niclas Sennerteg and Tobias Berglund, "Swedish concentration camps in the shadow of the Third Reich" - p.6-7, 2008

totalitarian goals.

Ganser argues that we need to ask ourselves - who are the governing actors or decision-makers? Traditionally, it has been said that nations are the governing actors. So we need to look deeper and ask - who governs the nations - is it oligarchic companies, politicians or is it the people?[201] In the case of Europe, many of the decisions are taken centrally in the EU, which also consists of a political elite. Those who govern - the elite, politicians and oligarchs - have an unequal power relationship with schools, institutions and hospitals. They want to take over and influence businesses, public services, electricity, the media, the private lives of civilians and their savings accounts. But also their dreams and desires and ambitions. They want to own everything that makes people consume - and they already do. The state they claim to run is called socialism, but it is actually *totalitarianism* - a totalitarian structure that is hidden, which in practice is harder to fight against than if the totalitarianism and power structures were open. The term 'socialism' is used to protect these power structures and make them appear "good" and "democratic". The term totalitarianism actually means a society where influence is one-sided and power is total.

> 1926, in reference to Italian fascism, "of or pertaining to a system of government which tolerates but one political party, to which all other institutions and all individuals are subordinated;" a word formed in English on the model of Italian totalitario ("complete, absolute; totalitarian") from total (adj.) + ending from authoritarian.[202]

---

201 Lecture: Daniele Ganser, *Ilegal wars* https://www.youtube.com/watch?v=vOuGpnORiwk

202 https://www.etymonline.com/word/totalitarian

Along with the big business leaders who hold a great deal of world political 'responsibility', the biggest power belongs to the countries that won the Second World War - the 'Allies'. The top leaders of these countries are also members of the so-called 'UN Security Council', a highly centralised bureaucratic body at the UN where many important decisions are taken. After the end of the Second World War, it was found that at least 60 million people had been killed. As a result, many world leaders signed a UN declaration proclaiming that all nations must refrain from violence in international conflicts.

The UN's work was to include imposing sanctions, intervening in military conflicts and keeping track of international relations. However, the UN's internal structure got unequal power over the course of time. Some countries sitting on the Security Council have more power than others. Of the 193 existing member states, there are five so-called 'permanent' members - the US, UK, France, Russia and China. These member countries retain the power they gained at the end of the Second World War, which has led to a global imbalance in the world. These five countries have a huge advantage over the others - they have a so called "veto power" to allow them avoid any consequences for military conflicts. For example, when Saddam attacked Kuwait, the UN ruled that the attack was illegal and Iraq was punished with various consequences including sanctions. But when the UK and France attacked Egypt in 1956, these countries used their veto power and did not have to face any sanctions. Another example is when the US tried to invade Cuba in 1961. Cuba went to the UN and complained but got no help, because of the US veto. So despite veto countries breaking the law over and over again, their military operations face no sanctions. Russia has used the veto on Ukraine and Crimea.

China has used the veto on Taiwan. The US has used the veto several times in the Middle East.

In the 21st century, the United States has troops and military bases in Germany, but Germany has no troops in the United States.[203] The same power imbalance applies to the other five veto countries and other countries. Other global aspects that affect the world's balance of power are: which countries have nuclear weapons, where is the oil, which countries have access to weapons?

Salil Shetty, a former secretary of Amnesty International says in an interview that the 5 permanent members Russia, China, France, UK and USA have exploited their veto power.[204] He says it's like a club; the most powerful members of the club make the rules and they don't change the statutes in a way that jeopardises their interests. The problem is that the United Nations is supposed to exist to protect people's interests - the interests of humanity as a whole. Mr Shetty says that when the UN says "We the people" - the voice of the people is missing from the actual decision-making process, which is why he is calling for true democracy on the issue.

A public account of this global imbalance is not desirable because governments and elites do not want to be described as an 'elite', or as an 'empire'. An empire aims to expand; it attacks and exploits in order to expand, like the Roman Empire or the Spanish Empire. The "elite", or world elite, is such an empire. But they don't want history books to write that "the US has military bases in 40 countries" or that "Swedish oligarchs make arms deals". Instead, those in power want the civilian population to have the experience of living in a free democracy, but in a democracy, such mili-

---

203 Lecture: Daniele Ganser, illegal wars, https://www.youtube.com/watch?v=vOuGpnORiwk
204 Salil Shetty former Secretary General of Amnesty International, The problem with the UN Veto Power, Now this interview

tary operations would never occur - they could only occur in a totalitarian society.

> All members shall refrain in their international relations from the threat or use of force against the territorial integrity or political independence of any state, or in any other manner inconsistent with a Purpose of the United Nations.[205]

The above quote comes from the Second Universal Declaration of Human Rights, written at the same time as the US attacked Vietnam. On 6 August 1945, the Americans dropped the first atomic bomb on Japan. In a few minutes, around 80,000 people died in Hiroshima. The US thus demonstrated to the world that it possessed a terrible weapon that gave it total military superiority. On 9 August, the second atomic bomb was dropped, this time on Nagasaki, and the following day Japan declared that it was ready to surrender. It was the US President, Democrat Harry Truman, who decided to drop the bombs on Hiroshima and Nagasaki. This display of power was part of the elite's strategy, while presenting the illusion of a socialist world order. The UN has been used repeatedly to achieve elite goals and the concept of the UN as an international authority has been abandoned - however, the laws that favour various large corporations and their economic interests remain. And academics - they are more interested in imposing even more Marxist and socialist ideology, than imposing freedom and real diversity and democracy[206]

Roast fishing

Elisabeth Wehling is a government researcher, who works for the government and has written a manual, an instruction manual for the purpose of convincing voters

205 UN charter chapter two, www.un.org
206 Antony C. Sutton - The Bolshevik Revolution Speech (1976)

to vote for a specific party. She has conducted research on why people vote specifically left or right,
which is then reported to politicians who use her research in their efforts to gain voters' trust. Wehling
believes that it is a matter of people's subconscious
and that the brain can only desire what it already
knows and has experienced – not new, abstract things.
According to her research, the most important thing in
a person's life is family and family values. If this is
used by politicians in PR campaigns, Wehling argues,
they can more easily persuade people to vote for their
party. She uses people's most valuable and private experiences - their family relationships - to give politicians a basis for getting even more votes and even
more power.

A key question, according to Elisabeth Wehling, is
how to persuade those who do not have a political position - those voters in the centre of the scale - to a
specific political view. According to her research, you
can get them to choose a direction - not by convincing
them of lower taxes or different political systems, no,
you just refer to their family values. You address
different groups in different ways - women, men, young
people, old people, the poor - based on their fundamen-
tal values, but using the same kind of methodology by
customising the content.[207] For example, many young
people are committed to animal rights; young people's
family values are to be kind to the weak. If a party
wants to get more young votes, they use slogans like
"No to animal cruelty".

Elisabeth Wehling has also conducted research on how
politicians and the media can effectively pursue the
concept of "framing" towards readers and voters. Framing means only providing information about one part of
an event, such as how fast a car is, but withholding
other parts of the information, such as the fact that

207 Political morality in your brain Ted Talk, Elisabeth Wehling,
    https://www.youtube.com/watch?v=ju6jHCKIOjg

138

the car is environmentally hazardous. If a senior politician does not want to lose power, it is important for him or her to maintain a positive self-image and thus necessary to keep out all facts that would appear ethically negative to the electorate and therefore "framing" is important to them. Politicians must be seen as positive role models and anything that is not as positive - must be kept behind the scenes[208]

A good example is the history of the Democratic Party. In the United States, the terrible event of the Trail of Tears took place in 1830-1850, because of the Indian Removal Act, a law signed in 1830 by Democratic President Andrew Jackson, which authorised the removal of thousands of Indians from their land. This is an example of a real event that they want to "frame" away from the history of the Democratic Party; they want to keep it out of the voters' image of the party, and only present a positive image of the Democratic Party's role in history. Another example is how, in the 19th century, a majority of Democrats were in favour of slavery, while Republicans like Abraham Lincoln were against it. Because of this, Abraham Lincoln was persecuted by the Democrats and the Democrats tried to depose and assassinate him. Despite the persecution, he freed the slaves. The Democrats were also the party where a majority supported segregation through large numbers of Ku Klux Klan members. Now the Democrats are "framing" that part of history to suggest that they have always been against racism. The Democrats were also the party that opposed women's suffrage - and fought against the suffragettes for a full 30 years on the issue. This has also been 'framed' out of the history available to the public. Now people talk about feminism and women's rights - as if it has always been a given.

In Greece, where the concept of 'democracy' was

208 Dr Daniele Ganser: Can we trust the media? (Basel 3 March 2018)
   https://www.youtube.com/watch?v=4bF-3ru1Jz0&t=155s

coined, democracy was supposed to concern only the upper echelons of society. The same greek top layer owned slaves who instead lived in terrible conditions. Democracy was not for them. Today, the matter is instead about consumerism and wage slaves and a population that is being misled.

Because every party needs a positive narrative for people to vote for them, they get rid of all the "shadows" and "slants". Instead, they transfer everything negative - onto their opponents. A method that Saul Alinsky, by the way, favoured[209] - as rule number 12 from "Rules for Radicals".

When it was not possible to depose Hillary Clinton's opponents, they called the opposing side racists, fascists and white supremacists. But who was actually connected to white supremacist organisations? Hillary Clinton, who calls herself a feminist, an anti-racist and a Democrat, whose two main role models, according to her, are the eugenicist Margret Sanger and a former leader of the KKK, Robert Byrd.[210]

The objective truth
In every genre of public information, be it election campaigns, news, or information coming from a government or an institution, there are generally three levels of facts, according to Professor Anthony Sutton:[211]

The first level is what most people *believe* to be true. It is the information the government *wants* people to take in. An example of this is that the Socialist government *wants* the Swedish people to believe that they were completely neutral during the Second World War. Therefore, they only publicise and draw attention to those events where the Socialist government acted neutrally - and gloss over the rest.

209 Saul Alinsky "Rules For Radicals",1971
210 Documentary: Dinesh D'Souza, Hillary's America, 2016
211 Anthony C Sutton "America's Secret Establishment: An Introduction to the Order of Skull & Bones", 1986

The second level is also a type of information that the government voluntarily provides to the public. This level challenges the first level but stays within what is necessary. The information still does not get to the bottom of the problem, as it often does not shed light on the full picture of what happened. Public access to the full picture of the incident is not the goal at this level, it may be classified information, and the real version may reach the public 100 years after the incident. An example is admitting that Sweden had labour camps during World War II, at the same time denying they were ever concentration camps.

The third level is the whole picture or the objective truth. Usually the political establishment has already had time to process the information, through PR consultants and the media, among others, before it reaches the public - therefore it is not often that such revelations are published, unless the revelation is made by whistleblowers or staff who go against the rules and disclose important or sensitive information. Such objective truth, according to Sutton, should have a basis or "evidence" and be based on actual documents.[212] The example is that Sweden actually established several concentration camps around the country, to which prisoners were sent because of their race, the evidence for which has been classified for many years.

This type of sorting information has been developed in several stages in the higher political circles and has been considered a necessity for many years.

> Some of the phenomena of this process are criticized the manipulation of news, the in-flation of personality, and the general bal-lyhoo by which politicians and commercial products and social ideas are brought to the consciousness of the masses. The instruments

212 Antony C. Sutton - The Bolshevik Revolution Speech (1976)

by which public opinion is organised and focused may be misused. But such organisation
and focusing are necessary to orderly life. [213]

As civilisation has become more complex, and
as the need for invisible government has been
increasingly demonstrated, the technical
means have been invented and developed by
which opinion may be regimented.[214]

Politicians, big business, oligarchs, and the government - all those under the power structure of the elite
have a need to maintain a facade, a living performance,
in front of the population, which means that only part
of the real story can be made public. One could imagine
that this necessity could belong to a Soviet communist
government or a dictatorship somewhere in Asia. But
these kinds of propaganda methods and information technologies are an essential part of the political structure of the West.

Furthermore, according to Charles Wright Mills, Professor of Sociology, there are three techniques for getting the desired information across - *Coercion*, *Authority* and *Manipulation* - the latter being the method
used when the other two do not work. The first two are
done in the open while the last method is practised behind closed doors. For example, war propaganda used the
technique of *coercion* to make people believe that
Afghanistan was the 'bad guys'. *Authority* was then used
to impose rules at airports and increased digital
surveillance after 9/11. And then, the technique of
Manipulation was used to make it seem that digital surveillance was only about terrorists, when in fact it
was becoming about the recording of ordinary people's
private digital information.[215]

213 Edward L Bernays, "Propaganda", page 12, 1928
214 Edward L Bernays, "Propaganda", page 12, 1928
215 Charles Wright Mills, Professor of Sociology, "White Collar: The American
    Middle Classes", 1951

It is the preferred form of power in modern societies as it relies on sophisticated methods rooted in science and technology.[216]

Power elites and social institutions seek legitimisation to gain the loyalty of the public. However when coercive and authoritative power fails to justify the legitimisation of authority manipulation takes its place.[217]

According to Mills, there is a concept called *"Sociogical imagination"*. It is a concept that allows the human brain to understand how major powers and institutions are represented in society and how they are linked to each other. The higher a person's capacity for sociological imagination, the more likely they are to be able to recognise a connection between different events in the higher political sphere. For example, thinking that media information provides access to only truth and reality, or that politicians never lie, is considered a lower sociological imagination.

Sociological imagination allows us to better understand what is going on and how various parts of society and the individual within society are affected.[218]

When social information and news undergo the abovementioned information screening processes and get stuck in the bureaucratic machinery, resulting in the public being exposed to only a part of the politics actions of the world - then the capacity for sociological imagination is lower and the contexts are less clear.
It is here, in this sphere, where the context be-

216 Charles Wright Mills, Professor of Sociology, "White collar", 1951
217 Ibid
218 Charles Wright Mills, Professor of Sociology "The sociological imagination", 1959

comes unclear and the picture of the outside world becomes distorted, that conceptual confusion is practised. It is therefore important to preserve authentic, truthful information about the world around us and to recognise the importance of real, truthful knowledge. Not only knowledge presented in public education but the knowledge of the whole picture of reality - "Knowledge is the key to promote social change. Knowledge has the power to challenge the status quo, disrupt oppressive systems, and foster social change."[219] Then, when you know the whole picture, you can also achieve real change. Otherwise, human judgement can eventually lose its footing, as people slowly move towards an increasingly distorted view of what is happening around them.

Another sphere where conceptual confusion frequently arises is science. Most people believe that all science is free from government interference, and free from financial funding of the corporate industry. But scientific research outside educational institutions is always commissioned in advance and many times sponsored. There is also no market in the public sector for science that is 'free' in the true sense of the word. When companies pay for and sponsor certain areas of research and choose to ignore others, the importance of the latter is diminished and an imbalance arises. Science thus becomes corrupt.

> The science delusion is that science already understands the nature of the reality in principle leaving only the details to be filled in. This is a very widespread belief in our society (...) But there's a conflict in the heart of science between science as a method of inquiry based on reason evidence

219 *Unleashing the Power of Knowledge: Transforming Lives and Shaping the Future*, Richard Mark Wood
https://www.interesjournals.org/articles/unleashing-the-power-of-knowledge-transforming-lives-and-shaping-the-future.pdf

hypothesis and collective investigation and science as a belief system or a world view. And unfortunately the world view aspect of science has come to inhibit and constrict the free inquiry which is the very lifeblood of the scientific endeavour.[220]

So what does it actually look like when a reader takes in news images, or 'social information' on a psychological level? Or even thinking about the power of politicians and oligarchs? There is an actual, real power imbalance between the masses and the elite, who are fewer in number, meaning that the ordinary people, because of their numbers, are actually more powerful than the elite. To begin with, this power imbalance is projected back onto the population. Thus, most people live in the perception that they are inferior to the state and "alone" in their perceptions. They further perceive themselves as "few in number" while the state and the others are more numerous and therefore superior in strength. Such an illusion is more effective for politicians and those in power - they do not want the revolutions of the 18th, 19th and 20th centuries to be repeated. If each individual feels alone and lives with the idea that "the others don't seem to protest", the power of the elite over the population increases - the individuals, of which the great masses are actually composed, cannot unite in consensus.

> *Luna Lovegood*: We believe you, by the way. That He-Who-Must-Not-Be-Named is back, and you fought him, and the Ministry and the "Prophet" are conspiring against you and Dumbledore.

> *Harry Potter*: Thanks. Seems you're about the only ones that do.

220 Rupert Sheldrake Ted talk The Science Delusion,
    https://www.youtube.com/watch?v=1TerTgDEgUE&t=79s

Luna Lovegood: I don't think that's true. But I suppose that's how he wants you to feel.

Harry Potter: What do you mean?

Luna Lovegood: Well if I were You-Know-Who, I'd want you to feel cut off from everyone else. Because if it's just when you are alone you're not as much of a threat."[221]

And when people try to broaden their horizons and learn about the news available in 'alternative' media, they are labelled as conspiracy theorists. In such cases, dismissing 'sensitive' information as 'conspiracy theory' has a calming effect. "Oh good, then there is not truth in the fact that Sweden is involved in weapon export or that politicians are lying to the voters. I'm sure they're honest and fair-minded, and anyway, we can go back to choosing the next sofa for the terrace - this year again!" It is precisely this safe image that politicians want you to live in, so that you detach yourself from free thinking and go back to a lifestyle where consumption and earning salary are central. Thus, people are involved in choosing their next car, their next wardrobe and which shopping centre to visit next.

When hearing the word "conspiracy theorist", the neural pathways are activated, due to manipulation in the form of conceptual confusion, and the brain automatically thinks that such behaviour - is outside the socially accepted narrative. At the same time, going outside the socially accepted narrative implies an unconscious, psychological threat of social exclusion. Humans, as social beings, become uncomfortable when faced with such a threat.

For example, if a newspaper claims that the West is constantly at war with various international actors, most people think it must be a conspiracy theory. But if you ask the western soldiers - who are in Afghani-

221 Harry Potter and the Order of the Phoenix, 2007

146

stan? - they say it's true.[222] That's why we need corroborating documentation, provided by whistleblowers like Assange, to enlighten people about what is actually going on. In combination, the above becomes one of many contributing factors that foster passivity and head-in-the-sand mentality in citizens, who stop opposing what the state powers are doing. The following quote can be related to the entire West:

> The hierarchical view of society was a vital part of the medieval soul. It was undermined in the West by the Renaissance, but in Sweden (as in Russia) it has survived more or less unchallenged. Accordingly, personal pride was the most reprehensible of medieval sins and in Sweden today it remains one of the most serious offences. Self-annihilation is the obligatory virtue.[223]

In the Soviet Union, a huge proportion of the population lived in fear of being reported to the KGB and knew they were being watched by the state. In North Korea and China, people still live in fear of the totalitarian regime and the knowledge of being watched. In the West, people live in peace and quiet, thinking that everything that is critical of society and that is expressed against the state is a conspiracy theory. In the West, freedom of expression and the right to a truthful view of the world are not as highly valued, which has meant that these values have lost their power and have been eroded. The anxiety, suspicions and negativity that may arise in individuals because of all the lies and because of the way society is structured is instead channelled through the method of divide and conquer - individual groups against individual groups, so that people's frustration is not turned against po-

222 Dr Daniele Ganser: Kennedy assassination in Dallas 1963 (Dresden 25.10.2020)
223 Roland Huntford, "Blind Sweden" (The New Totalitarians), 1971

liticians and the elite, and a new revolution is su-
pressed.

The state uses Marxist strategies, public relations
and psychological persuasion to maintain an omnipotent
power structure through conceptual confusion, identity
politics and information technologies. They use Marx's
theories to elevate the state above man, just as the
Church did with religion.

Demoralisation

The Communists' grand plan was to grow in Eastern
Europe first, then Asia and finally the West. In the
West, they would take over, not by revolution or by
using violence, but by infiltration over a long period
of time. The theory of infiltration was the brainchild
of Italian communist Antonio Gramsci. The Marxist
movement believed that the West must first be weakened
so that socialism could defeat the old traditions and
Christianity, which were seen as opposed to communism
and Marxism. Gramci's idea was that by infiltrating
institutions in culture and education - a weakening
would take place.

This is confirmed by the defected former KBG agent Yuri
Bezmenov, who in the late 1980s conducted an interview
- one of very few of its kind due to the risk it meant
- in which he claims that Russia has spent decades
trying to infiltrate the Western world through various
covert military operations. During the Cold War, according to Bezmenov, Communist intelligence conducted
several attacks against the United States and the West
in various ways, both overt and covert, including
through "ideological subversion". The term is inspired
by Gramci's idea of infiltration and means changing the
perception of reality in the human brain so that an
individual, despite an acute threat, is unable to de-

fend his family, his community and thus his country. Bezmenov describes the Russian technique as a slow brainwashing process. According to Bezmenov, it takes about 15-20 years to demoralise a nation for this purpose. Marxist-Leninist ideology is pumped into the heads of children and young students, for about three generations in a row, without being questioned or balanced by "ordinary" values. The result, according to Mr Bezmenov, was more than the Soviet top military could ever have expected. Part of the process, he says, is that those who graduated from university in the 1960s have gone on to achieve high-level positions in political science, journalism and culture - all with the same ideological background. They are, he says, "programmed" to respond to certain stimuli in particular situations. The aim was that, through brainwashing, everyone would become so convinced of Marxist ideology that no one would react to other information or be able to receive and process any other political views that were not Marxist. This state is called a 'demoralised' state. A person who is 'demoralised' cannot take in authentic information, even showing pictures of concentration camps can be dismissed as propaganda if they are in a 'demoralised' state. An individual who is "demoralised" cannot absorb certain types of information even if he has the evidence right in front of him.[224] Mr Bezmenov, who took refuge in Canada in connection with his testimony, was later found dead, as were other Russian defectors, 10 years after the interview.

> Subversion (from Latin subvertere 'over-throw') refers to a process by which the values and principles of a system in place are contradicted or reversed in an attempt to sabotage the established social order and its

---

224 Interview with Yuri Bezmenov, YouTube, https://www.youtube.com/watch?v=9apDnRRSOCk

structures of power, authority, tradition, hierarchy, and social norms.[225]

There are four stages or steps of "ideological subversion", which Bezmenov describes as one of the largest covert Soviet military operations in history.

1. "Demoralisation - Infiltration through institutions and culture. One ideology becomes the dominant one and the rest are pushed aside

2. "Destabilisation" - destabilising opposition, for example values that go against Marxism, economic conditions and defence policy

3. "Crisis" - A violent change in power structures

4. "Normalization" - a period of stability until the next cycle of ideological subversion reaches the crisis stage.

This programme was originally used by the Allied nations after World War II - when they carried out one of the largest mass influences on a population in the 20th century, known as the 'denazification' of the German people.

After the Nazis lost the war, the Allies not only wanted to bring the Nazis to justice, they also wanted to restore the German people from Nazi ideologies. A programme based on 'ideological subversion' was launched, in which the German people were trained to adapt to the premises of democracy and be deprogrammed from the Nazi views.

They wanted Germany to be transformed into a 'normal' socialist society and used schools, public information and the media to de-Nazify the German population.[226]

225 https://en.wikipedia.org/wiki/Subversion
226 https://en.wikipedia.org/wiki/Denazification

The "Information Control Division of the US Army" had by July 1946 taken control of 37 German newspapers, six radio stations, 314 theatres, 642 cinemas, 101 magazines, 237 book publishers, and 7,384 book dealers and printers. Its main mission was democratization but part of the agenda was also the prohibition of any criticism of the Allied occupation forces.[227]

Once the objective was achieved, the methodology was retained and proved useful in other parts of the Western world. Thus, the programme was not completely terminated. Instead, these techniques were applied to other parts of society.

The right schools

Through organised concept confusion, terms such as "capitalism" are used in socialist society in a way that is intended to foster negative associations. "Capitalists" are now associated with rich people who have high profits and do not want to pay taxes. But behind the scenes, the rich elite, the socialist political establishment and big business all use capitalism - when it suits and serves their own purposes. This makes the capitalism that ordinary people could benefit from more inaccessible to the public.

In today's world society, big business is allowed to make huge amounts of money in co-operation with politicians. Socialist and leftist leaders often live in opulence. They "live" out a wrongly executed capitalism that they "hide" behind a socialist curtain. They dont use Marx's ideas in the right way, if they did, mass-production would be curbed and return to a qualitative production. Although the elite powers outwardly pursue a left-wing policy, they exploit their position, just

227 https://en.wikipedia.org/wiki/Denazification

as the feudal lords did in their time.[228] Below follows a quote about the Swedish example, that could be applied to other Socialist states:

> From their first appearance, the Social Democrats (Socialists) have proclaimed the orthodox socialist creed of immediate nationalisation, together with income levelling and universal social welfare. But all this was just ideological pork for the orthodox. Behind the demagoguery of the election speeches, the party was directed by sober economists who thought they knew that reforms without resources paved the way for economic disaster. They considered it meaningless rhetoric to talk about the distribution of wealth until there was more to grab hold of in the first place. They therefore considered it their first task to create wealth and left radical newsmaking aside until the country could afford it. With industry mainly in private hands, the enforcement of state ownership must, for the time being, only halt progress. To build a welfare state too quickly would be to live beyond the country's means. Therefore, the Social Democrats (Socialistst) unscrupulously exploited the prevailing capitalist system and allowed the economic benefits to keep the slow pace justified by the natural tempo of economic development.[229]

Such an elite, using capitalism and a strong vested interest, exists in every country, whether the government is right- or left-wing. Kim Jong-il, North Korea's former leader, attended the right elite schools and learnt how to get to the top the right way - even

228 Ideologies 15 February 2019 - Left-wing ideas part 1 of 4: The roots of the Left, Engelsberg Mill, Ängelsberg - Svante Nordin, Professor of the History of Ideas and Learning, Lund University
229 Roland Huntford, "Blind Sweden" (The New Totalitarians), 1971

though the country's politics are thoroughly left-wing. He was the "great film director", whose films are considered unrivalled in North Korea. That's why film production has stopped in North Korea and the film studio has been turned into a museum - to prove that his legend is true. All other opinions are penalised. Those who do not have the 'right opinion', and the same opinion as the elite, are 'illogical' and discredited as such. Even those working in the UN have gone to the "right" schools and the same goes for the whole elite.

In fact, there are two approaches to capitalism, and two different concepts used by governments. One approach is used to show a negative, discouraging side of the private market and the "evil" capitalists. The other approach is used by the elites themselves, in their own interests, in big companies and investments, nice neighbourhoods and schools.

Those who vote for parties on the left most often believe that economic monopoly of big business is bad for the world. What they usually do not realise is that such monopolies can only be formed with the help of state support, which means that there can only be a socialist government behind it to support the corporate monopoly that the left ironically calls - capitalism. The national and international co-operation between state and corporate oligarchs is not official, which leads to the public not knowing this part of the information.

The common perception people have is that all forms of entrepreneurship are driven by the right side of politics, it is something conservative, profit-driven and capitalistic. But big business and the oligarchs are not on that side. They are neither right nor left. Their motive is to maximise their profits - regardless of politics. Many large corporate industries - support what benefits themselves. They don't make decisions based on political principles - like right or left. They co-operate with the state - when it serves their purpose. Big business is in favour of the free market if it believes it can cope with competition. If they can't, they are in favour of state protection and monopolies, which they achieve through a complex regulatory framework - developed by themselves.

Real capitalism stems from something else entirely. Adam Smith, known as the father of liberalism and economics, was the founder of capitalism in the 18th century. Smith did not intend for his theory to be exploited by large co-operatives. On the contrary - both Smith and Marx were against state intervention and greedy entrepreneurs.

Smith lived next to a market in the 18th century and marvelled daily at what he saw. Through his observations, he realised that natural and healthy competition helps people and at the same time creates the conditions for the free individual. He believed that an invisible hand guided people in trade, just like ants or other group creatures, and considered this to be natural for humans. This is because the free market implies a natural trust between people. Smith began to study people and their behaviour in other economic situations and deepened his studies at the University of Glasgow. Here, reason and free and open debate were highly valued and authority was instead resisted. Adam Smith studied morality and was admitted to Oxford. Compassion becomes a very important component of Adam Smith's theories of success, among other things, as well as his concern for the poor.

According to his theory, the free market also leads to a natural exchange of values and morals. In this natural economic environment, people learn the difference between right and wrong. Smith develops his theory from

the individual level, to the economy of the whole society. He believes that authorities should have a duty
to the people, rather than power, and that authorities
who control and move people around are dangerous because they think they are omniscient. The best thing
for everyone is when individuals are given freedom,
freedom to follow their dreams and develop. His theories on morality quickly became a success and he gained
followers.

They believed that the market must be free, without
state monopolies or oligarchs as found in mercantilism.
They believed that the wealth of society is created by
the citizens themselves and not by the state. Smith is
against mercantilism, monopolies and the high taxes
imposed on peasants by rich feudal lords. Businessmen
tend to be interested only in profits, which makes them
ruthless and excessively competitive, and creates monopolies, which in turn is not only bad for the economy,
but also bad for public morals, as the monopoly owner
may become an example for the common man. Instead of
violent revolution, Smith believes in slow, progressive
change. He also believes that the workload should be
shared among people. Whoever is most competent is given
the task where that specific competence is sought.

Smith goes on to say that the free market is
autonomous and driven by nature itself - the baker
makes bread to survive. There is no need for government
intervention, just like in the old barter system of the
old times. Therefore, he believes that the system of
governance or government needs to exist at the local or
regional level - because the state has little connection to, or insight into, the day-to-day events of
the population. Adam Smith believes in "The System of
Natural Liberty" which means that people will always
find ways to work and co-operate with each other.[230]

230 Documentary: The Real Adam Smith: Morality and Markets

Despite being labelled the father of capitalism and the fact that capitalism has been displaced as a right-wing concept, Smith was against monopolies because, according to him, monopolies put money in one person's pocket and only led to increased greed. Greedy businessmen trying to fleece consumers would fail - if consumers were allowed to turn to other sellers, Smith argued. Therefore, a free market curbs greed and selfishness - man becomes sociable, less greedy and less selfish. He did not believe that only the nobility, who kept capital in their own pockets through inheritance rights, should have an opportunity to earn, instead all working people should have that right.

> Laws and government may be considered in this and indeed in every case as a combination of the rich to oppress the poor, and to preserve to themselves the inequality of the goods.[231]

It is not how much silver the king can get into his treasury, it is how productive and prosperous his people are. Smith's free market theories imply that other nations are not the enemy, but an opportunity for trade. In these ideas, one can probably see an expression of the first anti-racism.

> Little else is requisite to carry a state to the highest degree of opulence, but peace, easy taxes a tolerable administration of justice; all the rest being brought about by the natural course of things.[232]

Adam Smith considered the East India Company to be an example of a greedy and unsound organisation. The com-

---

231 Adam Smith, "Lectures on Jurisprudence" p208, 1978.
232 "We do not know if Smith actually wrote the above and presented a paper in 1755, as we can only see them quoted in Account of the "Life and Writings of Adam Smith" by his student Dugald Stewart (1795). The original document that Stewart saw was destroyed, and we only have Stewart's quoted words to rely on." https://www.adamsmithworks.org/documents/tsang-1775-adam-smith-1776-prequel

pany employed 70,000 soldiers - an entire army, was powerful and had a monopoly over all trade with India. Smith also strongly opposed the massacre in India and the whole colonial system that involved England taking taxes from colonies because he believed that the colonies should be set free and free markets encouraged in colonial countries as well. Driven by a strong desire to do good, Adam Smith then became a professor of moral philosophy.

> ..the principle which prompts to save, is the desire of bettering our condition, a desire which comes with us from the womb, and never leaves us til we go into the grave. [233]

According to experts and economic researchers, Adam Smith's form of economics has never been practised in a society with a trusting population, even though some of his theories are rooted in modern society. Such an economic form would give man a trust: if the state gives the individual freedom and protects his rights, the individual can live his life and decide how it should develop. The state does not need to do things for the individual, it just needs to stop doing bad things to the individual. This way of thinking also means believing in the inherent competence and potential of people. Based on Smith's theories, one can understand Jeffrey Tucker, an anarchist writer, when he says that capitalism is love and making the world a better place.[234]

According to Anthony Sutton, a British-American author, researcher, economist and professor, it is true that big business finds it difficult to survive without state intervention when it comes to really big money. This started in the 20th century, when monopoly capita-

233 WN II iii.28, Adam Smith
234 Jeffrey Tucker anarcho-capitalist, https://www.youtube.com/watch?v=8OZGhHpWTSg

lists and mercantilists realised that they could not make really big profits within the framework of free markets and competitive laissez-faire societies. The only way to raise really big capital is through monopoly - first you drive out competition and open up state support and co-operation, so that you get the right protection for your capital and enterprise. The right approach leads to a legal monopoly. The strategy was described by Frederick C. Howe in his biography, "Confessions of a Monopolist".[235] There is a strongly held myth that "oligarchs" can only be Russian mafia or rich oil sheiks. This is not true. There are a large number of oligarchs who, through various methods, have entrenched oligopoly and monopoly in Western society. Instead, the myth has arisen through organised confusion of concepts, because Western oligarchs do not want to operate in public and would rather be incognito. This allows them to operate undisturbed and keep the population in the dark, unlike the revolutionary movements of the 18th century. In addition to those in power known to the public, there are many levels of the state apparatus that do not operate officially, such as the Triateral Commission. These bureaucratic bodies are involved in governance, but are not "elected" in the true sense of the word through the democratic right to vote. In a true democracy, only leaders elected by the people can govern the country and make decisions. In North Korea, totalitarianism is practised in the open, without being hidden, and the state is more truthful about the power imbalance that exists between the people and those in power. In the West, power is exercised behind closed curtains with a hidden agenda. Instead, they try to manipulate voters so that they remain unaware of the power imbalance. This creates different pictures of reality - what the civilian population know and what they are not aware of.

235 Frederic C. Howe "The Confessions of a Monopolist", 2022

According to the prevailing public perception, there is a political line running from left to right, with Nazism on the far right, although this line is based on incorrect historical presentation. Such a line only became possible after the great paradigm shift in which National Socialism was displaced from the left to the right. In this way, a false narrative has been constructed. According to Professor Sutton, the right vs left scale is not correct at all, it locks in opinions and intentions. The result is to sabotage natural, free political discourse and any new, as yet undiscovered political ideology. Rejecting this political line, or question it, is seen by those whose interest is to maintain it, as disingenuous or as supporting 'conspiracy theories'. The major socialist powers have long had an interest in not labelling Nazism as an inherently socialist ideology - in order to attract more voters to their side. Search engine algorithms are also shaping terms in line with the great paradigm shift. If you search for the word "right-wing" on YouTube, the channel suggests Nazi-biased clips for some time afterwards.

The discourse and free thinking are tightened by the "right-left" definition of concepts and by the biased presentation of history. It uses language and definitions that are loaded from the start. This creates an opportunity to direct political opinions in a particular direction. The system is structured for opinions to be directed against each other, so that 'right' and 'left' are always in conflict and can never agree, according to Sutton.

> They financed and encouraged the growth of both philosophies (right & left) and controlled the outcome to a significant extent. This was aided by the "reductionist" in

science, the opposite of historical "whole-ness". By dividing science and learning into narrower and narrower segments, it became easier to control the whole through the parts.[236]

Progress in the Hegelian state is through contrived conflict: the clash of opposites makes for progress. If you can control the opposites you dominate the nature of the outcome. [237]

Professor Anthony Sutton argues that it is in the interests of those in power to make it seem as if it is people who want individual freedom (left-wing politics) versus people who want centralised power (right-wing politics). In this way, misconceptions are kept alive. This is because capitalists and the true right-wing have never historically sought centralised power - either political or economic. The free market for the population is in no way centralised, as we have seen with Adam Smith. There is also a false image, originally created by Karl Marx and then maintained by the elite, that capitalists and Marxists are enemies, which is also not true, as revolutionary Marxists and capitalists, in a higher level always cooperated for their mutual benefit. Through organised conceptual con-fusion, they try to convince people that the concepts of "monopoly" and "capitalism" are on the same side - they belong to right-wing politics, just like "capita-lism" and "Nazism". Actually, the biggest companies, the monopolies, the oligarchs and the socialist state (with full state intervention in all areas of society) - are on the same side. However, this alliance is not visible to the public.

236 Antony C Sutton, "America's Secret Establishment: An Introduction to the Order of Skull & Bones", p 14, 1986
237 Ibid

Because many historians and other prominent academics who have served in the institutions have held socialist or Marxist-coloured views, the mistaken notion that an alliance of a socialist government and monopolistic big business is not possible has been perpetuated. But the truth is that state-supported big business is opposed to the free market because competition is undesirable to them. Simply put - a totalitarian socialist state is the most fertile environment for the largest corporations. An example of how big corporations turn against the principle of the free market and get rid of competitors is the following: Jeff Bezos advocates for raising the minimum wage at his big company Amazon. This in turn pushes his competitors out of the market, as they, unlike him, cannot pay higher wages. This makes Bezos look better and his employees richer. The fact that the other competing companies and small businesses go bankrupt and the employees lose their jobs is a flip side that is not recognised. This is not a new method. The same technique was used by Henry Ford to get rid of competing car manufacturers.[238] How does globalisation, as advocated by both Rockefeller and the other big businessmen, come into the picture? Apart from being able to tinker with complicated corporate rules, which most companies would not be able to fulfil, it elevates the control and responsibility of the largest capital and the most important global issues - above the heads of the population. In other words, the opposite of what Adam Smith wanted to achieve in his time.

This globalism or internationalism is further based on cooperation between socialism and monopolism as the common goal is to have a more centralised state and power - both gain from this. Profit for monopolists and financial support for the government. The last thing

238 Documentary: Did Wall Street fund FDR, Hitler and the Bolsheviks? Looking at Prof Antony C Sutton's theory https://www.youtube.com/watch?v=SnbFpR1m0zA&t=1602s

the banks, politicians and rulers want is decentralised power as they would then lose their power.

Tom McDonald's "Brainwashed"
Step one, train the people only to consume
Step two, infiltrate adults with the news
Step three, indoctrinate the children through the schools
And the music and the apps on the phones that they use
Step four, separate the right from the left
Step five, separate the white from the black
Step six, separate the rich from the poor
Use religion and equality to separate 'em more
Step seven, fabricate a problem made of lies
Step eight, put it on the news every night
Step nine, when people start to fight and divide
Take control, this is called "situational design"

Bernays, Freud and the elite

In Vienna, just before the Second World War, there was a big crisis and Freud turns to his now rich and famous relative Edward Bernays for help. He organises a campaign to get Freud's work published in the US for the first time. Edward ensures that the books become controversial and that it becomes known that the books are about sex. Freud is accepted and more than that - his theories become a big success.

However, Freud falls into a state of prolonged depression and his new work takes on a pessimistic character. In his new book, he writes that man is a race of bad character and, as such, unchangeable. According to Freud, he is both immoral and sadistic by nature. Everything is published and becomes hugely popular

162

among the intelligentsia, journalists and politicians of the time. The image arouses both fascination and fear. It evokes the idea that people are capable of forming a mob and destroying governments, and the associations go back to the Russian Revolution. People are no longer considered as individuals, capable of making their own decisions in a democracy. Walter Lippmann, one of the West's most influential political thinkers, is inspired by Freud and writes that if people are, as Freud describes them, driven by irrational forces on an unconscious level, then democracy needs to be rethought - completely. A new elite is needed, according to Lippmann, which can curb and control the wild masses. This, he says, can be done through psychological techniques that can control unconscious emotions. These ideas are echoed by politicians of the time who begin to seek psychological knowledge to understand how the public psyche works. With a single goal - to understand how to apply the new psychological theory to social control strategies - control of the masses.

Edward Bernays, in turn, became fascinated by Lippmann's arguments and wrote books incorporating Lippmann's theories. By first stimulating people's inner desires and then satisfying them with products, new ways of controlling the irrational urges of the masses was created. In this way, the masses are 'pacified'. Bernays calls it "the engineering of consent". While he has nothing against democracy, he believes that people are not trustworthy enough in their judgement - they could vote for the wrong political candidate or choose the wrong products. That's why he believes they need to be guided from above. If you can tap into people's deepest desires, wishes and fears, this can then be used for different purposes.

> The conscious and intelligent manipulation of
> the organised habits and opinions of the
> masses is an important element in democratic
> society.[239]

In 1928, Herbert Hoover comes to power, the first president to fully embrace Bernays' theories that consumption should be the central engine of the American nation. After he wins the election, a team of public relations consultants is hired, instructed by the government to elicit and create desire. The population was to be transformed into consuming happiness machines that were constantly on the move. This would become the great key to economic success in society.

A new vision is born - mass democracy would have at its heart a consumerist self that would stabilise the economy and be cheerful and easy to cooperate with (instead of the irrational savage that Freud warned against). Like Julius Caesar of the Roman Empire stated, Bernays and Lippmann want to make people happy - and thus more easily governed. The basic view of democracy, which was really there to equalise power relations in the world - is instead reformulated and consolidated in a new, completely distorted version through Lippmann's, Freud's and Bernays' theories.

Edward Bernays is now part of a new elite, made up of politicians, socialites and newly rich business owners, who dominate American politics and society in the 1920s. He becomes immensely wealthy, living in a suite in a five-star hotel and hosting constant parties and gatherings for politicians, powerful business leaders and film stars. He establishes many contacts.

Despite all his success, in private - he says that people are stupid and gullible.[240] He uses the same

239 Edward L Bernays, "Propaganda", page 9, 1928
240 Documentary: The Century of the Self 2002 British television documentary
    series by filmmaker Adam Curtis, Bernays daughter, Anne bernays Interview

pejorative words about the crowds. But his success doesn't last long and what stops him in his tracks is the biggest stock market crash in world history. Millions of consumers, whom Bernays works so hard to convince, suddenly stop shopping. Unemployment spreads. In crisis-hit Europe, the civilian population begins its fight for survival.

Freud, who is in the Alps to cure cancer of the jaw, writes that civilisation is not an expression of human progress but is designed to control the dangerous animal instincts of human beings. A few hundred miles away, Hitler also believes that democracy is dangerous because, according to him, people cannot be trusted. When the National Socialists take over Germany, one of their first steps is to take control of businesses and make them state-owned. The National Socialists also begin to focus on the emotions of the masses, but instead of striving for a consumer society, they channel technology to create a unified Socialist state. Goebbles organises events with the aim of uniting the feelings, thoughts and desires of the German people - into one. His greatest inspiration was - Edward Bernays.[241]

> While Bernays has been lauded as the "father of public relations" and "the PR profession's first philosopher and intellectual", Goebbels is remembered as a "master manipulator", "probably the most overt and arguably the most important, exponent of propaganda in history".[242]

Goebbels is later portrayed in history books as a villain for his propaganda work in the German Reich, while Bernays is instead given the epithet of "Father of Public Relations" - although their views on how peo-

241 https://www.historytoday.com/miscellanies/original-influencer
242 Kerrie Milburn "Bernays and Goebbels: The strange case of Dr Jekyll and Mr Hyde", 2023

ple should be exploited through propaganda, advertising and PR - are similar.

> If you tell a lie big enough and keep repeating it, people will eventually come to believe it. The lie can be maintained only for such time as the State can shield the people from the political, economic and/or military consequences of the lie. It thus becomes vitally important for the State to use all of its powers to repress dissent, for the truth is the mortal enemy of the lie, and thus by extension, the truth is the greatest enemy of the State. - Joseph Goebbles[243]

Meanwhile, in the United States, there are violent riots. In 1932, a new president is elected - Franklin D. Roosevelt, who wants to find a new way to deal with the angry masses. He gathers new advisors, experts and public relations consultants who launch government projects to calm the masses. Roosevelt is convinced, after the failure of the stock market crash, that the free market cannot be realised and that, as in Germany, the state must control the economy instead. However, business leaders and the elite are initially reluctant to give up power. At first, they see state-controlled companies as a disadvantage. When they realise they cannot be free of state power, they decide to use it to their advantage - and become one with the state.

Suddently, big business on Wall Street is launching a new PR campaign that takes matters into its own hands. This PR campaign claims that it is the big corporations, not politicians, that have built modern America. They work hard to get their campaign into the media, preferably on as many pages of newspapers as possible. Now Bernays' work is multiplying and a host of famous

243 https://www.jewishvirtuallibrary.org/joseph-goebbels-on-the-quot-big-lie-quot

firms are working with the new tool - public relations. Among the names are Rockefeller and General Motors - two of the biggest companies in the West. The government wants to curb this conflict, gives in and agrees to co-operate.

A major gala, which is part of the PR campaign Bernays is responsible for, aims to link democracy, politics and big business. Everyone from the establishment, celebrities and politicians are invited. General Motors contributes a miniature model of a city. The gala seeks to demonstrate the benefits of socialism/democracy working in partnership with business/consumption. The new society will be borderless, with new pathways and innovations, and will operate on a global scale - a "World Society". A new world democracy where entrepreneurs and the elite would respond to people's innermost desires and the role of man in this utopian society is the happy consumer. Such a view of humanity values people no more than cattle. But politicians are finally convinced during the gala, and Wall Street and the powers that be agree to work together - once and for all.[244]

The outbreak of World War II changes the course of events. Freud manages to escape to London through his contacts in 1938, but dies three weeks later, cared for by his daughter and heiress - Anna Freud.

The barbarism of the Nazi Germans confirms to the elite that Freud's theories are true. This becomes the proof that man is not to be trusted, and politicians seek further ways to control the masses. They start to take Bernays' and Freud's ideas even more seriously and begin to mass-incorporate them into society - through corporations, public information, government and the CIA - to develop an all-encompassing system to manage the civilian population. What they don't realise is that they are dealing with the ideas of a cocaine ad-

244 Documentary: The Century of the Self 2002 British television documentary
    series by filmmaker Adam Curtis

dict. Sigmund Freud had developed an addiction to cocaine for much of his life. - This gives a cocaine ad-
dict the confidence to influence a whole nation if not
the whole world.

In Germany, denazification begins with 'ideological
subversion', but the rest of the West also wants a
human being who can internalise democratic values. Psychoanalysis, the new method, is believed to be able to
open up the human psyche and help it to uphold democratic values. Anna Freud will now continue the work of
the late Sigmund Freud - as the head of the World
Centre for Psychology. Her mission is to educate and
'train' people to keep their animal urges in check.
Anna and her colleagues offer psychological techniques
to create these 'new' people. She is practising on the
children of an acquaintance, a case named "The Birmingham Children"[245]. The project aims to teach and
manipulate these children to adapt to the rules of
society while submitting to authority. It is more than
just 'moral' guidance. The theory is that if children
follow the rules of what is acceptable, within the
norms of society, they will be well-adjusted, happy and
in control as adults. But if they cannot submit, they
may fall prey to the unconscious irrational urges. What
was not known at the time was that this experiment
would serve as the basis for thousands of institutions
in the United States - through the US government. From
this, in 1946, the National Mental Health Act was
developed - a major national health programme. It was
designed to address the threat Freud saw before him, on
a large, national scale. A lot of money was spent on
training psychologists. Many clinics were opened and
psychologists were to help people submit to the norms
of society and family life and control dangerous
emotions.

245 Documentary: The Century of the Self 2002 British television documentary
    series by filmmaker Adam Curtis

To make America work as a welfare society, it became necessary to use psychological techniques to control mass rationality. Those in power did not believe that this undermined the capacity of citizens - on the contrary, they believed that it ensured the survival of democracy.

Anna Freud and her colleagues had succeeded in reaching out to the world. However, the experiment, the 'Birmingham Children', had not become well-adjusted adults, despite all the therapy. They had become alcoholic, divorced and had mental health problems.[246] Because they were considered the world's living proof that psychoanalysis worked, the real results were kept quietly. The news of their fates was not allowed to get out. Politically and scientifically, Anna Freud's theories became more and more embedded in society and it became harder to admit that something was wrong. And the influence of the Freud family, including Edward Bernays, would only grow.

> Voddie UTII: You just ave to understand the spirit of the age. Marx is doing the science of economics. Freud, the science of psychology. Darwin is operationg within the realm of biology. [247]

Anna Freud's ideas were passed on to the intelligence community. The CIA begins conducting secret experiments to access and control people's minds, according to Dr Jake Gittinger, the CIA's chief psychologist from 1950 to 1974.[248] The experiments involved reprogramming people to achieve a desired outcome. And the project was funded. Millions were paid to several universities

---

246 Documentary: The Century of the Self 2002 British television documentary
   series by filmmaker Adam Curtis
247 Documentary: Uncle Tom II: An American Odyssey,2022, Voddie
248 Documentary: The Century of the Self 2002 British television documentary
   series by filmmaker Adam Curtis

to conduct the secret research. The experiments focused on memory, electrotherapy, drugs, and were also conducted on a larger scale in mental hospitals.

The new psychological perspective had now become indispensable; it was felt that psychologists should be present in every government department to advise politicians. However, there were critics who felt that the methods of Bernays and Freud were controlling people rather than helping them, that everything was done for the sake of power, and that 'puppets' were being created to fulfil new desires and needs, thus disempowering people and turning them into children. This was seen as power corrupted and used for the wrong purposes. Forcing people to choose what they wanted was not democracy. The debate on the imbalance between the state and the individual was more open and free in those days than it is today.

The student revolt that was suppressed

A revolution was attempted in the 1960s, with ordinary people trying to free themselves from the shackles of society. Young people and students were against brainwashing and the consumer society, and protests took over the streets and squares. Some of the groups even carried out bomb attacks against several large companies. The wave of revolution was a serious one, and teenagers, Hippies and students worked to liberate people and society from what they saw as state control. The personal became the political. If you could change yourself, you could change the world.

Students did not behave like the typical, predictable consumer. In business world, this was seen as a major problem. Sales figures had dropped, radically. The new, rebellious generation was not buying life insurance. Customers who buy life insurance worry about the future and don't live as much in the present. Wall

Street was in crisis. The solution for big business was to hire psychologists and, once again through observations, interviews and statistical surveys, follow and study the new generation. Clothes, cars, everything would now be moulded to the 'new' consumer. This was done against the wishes of the new generation - they did not want to be interviewed, observed or manipulated. The big companies didn't give in and continued their research, trying again and again to understand the language and the music the Hippies listened to. All statistics were recorded to create a new picture of the new consumer.[249]

The Stanford Research Institute at the University of California, one of the institutes researching "psychology and influence" at the time, collaborated with businesses, politicians and the armed forces. Together, they wanted to satisfy the desires of the new generation and save economic growth. Eventually, they managed to identify the lifestyle and values of Hippies, and started to categorise people into groups, based on values, wants, needs and desires. The statistics were then categorised so that the right target group could be paired with the right company, so that companies would know, exactly who to target in advertising and magazines. People were categorised into sports enthusiasts, intellectuals, parents, children and so on. This was the beginning of 'lifestyle marketing', a concept that lasted well into the 21st century. Eventually, companies managed to hook even the Hippie generation - after their dogged research, they knew what these young people wanted, what they thought, where they lived and how they wanted to live their lives. The link, between Maslow's hierarchy of needs and self-actualisation to status products was made.

249 Documentary: The Century of the Self 2002 British television documentary
    series by filmmaker Adam Curtis

In their attempts to ensnare and involve new audiences, advertisements began to use words that appealed to young people who were in the process of self-actualisation. The written and spoken word, now became a tool for multi-business and the organised confusion of concepts grew. Through research, advertising phrases were adapted to class, age and gender - to make products more appealing. This is how revolutionaries were customised for consumption. The Wall Street crisis was solved.

Sales figures exploded, as did demand. Producing the same kind of products was easy, as it involved 'mass production' via automated, robot-controlled factories. Customised products, appealing to *different* types of consumers, were much harder to produce. Therefore, production moved to other parts of the world where labour was cheap and factories were still run by human labour. This forced those countries to stay in the industrial age.

Instead of *creating* their own identity and thus *changing* the world, young people would now 'buy' an identity. Consumption no longer had any limits. The new man felt freer than ever before, but at the same time became more dependent on maintaining his identity through department stores. The focus shifted from social revolt and the power of change - to creating and re-creating one's identity with money, while the 'rebellious' spirit remained, but had been skilfully manipulated to be expressed through a pair of jeans instead. Companies now realised that consumer autonomy was not a threat but simply another opportunity - for themselves.

This type of intrusion into human culture, especially into various youth cultures, has since expanded greatly in the 20th and 21st centuries. When a new culture is born among young people, a culture that emerges 'naturally' from human enviroment, such as a new style of music or a fashion of clothing - corporations are there immediately to take over or 'hijack' the culture - in order to sell more products. When corporations hijack a culture, by starting to produce the music or manufacture the garment in question, a psychological process begins between consumer and company. For this purpose, the existence of specialised professions known as "trend spotters" or "business intelligence" has emerged. One such company, which looks for cultural seeds that arise naturally among people, only to sell them to big business and oligarchs, writes as follows on its website:

> Guiding our work is our proprietary Purpose-Driven Innovation (PDI) methodology: a core analytical framework that turns trends into meaningful business opportunities. It's designed to guide professionals and the wider world in both identifying and acting on them.
>
> We've embarked on an exciting multi-year journey to assist future-focused business professionals in every possible way to identify and run with meaningful business opportunities.[250]

When a naturally occurring culture is used for the purpose of achieving economic power - the natural drivers of that same culture are stifled. The artificial layers make modern man unable to live out his authentic culture; instead humans are repeatedly deprived of this right. Natural cultural development is constantly interrupted and hijacked by the elite, the media and big business. Cultural movements are hijacked and replaced with consumerism, in the same way bankrupt companies are bought and sold.

---

250 https://www.trendwatching.com/careers

A new type of political class is emerging

> Don't tempt me Frodo. Understand that I would
> use this Ring from a desire to do good. But
> through me... it would wield a power too
> great and terrible to imagine.[251]

Throughout history, there have been numerous individuals as well as organised groups striving for change and development. The politically active, especially those in the 1960s and 1970s, had a spirit of activism and real enterprise, when it came to political organisation and community building. They knew how to move from words to action; to take action.

How many basement rooms were not filled with committed Hippies and, two decades later, equally committed Punks, discussing politics, bonding and demonstrating against injustice? Where the power-hungry state was discussed and a real fire was lit in the hearts of the many young people. They dared to go out and demonstrate and they dared to protest. They didn't take what the state said and swallowed it easily; instead, they wanted to think for themselves and cultivate their own opinions.

This fervour is now conspicuous by its absence in the Western world. It has been hijacked and channelled by governments and big business - into the dull, endless squirrel wheel of consumer society. If you compare the revolutionaries who once carried the fire at the barricades in the 1960s, 70s, 80s and 90s with today's politically engaged among the adult establishment, the difference could not be greater. This heard of "culture-workers" have grown up with middle-class parents and had everything handed to them on a silver platter - during a time when life was, in a sense, at its best -

251 Gandalf, Lord of the Rings, 2001

and went straight to college, where they were drilled in the usual unoriginal political ideas. These ideas have often remained - theoretical commitments, and after years of rosy dreams of social justice, they have utterly failed to act on them, instead allowing middle-class tendencies, convenience and their own needs to come to life when adulthood arrives. The generation described here, which grew up in the 21st century, is one of the most affluent generations of all time.

> How has this unfavourable relation of forces come about? How did the West decline from its triumphal march to its present sickness? Have there been fatal turns and losses of direction in its development? It does not seem so. The West kept advancing socially in accordance with its proclaimed intentions, with the help of brilliant technological progress. And all of a sudden it found itself in its present state of weakness.[252]

As the resistance movements of the old left have declined in the 21st century, a new type of political class has emerged. The next chapter will describe how Marxism went from infant 19th century communism to 21st century WOKE culture and how the Marxist legacy is being utilised by big business in modern times.

Marxism - the beginning

Who was Karl Marx? This big thinker who has managed to influence world politics for over a century was born in 1818, came from a wealthy upper-class family and had an idyllic childhood with a solid bourgeoisie education. His father supported the French Revolution, which inspired Marx to become a revolutionary - despite upper-class fears of further revolts and bloody raids in the

252 Alexander Solzhenitsyn, "A World Split Apart", 8 June 1978, Harvard University

175

wake of the French Revolution. As was customary for the upper classes, Karl Marx studied at the University of Lyon. Unfortunately, the hot-tempered Marx got into duel and fight after fight with the young aristocracy and ended up in prison. Because of his escapades, his father said he had to move to Berlin.

There he continued to create provocations. Above all, he criticised the state and, as those in power in Berlin did not tolerate opposition, he was not allowed to study further. He moved again, this time founding the 'Neue Reihnische Zeitung' in Cologne, a newspaper that became known for its angry and sarcastic tone, attacking the old aristocracy. Marx began to gain popularity in this context and at the same time took an interest in wine merchants who had gone bankrupt and wanted to be heard. These growers blamed the state for their plight and Marx publicised how they were not given the freedom they were entitled to. The ruling powers now shut down his newspaper. His reputation grew and he now became notorious for his ideas. Political circumstances forced him into exile and he fled again, this time to Paris in 1843. Here he found inspiration and a sense that the French Revolution had never really been buried.

Paris was back then swarming with anarchists and communists. His wife, who had kindly moved in with him, was given a lower standard - being the daughter of a baron and originally belonging to the bourgeoisie. Here, in Paris, Marx discovers that part of the problem of society was the economy and productivity of the state, and that workers in factories are given only repetitive tasks, things that humanity is not really meant to do. He also discovers that both the workers and the capitalists are taken over by higher, elitist powers. Marx meets Engels, who works as a superintendent at a textile factory owned by his father. There, the well-off Engels gets a mistress who shows

him the slums and the hard working life. Marx and
Engels begin to co-operate, but don't get very far
until Marx is once again expelled from France. In their
new home in Brussels, they reunite and form a communist
organisation.

In Brussels, they also write one of their famous works,
'Das Kapital'. Because of Marx's criticism of the state
and his excessive drinking, he is arrested and forced
into exile again. Now the problems pile up, he drinks
even more and writes in total poverty. His wife and
children struggle to survive in the slums and the
family pawns all their possessions. In addition, Marx
gets his housekeeper pregnant, which only exacerbates
the crisis. His own children perish from poverty, dying
of disease and starvation one by one. Engels also tires
of their cooperation and goes back to his wealthy
father and the bourgeois life where he is most comfortable.

This "Left" that Marx is now considered to have fought
for, first really emerged in 1789, when King Louis XIV
of France convened his National Assembly. The nobility
and clergy ended up on the right side of the king and
the bourgeoisie on the less honourable left. Shortly
afterwards, the bourgeoisie carries out a bourgeois
revolution and the workers carry out the socialist
revolution, and it is this revolutionary tradition of
France that Marx and Engels capitalise on. Marxist
ideology is initially called 'scientific socialism'
because socialism and Marxism are considered so similar.

> Marx and Engels drew from these socialist or
> communist, ideas born in the French revolu-
> tion, as well as from the German philosophy
> of Georg Wilhelm Friedrich Hegel, and British
> political economy, particularly that of Adam

Smith and David Ricardo. Marx and Engels developed a body of ideas which they called scientific socialism, more commonly called Marxism. Marxism comprised a theory of history (historical materialism), a critique of political economy, as well as a political, and philosophical theory.[253]

In the beginning, Marx and Engels do not speak of the "Left", nor does Lenin; the "Left" is looked down upon and held up as a bad example. Yet the "Left" movement, homogeneously invoked Marx and Engels as great their role models, lifting a legacy from them. Instead of adopting Marx and Engels' ideas outright, the left misunderstood them. Marx, for example, believed that capitalism must carry the proletarian revolution and Marx and Engels believed that communism should only arise in societies with a strong bourgeois economy. Revolution does not break out in bourgeois countries, contrary to what Marx and Engels wanted for the population. The first revolution breaks out in a capital-rich but imperialistic Russia. The widespread Russian peasant class - which has no role to play in communist society - is consigned to starvation. Lenin therefore had to reinterpret Marxist theory with Trotsky and Stalin to make it work. The new 'Leninism' offers an anti-capitalist, anti-Western revolution in which traditional Western culture and capitalism are confused and become one. In the wake of this, the idea of fighting Western culture and Western traditions is reinforced. The intellectual "Leninists" are to "bestow" this transformed Marxist theory on the working class, through a mission of salvation. Because of the intellectual language, "Capital" and Marx can only be read by intellectual academics.

253 Jean Jauré's "A Socialist History of the French Revolution", 2022

Another aspect of Marx and Engels that the "Left" misunderstands, is the theory that development can only take place in a worldwide perspective, under a world market where colonialism is celebrated as something progressive. Marx and Engels were thus in favour of colonialism. At the same time, Marx and Engels criticise religion, and Marx transforms this criticism into a critique of society and political structures. According to Marx, society and the reality in which people live, are distorted. He believes that man needs to free himself from the shackles of society in order to be able to realise himself, otherwise he will become alienated from the world and exploited by the feudal lords. The Western tradition of knowledge, which is born in the ecclesiastical environment, which is why older universities in England look like cathedrals, including in the film Harry Potter, and has a long history, must also be renewed. To transform theory from idea to reality, Marx believes that the proletariat needs to make a revolution against society, contribute to the dissolution of the world order and abolish all private property. He also sees consumption as something useless.

In *Das Kapital*, Marx's *magnum opus*, the first part of which was published in 1867, similar ideas were expressed in the theory of 'commodity fetishism'. Under capitalism, commodities are produced not because of their use value but because of their exchange value. Their concrete natural properties become unimportant. The important thing becomes that they can be exchanged for money. The abstract property, the exchange value on the market, becomes decisive, products become fetishes that are worshipped because of their inherent power. The capitalist economy appears to Marx as a regiment of abstractions. The economy becomes the new mysticism, the new religion.[254]

Much of modern politics is based on the theories of Karl Marx from the 19th century. The phenomenon of using old political ideology that is more than a century old is not only conservative, but can be considered highly outdated. The political situation back then is very different from the social structure we live in now. Back then, people were caught up in a real tyranny in a very different way, especially the less well-off classes. The streets were full of a large amount of homeless people, many of them children, until the establishment of children's wards and orphanages. Disease and deprivation and unsanitary conditions were common and life expectancy among the population was very low. The need for radical change was enormous. A large part of the population suffered, both physically and mentally, on a completely different level than people in the West do today. The theories of Marxism are used today as if we lived and suffered as they did in the 19th century. The ideology has certainly found new ways and forms, but as long as the foundations are used, human political development cannot move forward.

According to Karl Marx, part of this misery was due to religion; he wanted to create a religion that would surpass all other religions and give man back his individuality. He separated the classes into two, those who have and those who have not.[255] However, he wanted the working classes to use violence to bring about change, so that justice would be done.

That Marx himself did not live as he taught, with secret mistresses and an illegitimate son whom he did not want to recognise so as not to tarnish his reputation, must probably be attributed to the harsh reality of the time. Despite his own life and bloodthirsty the-

254 Svante Nordin, "History of Philosophy", 2017, p. 479
255 James Lindsay | WOKE Culture HAS NOT Gone Too Far - 6/8 | Oxford Union

ories, he inspired much of the world, including the Chinese government in Asia. The Communist Manifesto states:

> In short, the Communists everywhere support every revolutionary movement against the existing social and political order of things.
>
> In all these movements, they bring to the front, as the leading question in each, the property question, no matter what its degree of development at the time.
>
> Finally, they labour everywhere for the union and agreement of the democratic parties of all countries.
>
> The Communists disdain to conceal their views and aims. They openly declare that their ends can be attained only by the forcible overthrow of all existing social conditions. Let the ruling classes tremble at a Communistic revolution.[256]

Out with the old, in with the new.

A Communist Party is formed in China in 1921, around the same time as the Communist parties in Europe and the United States. Mao Dzedung, who becomes party leader, is inspired by Karl Marx to create a new political class system in China. He renews Marx's theory of class division and instead establishes different identities into which the population will be divided. The establishment of the Chinese Marxist caste system requires first creating a desire for community among the masses through public relations campaigns and political influence. The project is initially sabotaged by the regime itself so that the community will "fail" and give rise to an even greater desire. Subsequently, a

256 Manifesto of the Communist Party (1848), chapter 4

long-awaited unification takes place - now in completely new forms, under Marxist forms.[257]

Under the cover of Marx and Engels' theories, all of
society's problems are blamed on the old and traditional. All old culture, old thinking, old habits had to
be destroyed under the rule of Mao and the Communists.
Instead, the 'new' identities, 10 in number, would now
define and govern the Chinese people. People are categorised into different colours. For example, there are
'red' and 'good' and 'good' identities, and 'black' and
'bad' identities, such as anti-revolutionaries and
anti-communists. 'Bad influence' and 'Counter-revolu-
tionary' are just some of the terms used to classify
people.[258]

> In the cities, the most favourable categories
> were "revolutionary cadre," "family of a re-
> volutionary martyr" and "industrial worker."
> At the other end of the spectrum sat cate-
> gories such as "capitalist," "rightist" or
> worse still "counterrevolutionary."(...) In
> the countryside, "poor and lower middle peas-
> ants" were regarded by the party as its most
> reliable allies, while "middle peasants" who
> had more to lose from the collectivisation of
> agriculture, were to be neutralized. "Rich
> peasants," "landlords," "counterrevolutionar-
> ies" and "rotten elements," meaning crimi-
> nals, were viewed as enemies to be isolated.
> These foes, collectively known as "the four
> elements" (*silei fenzi*), were attacked in
> various campaigns and placed under "the
> supervision of the masses." Cadres would fre-
> quently assign them undesirable or dangerous
> work such as cleaning out village latrines.[259]

257 Helen Pluckrose and Helen Joyce, The Ideological Roots of WOKEness
258 Critical Race Theory, Queer Theory & Maoist Education, James Lindsay, New
   Discourses
259 1 - Chinese Society under Mao: Classifications, Social Hierarchies and
   Distribution. Published online by Cambridge University Press: 21 March

China's children and young people were also to be brought into line with the 'good' revolution and become part of the same identity policy. Those children who excel in 'better' behaviour receive praise and gifts, which are shown to the outside world as the 'good example'.[260] At the same time, this theory separates generations from each other and separates the younger from the older, those belonging to the old culture, thus creating further division. The old culture had to go and the young were seen as the tool to make it happen.[261]

In North Korea, the Communist Party is founded somewhat later, in 1945, with the party leader Kim Il Song, an ancestor of Kim Jung Un. The caste system is also established in North Korea, initially to convince the people that the caste system and the new communism are a long-awaited and positive reform. The electoral strategy is this - if the people give up property rights, freedom of speech and freedom of movement across borders, the communists would make everyone equal, create access to free education and free healthcare. As soon as the population voted in and accepted the Communist Party, the entire nation was divided into 51 different castes, in a system of harsh, hierarchical 'identity politics'. The castes, in turn, are divided into three classes. One third is the 'royal' class, one third is the so-called 'wavering' class, which needs the constant supervision and guidance of the state. The last third is the 'hostile' class. The families belonging to this class are persecuted by the state in various ways - until they die. Generation after generation

2019 "Class Status" (A Social History of Maoist China, Conflict and Change, 1949-1976) by Felix Wemheuer

260 Critical Race Theory, Queer Theory & Maoist Education, James Lindsay, New Discourses

261 Critical Race Theory, Queer Theory & Maoist Education, James Lindsay, New Discourses

is subjected to cruel persecution because the class system - is hereditary.

Frankfurt School and the new era

In 1921, a Marxist institute opens in interwar Frankfurt. Researchers and academics work there with the mission to further spread the Marxist revolution. Its researchers aim to transform Marxism from an economic ideology into a theory that can also be incorporated into culture, as Gramci intended. A new kind of Marxism is therefore being developed that differs from the Soviet one. Following the research carried out, it was decided to no longer focus on the working class. Now they want to reach out to other groups of people and social strata. A major step in the new strategy is to cross-fertilise Marx's theories on society with Freud's theories on psychoanalysis. Here too, they are influenced by his ideas.

One of Freud's great theories is that everyone in Western society lives under constant psychological oppression. This theory is now to be incorporated into society through Marxism and, together with Marx's ideas, the researchers have sufficient basis for an ideological new start. Following in Gramci's footsteps, it is decided that not only an economic revolution is needed, but also a social and cultural revolution. In this context, a new kind of social psychology is developed, based on Marxist and Freudian theories. The Institute invents the theory that gender is not biologically rooted but a result of how the two sexes actually live - in other words, a social construction. The term 'Critical Theory' is also used for the first time. The term is invented as part of the tools to support the revolution or 'infiltration' against Western society. "Critical Theory" is based on the idea that the revolutionary should always be critical of

traditional society and that the goal is to deconstruct, or crush, traditional society piece by piece
through constant questioning. The Frankfurt Marxist
Institute writes that Marxism, with the help of
"Critical Theory", would even obliterate logic - if an
argument was in favour of the communist ideology, it
was "logical", if it was against, it would automatically be "illogical". "Critical Theory" became widespread
and is now used in all universities and most humanities
departments in the West and around the world. When the
Nazis seized power in the early 1930s, the Institute's
researchers fled Frankfurt for the United States. There
they found a welcome and steady financial support, and
were able to work undisturbed, shifting their focus
from Germany to America.[262] Because Marxism, in its
ideological form, is so close to socialism, the
Institute's research is widely accepted and embraced by
the US government. Socialism was a social movement that
originated in the 19th century and lacked clear practical tools. The Frankfurt Institute, and Marxism, gave
socialism its actual tools.

The sweet 1960s

At the newly opened Frankfurt Institute, research had
begun on American people. Scholars Herbert Marcuse and
Max Horkheimer are two of the initiators who later play
an important role in all educational institutions in
the United States. Marcuse comes from the upper middle
class and Horkheimer is the son of a rich businessman.
Their research results show that the whole of the
American people are, as they put it, "fascist" at
heart, and the thesis is that if one subscribe to the
traditional beliefs of the American people, one is
mentally unstable, a view of human nature not unlike
Freud's. This is published in books and is widely di-

262 Documentary: The History of Political Correctness, 1994 C-span

sseminated in socialist America.[263] Marcuse writes the book "The One-Dimensional Man" in which he further develops Marxism to suit the revolutionary students of the 1960s. The Marxism of the 1960s is based on Freud's theory of oppression, which leads to the birth of Western "identity politics" that divides people into identities where only the victim roles suffer from social oppression.

Now the question is finally being answered - who can replace the working class in the revolutionary struggle? Those best placed to carry this ideology forward are the students and the fight they will wage is fierce. Socialist politics is becoming narrower and the new wave of communists has tolerance only for left-wing ideas and nothing else, which will be called 'Repressive Tolerance'. All other theories, especially traditional ones, come under heavy criticism. Through thinkers like Marcuse and Horkheimer, who become the students' political role models and gurus, the ideas of the Institute spread like wildfire.[264]

In the 1960s, Marxism begins to influence entire societies in the West. Beginning with the student revolt among young people, it escalates to the infiltration of Marxist ideology into institutes, medical institutions, education, the media and the political arena.

> It is not unusual to be a conservative. But it is unusual to be an intellectual conservative. In both Britain and America some 70 percent of academics identify themselves as "on the left", while the surrounding culture is increasingly hostile to traditional values, or to any claim that might be

263 Documentary: The History of Political Correctness, 1994 C-span
264 Documentary: The History of Political Correctness, 1994 C-span

made for the high achievement of western Civilisation.[265]

It uses educational giants such as John Dewey, whose theories influence generations of young people, so that students trained in socialism or Marxism become leaders and in turn representatives of left-wing ideology.

> Dewey was ardent statist and a believer in the Hegelian idea that the child exists to be trained to serve the State. This requires suppression of the individualist tendencies and a careful spoon-feeding of approved knowledge.[266]

But the Western Marxists have one thing in common. An upper-class socialite named Mabel Dodge throws parties and gatherings to which she invites radical and famous socialists such as Walter Lippman, Hutchins Hapgood and Carl Van Vechten. These are established figures in politics, the entertainment industry, the media and educational institutions, whom Mabel calls 'Movers and Shakers'.[267] All of them, without exception, come from a higher social strata with an educated background. Yet they want to overthrow society based on an ideology created for a distressed working class during 19th century industrialisation. Why is this? Is Freud's social theory of psychological oppression better suited to the affluent society? In the post-war period, the following changes take place: Marxism stops generating poverty and instead generates wealth. It does not generate misery but prosperity. It does not produce unfreedom but freedom and democracy. The working class is bribed by an abundance of products and is transformed into a consumer class, and so the students are

265 Roger Scruton "How to be a concervative", 2014
266 Antony C Sutton, "America's Secret Establishment: An Introduction to the Order of Skull & Bones" p 14, 1986
267 Documentary: Uncle Tom II: An American Odyssey, 2022, Chad Jackson

made to rebel instead.[268] More and more, the Marxist tactics end up in the hands of the educated class.

Saul Alinsky and his students

> The pressure that gave us our positive power was the negative of racism in a white society. We exploited it for our own purposes.[269]

As in the above example, various Marxist tactics and strategies have been fully exploited for various purposes and ends. One man who develops it into pure art, is Saul Alinsky. He calls his art "Community Organising" which he describes in his book, "Rules for Radicals". In it, he compiles aggressive and unscrupulous political methods to bring down the opposition. This unscrupulousness is something he learnt when, as a young orphan, he was taken in by the Mafia in the 1930s.

If you come to an organisation or a society and want change, then according to Alinsky you have to *disorganise* it first. "There is no nice way to getting things changed"[270] .

> Saul Alinsky, mentor to Obama and Hillary, learnt his political lessons from the Al Capone mob in Chicago. Mobster Frank Nitti was impressed with Alinsky because he found Alinsky to be more ruthless and callous than he himself was.[271]

> Obama, like Hillary, learnt the art of the "shakedown" from their political godfather,

---

268 Ideologies 15 February 2019 - Left-wing ideas part 1 of 4: The roots of the Left, Engelsberg Mill, Ängelsberg - Svante Nordin, Professor of the History of Ideas and Learning, Lund University
269 Saul Alinsky, "Rules For Radicals" p 144, 1971
270 Saul Alinsky "I'd Organize Hell" - TV interview 1966 https://www.youtube.com/watch?v=OfAyNrEsqic
271 Dinesh,D'Souza, "Stealing America: what my experience with criminal gangs taught me about Obama, Hillary, and the Democratic party," page 201, 2015

> Saul Alinsky. Here Obama teaches other com-
> munity organisers how to extract money and
> power from corporations and the rich by (in
> the words of the Don Corleone) "making them
> an offer they can't refuse."[272]

After Salinsky's ideas spread to universities and colleges, he is called The Father of Community Organising. His book "Rules for Radicals" becomes famous and is studied in educational institutions around the world. One of Alinsky's tactics is that a group of people who need to be convinced must be in a "frustrated" state and feel "futureless" in order for them to embrace change.

> People are naturally fearful of change they
> avoid and resist it and must be frustrated
> and defeated lost and future-less in the
> existing system so that they let go of past
> and change future.[273]

According to Alinsky, infiltration is better than a bloody revolution, and instead of using Gramci's old concept, he coins a new one called "Gradualism". Revolution is thus a gradual process and reform must take place through institutions - first, according to Alinsky, one needs to observe and understand, and then infiltrate from within. Another rule from the book is to "portray" the political opponent as evil, mean and bad and there, according to Alinsky, all means are allowed. Below are more famous rules from "Rules for Radicals":

> - The organiser must stir up dissatisfaction
> and discontent in the community

272 Dinesh,D'Souza, "Stealing America: what my experience with criminal gangs
   taught me about Obama, Hillary, and the Democratic party," page 202, 2015
273 Saul Alinsky "I'd Organize Hell" - TV interview 1966
   https://www.youtube.com/watch?v=OfAyNrEsqic

- The opposition must be portrayed as the personification of evil, against whom any and all methods are a fair game

- Unless there is commotion people wont act

- Power is not what you have but what the enemy thinks you have

- Never go outside the experience of the people

- Always go outside the experience of their enemies

- Make the enemy live up to their own rules

- Ridicule is a weapon[274]

After the revolt of the 1960s, infiltration was slow and the new, educated academics took over important positions. The fact that Marx himself strongly disliked professors, did not seem to matter. Universities claim to teach 'social' or 'economic' theory, but what they fail to realise is that everything has a Marxist angle. A telling example from a contemporary, not uncommon, academic publication from Harvard University:

> Karl Marx (1818-1883) was the most important of all theorists of socialism.[275]

At the same time, during the 1960s and onwards, a cultural environment is created in which conservatives are pushed out and the communist left is welcomed in. This also applies to the entire education system as such - institutions that are supposed to be neutral and for "everyone". [276]

274 Saul Alinsky "Rules For Radicals", 1971
275 "MARX, KARL" - Michael Rosen -
     https://scholar.harvard.edu/files/michaelrosen/files/karl_marx.pdf
276 How the left took over everything, James Lindsay,
     https://www.youtube.com/watch?v=q_NTXZymro8&t=1070s

Its unfortunate but history is written by academics and academia is a toll of the left.[277]

A well-known tool used by the left to infiltrate institutions is the criticism of all that is old and traditional. They want to overhaul all history of ideas, literature and humanistic theory. Every text is to be countered by a counter-text, and all classic fiction, all great works are to be discussed and accused of one-sidedness and lack of awareness. Instead, they make up their own versions of old classical culture, thereby undermining great works. [278]

Here is an example of the firm grip of Marxist theory on the educational system. The example is taken from a literature course at the English Department of Washington University, where a Marxist critique and reworking of cultural practices, is seen as "expanding" culture.

> Our study of Marxist theory will necessarily involve close, intensive reading of dense and often highly philosophical texts. Through engagement with these texts we will seek understand how a *materialist method* indebted to Marx and Engels emerged as dominant (if often unnamed or acknowledged) within contemporary literary and cultural studies scholarship, and how diverse critical practices (given labels such as "critical theory," "feminist theory," "critical race theory," and "cultural studies") sit within an expansive Marxist intellectual tradition.[279]

277 Documentary: Uncle Tom: An Oral History of the American Black Conservative, 2020, R.C. Maxwell
278 Anna Hallberg Phd Södertörn University, Axess TV, https://www.axess.se/tv/en-ny-bok/vansterns-ideer-med-anna-victoria-hallberg/
279 ENGL 308 A: Marxism and Literary Theory, Alys Eve Weinbaum - https://english.washington.edu/courses/2021/winter/engl/308/a

Compulsory state education did not exist before 1950. Instead, all education, such as literacy, is localised and regional. Once compulsory education conquered the masses, state influence could be introduced, including through textbooks. History was written from the perspective of political educational institutions and thus standardised. In the new socialist society, influence and control over education was necessary to indoctrinate Marxist ideas into society.[280]

> It is the victor who writes the history and counts the dead - Sir William Francis Butler[281]

Marxism = WOKE

Marxism has, from the class divisions of the 19th century, through the barricades of the 1960s, travelled the long road of transformation to the postmodern leftist politics of the 21st century, also known as "WOKE". Such politics is not the kind of politics that takes over at the top of political organisations. Instead, it influences schools, libraries and cultural institutions. Since the 19th century, Marxism has remained in the political system, disguised as socialism or leftism. One strong remnant that remains, but in a new guise, is so-called 'identity politics'. The principle is not unlike that used in Asia. Instead, identity politics has taken on new forms - and new roles.[282]

The generation practising the new identity politics has been given the name 'WOKE' in Americanised culture. This term, initially intended to mean being 'woke' on important issues such as racism and gender equality, instead became a name for the new Marxist left culture. According to Professor Victor Davies Hanson, the term WOKE originated in a Protestant movement where, in the

280 Documentary: Uncle Tom II: An American Odyssey, 2022
281 Sir William Francis Butler "Charles George Gordon", 1892
282 Why Marxism is so appealing, Jordan Peterson and Thomas Sowell, https://www.youtube.com/watch?v=4yowxcqdM7E

late 19th century, in an agnostic society, people considered themselves 'waking up' to Christ. Later, it became about fighting oppression and injustice in society with the support of the state. With Barack Obama, the class struggle was replaced by anti-racism, according to Hanson. Marxism failed to invoke a real underclass in the US in the early 20th century because the class system was so fluid - anyone could make a fortune, but race and colour were harder to replace. Marxism gained a stronger foothold amongst the "anti-racists" and the issue of victimhood became stagnant. Although Barack Obama wakes up in a large mansion at Martha's Vinyard in the morning and is served his coffee by a servant, according to the new WOKE-ideology, he still has the right to lecture thousands and thousands during the day about what real sacrifice is. Before the rise of the WOKE ideology, society was based on a meritocracy that was blind to skin colour and origin. Hanson argues that dividing people into external attributes in this way reverts to a tribalistic perspective. He goes on to criticise the WOKE-generation for first taking courses in art, music and literature and then taking old classical works and recalibrating them to fit their new political standards.

On the one hand, Shakespeare, Tolstoy and Verne are undermined; in the modern version, Boris Godunoff sits like a CEO at a computer; he can be anyone, he and his job are interchangeable in the modern version. Contemporary versions are created without respect for traditional, classical literary and musical creators who built their works on ideas of faith and conviction. Tarkovsky was a modern filmmaker who instead sought to elevate and honour traditional, classical works and their creators.

In doing so, the WOKE-generation believes that they have reached the end of history and that no generation after them will want access to classical culture as it has been preserved for thousands of years. Hanson calls for a thought experiment to ask: if the generation living in 50 years says "You, the WOKE generation, had millions of homeless and abortions, and therefore we will destroy everything you have created" and so would every generation henceforth. Then there will be no traces of culture left. Instead, the classical works will be contextualised and remind us of what was good about history and what was not. If the WOKE-generation is confident enough to say that all these works are bad, Hanson says - they are in good company. Because so did also Hitler, Stalin and Mao.[283]

North Korea

In North Korea, communist ideas are firmly entrenched in modern society. Below is the testimony of a North Korean woman, Yeonmi Park, one of the few to escape North Korea - one of only 200 survivors who managed to escape. At a Western university where she started studying after her exile, all the students wore expensive technology gadgets and drank lattes, and the professors said that - if a Marxist left-wing revolution were to break out in the West, everything would be much better. Yeonmi Park understood that to be the goal of the teachers' teaching. And from a North Korean point of view, she could not understand this.

She says that in North America they teach about the history of slavery and the injustices suffered by slaves. But what people in the West don't fully realise is that the real oppression is still going on elsewhere in the world. The victims of communism are up to 120 million dead so far. Slavery has ended, but not the oppression and persecution of communism.

---

283 Origins and History of Woke | HISPBC Ch.1, Victor Davies Hanson, American classical and military historian and professor emeritus at California State University at Fresno https://www.youtube.com/watch?v=FX5Jv2Y1dmw

In North Korean schools, there is still no electricity or internet. There is no freedom of expression - they don't know the concept of freedom of expression and simply don't know what it means. Yeonmi Park's mum told her when she was little: "don't even whisper, the birds and mice can hear you". If she had said a single 'wrong' word against the North Korean regime as a child, it would have resulted in certain death, not only for her but for her entire family - up to three generations of her family would be rounded up, thrown in prison or executed. Her relatives were probably imprisoned or executed after her escape and she herself is on a North Korean death list. But those who most often die for political reasons in North Korea don't mind - their fate is otherwise to die of starvation.

And this destiny is decided even before you are born. In North Korea, there is a caste system with different 'classes'. It is a kind of hierarchy where the highest classes enjoy a privileged lifestyle and the class at the bottom of the scale is not even allowed to eat and must fight for survival - daily. In 1990, a famine broke out that contributed to one of the worst disasters of modern times. Over three years, 3 million of the 20 million North Koreans belonging to the lowest 'class' died due to lack of food. According to Yeonmi Park, the famine was organised by the state, as the government felt it was easier to practice socialism and control the population when they were fewer in number. It was also due to the collapse of the Soviet Union - the Soviet state could no longer provide aid to North Korea.

In North Korea, as in the former Soviet Union, there are neither human rights nor the protection of the law. Yeonmi Park and many other children from her 'class' ate grasshoppers and dragonflies for lack of other food. When she played as a child, she did not play with Lego. In North Korea, she and the other children caught cockroaches and ate them.

This is one of the reasons why North Koreans are generally 11 cm shorter than South Koreans. Men are allowed to attend military training, which lasts 10 years - if they are over 1.2 metres tall. Women undergo 7 years of compulsory military training regardless of height. In the unlikely event that you manage to fly over North Korea in an aeroplane or helicopter, it looks very dark from above. This is because there is no electricity and what electricity there is has to be switched off at a certain time in the evening. The lowest classes do not have access to electricity. For the lower classes, doctors do not use anaesthesia when performing operations and Yeonmi Park herself underwent such an extremely painful operation. Dead bodies can be found everywhere, especially outside the hospitals.

Her friends and colleagues in the US talk about how bad the capitalist West is. They are interested in the political LGBTQ struggle and they ask her how this struggle is going in North Korea. She replies that the word "gay" doesn't exist there, either as a concept or a reality - you can't be gay in North Korea. The rules are very strict. For example, you have to ask for police permission to sleep over at a neighbour's house. However, the biggest crime in North Korea is criticising the Communist Party. So the worst offence is not killing your fellow human being. Criticising the Communist Party carries a higher penalty than murder. Wehen Assange criticized the US government, he got a long penalty, while the people who comitted the crime — no consequences.

Yeonmi Park is now fighting to save her country by spreading these images of what's really going on and raising awareness of how Marxism has destroyed North Korea.[284]

Identity policy

Part of the basis of the theory behind identity politics comes from Marx who divided social groups into two classes, the bourgeoisie and the proletariat. Part of it comes from Freud, who believed that people are constantly oppressed. Post-colonial thinking also contributes to the theory of identity politics. Together, the above form a powerful political tool that is spreading in society.

'Post-colonialism' originated in higher education and aims to problematise the Western tradition of knowledge, as well as to demonstrate historical links between past colonialism and contemporary racism. Areas where this approach has gained strength are in educational institutions, culture, literature and the history of ideas.[285] This includes attempts to consolidate dominance and subordination in the form of charged identities, such as 'white' and 'black', arguing that these identities were created during colonialism and persist globally today. Among the majority of those who subscribe to this line of thinking is the idea that the West is 'indebted' to the former colonial countries:

> The old colonies want to be vindicated and by discussing themselves in relation to the "white" they want to create a clearer identity where they also believe that culture and society and politics have been characterised by a very colonial way of thinking and they want to change that.[286]

284 What I Learned about Freedom After Escaping North Korea, Yeonmi Park LIVE at NCSC, https://www.youtube.com/watch?v=fZGYbTgRpr8&t=873s
285 Ideologies 2019 - Ideas of the Left, Part 3 of 4: A New Left? - Anna Hallberg PhD Södertörn University

Post-colonialism has made a big impact on the WOKE-generation. At the individual level, the WOKE-generation has a postcolonial Marxist outlook, but only in theory, as the practical-economic conditions are different. According to this theory, WOKE identities are in a constant state of oppression through a symbiosis with the corresponding 'oppressors', partly because Marxism originally stems from an outdated political ideology of the 19th century when the working class was in great distress and thus subjected to real oppression. Note that the Marxist "oppressed-oppressor" relationship exists only in Western countries, where Freud's psychoanalytic social theory has gained great power.

It could be said that Freudian repression in the West is now imagined and theoretical. There are other societal factors that can contribute to victimhood. But one should distinguish between real social problems and the theoretical oppression described here. Otherwise, a lie is created when people make themselves 'victims' when they are not - in the 'real' sense. Instead, you end up in a self-fulfilling prophecy. The striving towards the ideal society, towards the utopia, also creates a dissonance, between the idea of the perfect society and the actual reality. This leaves an emptiness, a longing that is filled by the role of consumption.

We're on a road to nowhere

Come on inside

Taking that ride to nowhere

We'll take that ride

I'm feeling okay this morning

286 A new book in 2020 - Ideas of the Left with Anna Victoria Hallberg (PhD Södertörn University) - Axess TV

And you know

We're on the road to paradise

Here we go, here we go[287]

The alternative is that this emptiness is filled with the idea of the perfect society, which leads to a vicious circle. Thus, Marxist ideology blames the emptiness on capitalism and social oppression, but at the same time fills it with even more desire and consumption, which in turn only creates even more emptiness. This is not surprising, as the word utopia actually means - "emptiness", "nowhere" or "no man's land":

> Epistomology: 1551, from Modern Latin Utopia, literally "nowhere," coined by Thomas More, from Greek *ou* "not" + *topos* "place". [288]

If one observes identity politics, one can clearly discern power structures. These power structures are maintained by a role hierarchy. In order to clarify the role hierarchy and consolidate the power structure, loaded words such as "patriarchy", "heteronormative" or "racism" are used. "You" are "racist" while "I" am a "victim", "you" are "patriarch" while "I" am a "victim" and so on. This indicates that Marxism lives on in modern political movements, for example in contemporary feminism or anti-racism. And in line with the theories of post-colonialism, Sigmund Freud and Karl Marx, the questioning of the traditional is indispensable. Freedom and traditional culture are incompatible - according to Freud:

> The liberty of the individual is not a benefit of culture. It was greatest before any culture, though indeed it had little value at that time, because the individual was hardly

287 Talking Heads, Road to Nowhere
288 https://www.etymonline.com/word/utopia

in a position to defend it. Liberty has undergone restrictions through the evolution of civilisation, and justice demands that these restrictions shall apply to all. The desire for freedom that makes itself felt in a human community may be a revolt against some existing injustice and so may prove favourable to a further development of civilisation and remain compatible with it. But it may also have its origin in the primitive roots of the personality, still imfettered by civilising influences, and so become a source of antagonism to culture. Thus the cry for freedom is directed either against particular forms or demands of culture or else against culture itself.[289]

The WOKE-culture believe that they are striving to achieve equality between different communities and identities. What they do not understand is that by categorising people in identity politics, they create the very divisions that they want to stop. In many of the victim roles, where the individual is considered to be oppressed, one can see that the victim experience is theoretical and visualised in advance, compared to the social power structures in many non-Western countries. Here too lies a dissonance between experience and reality. An example of such a dissonance is if the WOKE-generation were to find themselves in place of those participating in the war in Ukraine and the actual suffering of both Ukrainian and Russian soldiers. These soldiers, these real victims, have not asked for the war either.

There is no need to go to war to show that the suffering of the WOKE generation based on actual-practical world conditions remains theoretical - real poor and suffering people exist all over the world. 20%

289 Sigmund Freud, *Civilisation and Its Discontents*, page 60, 1929

of the population in Russia still have outdoor toilets. 120 million people in China live in extreme poverty and suffer from malnutrition. They struggle to survive, to avoid imprisonment and torture. Most people in the world *want* economic growth - to eat and to feed their children. One third of all poor children living in India die of poverty-related diseases. There is, of course, psychological suffering that can affect anyone; the difference is that within the WOKE culture, a whole generation *is indoctrinated* to believe that they are the real victims.[290] And this is done, among other things, through conceptual confusion.

In practice, these young people have little to compare with - war and hardship have long stayed outside the borders of the West. As a result, the WOKE-generation is placed in a kind of psychological 'captivity' - by the same identity politics they want to invoke. This 'captivity', or bubble, makes it harder for them to find a realistic relationship within their life and the world around them. Instead, the WOKE-generation focuses on themselves and practises what could be called "Oppression Olympics" where the key question is "who was most offended"? And where victimhood becomes a virtue, a way of life.

If you were to compare this lifestyle with the standards of previous generations and what they had to struggle against, it becomes obvious - the current generation is the best off in the history of the world, in terms of education, access to food, hygiene, access to technology, access to medical care and the ability to realise personal projects, such as a career. Has anyone been worse off than their grandparents? This again shows that the ideology of the WOKE-generation is partly based on an illusion, an imagined struggle. Here again, a distinction needs to be made between people's personal experience of problems, and an imagined social

290 Konstantin Kisin: WOKE Culture HAS Gone Too Far - 7/8 | Oxford Union

or societal oppression.

Marxist ideology pits different identities against each other, makes people see oppressors among themselves and inhibits people from uniting across political boundaries, in line with Saul Alinsky's 'community organising'. The WOKE-generation turns against each other, through different identities in their struggle, such as women against men and 'black' against 'white'. Instead of fighting against individuals and groups, the focus could on improving society by fighting against centralised power - big business running a totalitarian global economy, fed by people's over-consumption; elite politicians going to one war after another; and the media PR community treating readers like children and standing in the way of real social information and real social development. These rulers are the only ones with enough resources, means and power to oppress the entire West, and they are the elite. [291]

> Well, we know where we're going
>
> But we don't know where we've been
>
> And we know what we're knowing
>
> But we can't say what we've seen
>
> And we're not little children
>
> And we know what we want
>
> And the future is certain
>
> Give us time to work it out[292]

When an individual lives in models of identity politics, there is a restriction of real, natural and personal views. Belonging and loyalty to one's 'role' be-

291 The Ideological Roots of WOKEness, with Helen Pluckrose and Helen Joyce
292 Talking Heads, Road to Nowhere

comes personal, emotional and more important than the issue itself. It is more important that you identify as a "feminist" with the mandatory set of opinions that belong to that role, than what you actually think about leaving children in kindergarten at a young age. It is perceived as highly problematic if you are suddenly not considered to "live up" to your role, if you want to take your own path on a political issue; this to the extent that you would rather continue in the same track. You have already bought the whole package of opinions, whether you knew them beforehand or not, and so you are stuck in identity politics.

> Being left is more an identity then anything else, its the way I think of myself as a decent civilised human being.(...) It works on a cultural level.[293]

Eventually, these "bubbles" turn into restrictive opinion prisons where you "have" to buy the whole role, i.e. the whole "opinion package" in order to be able to identify with a political group; to gain social group membership. If you change your mind, you can lose friends and acquaintances, even family members. To be considered as belonging to the "left", you must hold the same views that the left serves, without much exception. Also included is the opponent or oppressor that you "must" oppose. Otherwise, you cannot belong to the category "left" and then you become politically and opinionally "homeless" at best, or otherwise labelled as "radical right", "racist" and turned into an opponent.

The above perspective is hidden from public view and, when people do not have the full picture, they find it more difficult to think 'independently'. Instead, a discourse emerges in which 'our' ideology is pitted

293 Shelby Steele - White Guilt and the Identity of Innocence
    https://www.youtube.com/watch?v=JLkJpCj42iQ

against 'their' ideology, the 'right' against the 'left'. This leads to criticism and finding "fault" in the other's perspective - which is also part of the "package" - I am "left" therefore I cannot agree with the "right". In this way, people can never be united enough to be able to implement comprehensive changes in society and allow real development to take off. This leaves the "elected representatives" to make the decisions for humanity, because the hummanity cannot unite - and these "elected representatives" do not mind at all. This makes it even easier to foist consumption and products on people.

Not only that - most people walk around with the idea that people who don't think like us - are alike, are not like us - at all. If we instead put ourselves in different interpersonal contexts, we could find much in common with individuals we think are our opponents. This would be in opposition to the 'divide and rule' approach and could instead unite people.

Nazis are the New Right

In the new Marxist role hierarchy, if you belong to the left or to the feminist movement, you are automatically considered more sympathetic. According to this model, you also have *more* right to speak out and *more* right to form opinions and engage in activism - if you belong to the left. Then you are one of the "good guys".[294] If you belong to the so-called 'right', you are automatically suspected of harbouring racist views.

In this way, the use of words has been swapped and conceptual confusion has been created, with some concepts and words belonging to the 'good' concept and some concepts belonging to the 'bad' concept. It also has to do with the paradigm shift where the National Socialists were displaced from the socialist left side of

294 Why Marxism is so appealing, Jordan Peterson and Thomas Sowell

the scale, to belong to the "extreme right" side. The left is thus entitled in its arguments to compare the right and their role models with Hitler and Mussolini. It also became easier to blame negative phenomena on the 'right', which became the 'bad guys', following Saul Alinsky's model; the post-war 'narrative' facilitated such an approach.

If we start from the overall picture of history and take the National Socialists and the events of the Holocaust, shouldn't these historical events influence the image of today's socialist parties and their narrative? Shouldn't the same apply to communists and the events of the Holodomor? Why is it that the Holocaust and the Holodomor are not "given" their proper connection to socialis, and communism in a realistic way? And that today we are allowed to slander the "right" and the "conservatives" with terrible and unfounded words like "racist" and "Nazi"? When more people have been murdered in the name of National Socialism and Communism than in the name of conservatives or the 'right'?

Conceptual confusion

The WOKE-generation creates a relationship between ideas and reality where ideas become a substitute for reality. If you have an idea of what your conservative neighbour thinks about immigration policy, you assume that it is true, and thus become surprised when he is married to an immigrant. The 'left-wing' rhetoric and conceptualisations leads to the automatic formation of prejudices and judgements, without looking at the *reality of the situation*. It is assumed that all people in a group hold the same kind of opinions. There is a difference between what the opponent actually says - and what the listener *imagines* the opponent is saying. This can easily lead to a false moral perception, where the left is seen as 'good' and the right as 'less good'.[295]

Part of the communicative dilemma is that those who stick to their left-wing political views, the "good" views, find it difficult to absorb information or facts - even if they are presented to them in black and white - facts that contradict the "left-wing identity" or "set of views" and the ideals that have been indoctrinated with it. Instead, they dismiss facts, other people's opinions and information that do not fit into the opinion package, as conspiracy theories, "right-wing" opinions or excuse it in some other way. The words "left" and progressivism are loaded with something positive and "good". Reality becomes entangled in the concepts and the experience of reality becomes trapped in the Marxist model. Left-wing coffee *must* be good, etc. Even the big business corporations have the same jargon. When the left lost the 2016 US election, the owner of the big company Google started a meeting by saying "I know this is not the most joys meeting we have had. Lets face it most people here are pretty upset and pretty sad about the election." The meeting was purely internal and no opinions were expressed publicly.

Instead, Google claimed that the left was losing because of fake news and all the conspiracy theories that made Americans vote for the Republicans. Therefore, it wanted to use algorithms to remove from search engines all information that it considered "conspiracy theories" and "fake news":

> He told the British broadcaster "From our perspective, there should just be no situation where fake news gets distributed ... I don't think we should debate it as much as

295 Ideologies 2019 - Ideas of the Left part 4 of 4: A new left? - Björn Östbring (PhD in Political Science, affiliated to the Department of Political Science)

work hard to make sure we drive news to its more trusted sources, have more fact checking and make our algorithms work better."[296]

Google's algorithms were developed after the election to reflect the company's internal views. Large mega-corporations that play such an enormously important role in society should always be able to claim political neutrality above all else. But that's not what they did - at Google.

Instead, it helped perpetuate an outdated 19th century political model - in order to constantly recreate a 'narrative' that corresponds to the post-colonial Marxist view - for millions of users. This narrative involves imagining how the various 'identities' think and how all the 'oppressors' and 'oppressed' feel. The defence is that the opponent is a racist and knows it, or a racist without knowing it. [297]

Something similar happened at the Times. Journalist Nellie Bowles was hired by the Times for her dream job as a reporter. At first, everything went well. After a couple of years on the job, she was asked to write an article about the conservative YouTube channel PargerU. The mostly positive article was not approved, and when she asked why, the Times said she was trying to spread "disinformation". But the real turning point came when she wrote a negative article about Antifa. Her colleagues then began to oppose and criticise her in various ways. They questioned her and said she was "racist" and anti-feminist. Bowles, who openly lives with her wife as a homosexual, was shocked. However, colleagues spread rumours and comments that she was out of the 'tribe' and spread 'fake news'. This affected her reputation, but despite being alone and ostracised,

296 https://fortune.com/2016/11/16/fake-news-election-google-sundar-pichai/
297 The Ideological Roots of WOKEness, with Helen Pluckrose and Helen Joyce

she did not give up and wrote articles on other Marxist phenomena.[298]

These loaded concepts, ideas and ideology are part of the WOKE-generation's "narrative", the story formation through which they interpret the world around them. A child has a different image and vision of what a circus is than an adult. This creates two different narratives. The right narrative can influence and change the world around us. The political narrative used by the WOKE-generation becomes a means of power and is utilised when it is filled with loaded words and concepts.[299] Identity politics and the forces behind Marxist ideology make the narrative more acceptable than reality - even actual statistics. At the same time, the 'good', 'innocent', 'non-oppressive' identity, regardless of real actions, is turned into an goal in itself:

> The pursue of innocence specifically ugly American past(...) because I'm innocent of this past you should vote for me, that's why you should let me change this aspect of the university system (...) not because I have better ideas or that I'm a better problem-solver, but because I offer this identity of innocence.[300]

All this results in both the disappearance of freedom of expression and actual, individual diversity. The proliferation of conceptual confusion and desire to revolutionise language helps. Students at the School of Journalism and other institutions are being radicalised in this way. The aim is to influence all organisations,

298 Nellie Bowles, Ex-NYT Reporter: The world went crazy! https://www.youtube.com/watch?v=wKHSE9eISRg&t=884s
299 Ideologies 2019 - Ideas of the Left part 4 of 4: A new left? - Björn Östbring (PhD in Political Science, affiliated to the Department of Political Science)
300 Shelby Steele - White Guilt and the Identity of Innocence, https://www.youtube.com/watch?v=JLkJpCj42iQ

research institutions, students and teachers, and thus also the future.[301]

> Blind ideological conviction disguised as academic perspective tears apart democratic discourse and radicalises concepts. This is incompatible with the basic idea of universities.[302]

The term freedom of expression has undergone a transformation in the 21st century that began in the 1990s. Freedom of expression, which is a human right, means that anyone can speak openly about anything, provided it does not cause harm. Freedom of expression is an extremely important element, not only on a political level, but also of the psychological development of a human being. Research has been done on the Chernobyl disaster and found that in Russia there were certain professional hierarchies that prohibited and curtailed free speech. As a result of these hierarchies, Chernobyl employees were unable to obtain information about the disaster in time. They did not dare to communicate the real events of the disaster with their superiors, because of the instructions they had received. When you make things unspeakable, you create dangerous restrictions. One such linguistic restriction is conceptual confusion, which leads to less exchange of ideas, locks down debate, and prevents further development

Political correctness is an example that has been subject to conceptual confusion. The concept is, so to speak, "hijacked" by Marxism; political correctness has now become part of the Marxist ideology, and part of the tools used to curb free speech.

Another example is that 2-3 generations of students

301 James Lindsay sounds the alarm on the 'national danger' of Marxism in schools | Liz Collin Reports, Alpha News https://www.youtube.com/watch?v=1AFRtSWQHPg
302 Ideologies 2019 - Ideas of the Left, Part 3 of 4: A New Left? - Anna Hallberg Phd Södertörn University

have been taught in school that the West has been the most "evil". Which countries have not been? Why should the West dislike its own nationality? And belittle it? The West can no longer express values in which Western culture is appreciated in a positive discourse, which has materialised at various levels through our educational efforts. All cultures are worthy of being kept and remembered and preserved.[303]

A totalitarian culture

If you do not fully accept the views of the left, you are excluded or "cancelled", also known as "Cancel Culture". People would rather exclude, change or even reprogramme those views that do not fit into the WOKE-culture's set of views than show understanding, open up for debate or compromise.[304] This culture of exclusion can have a very harsh effect on the individual who is subjected to it; he or she becomes a victim of character assassination, slander in the legal sense - loses a good reputation or part of the circle of acquaintances. This is a sign that in today's society, social cohesion is more important than freedom of expression and the right to one's own opinion.

> You see reasonable civilised, decent people just fold up when the charge of racism is even hinted at and they begin to sell out the quality of the university but they end invariably i lower standards - removing Western Civilization from the curriculum - what are you doing? You think its going to make you innocent? You're keeping us from it saying its just a bunch of white guys, I don't care I need to know! I need to identify with West-

303 Restriction of speech, Konstantin Kisin
304 Critical Race Theory, Queer Theory & Maoist Education, James Lindsay

ern Civilisation! Black Americans are a Western people we evolved here in the west![305]

The old Marxist belief is that anything that can be
described as traditional and part of the 'old society'
should be controlled, overthrown and revolutionised.[306]
The "victimhood" they believe they carry gives them an
automatic right to destroy what the supposed "oppressors" have built. The WOKE-generation imagine that they
are so wise, knowledgeable and wealthy that they can
destroy 20,000 years of human history and come up with
something completely unique and new - which would be
better than what men and women have developed over
thousands of years. All the foundations on which
society rests, the right to freedom of expression and
the right to be presumed innocent until proven guilty,
are old and have evolved with civilisation. Yet they
believe they can build something that no one else has
ever done.[307]

For example, when the indian-american lecturer,
Dinesh D'Souza, suggested trying redistribution policies and giving away all the students' mobile phones to
the poor, most of the students said no and squirmed.
What these students did not realise was that it was
Western society that had given them the opportunity to
own a mobile phone. In theory, the Marxist idea was
good, but in practice it did not work as well.

The WOKE-generation claims to be fighting against
the oppressive patriarchal system of the West. This
worldview is a straightforward black-and-white thinking
without nuances.

If you look at history, many historical periods are
full of bloodshed; many works have been created that
have brought progress. You don't throw away the whole

305 Shelby Steele - White Guilt and the Identity of Innocence
306 James Lindsay talks of National Danger of Marxism
307 The Absurdity of Socialism, Jordan B Petersen and Dave Rubin
    https://www.youtube.com/watch?v=QpjCca9Beww

book of Nietzsche just because you find something you
don't agree with, this legacy of great writers humanity
has inherited, those writers who in their lives suffered more than us. Nowadays, this is dismissed in the
WOKE culture, unable to separate the wheat from the
chaff. There are endless inventions and old concepts
that are both necessary and good, such as our laws,
which date back to the ancient Roman Empire. The right
to property and innocence before the the law. The
rights of the individual. It would not be good to overthrow an entire system that is, after all, based on
many good values.[308]

> Of course there are things that are wrong
> with the world but there are also things that
> are beautiful and right and youve got to go
> through this and come back and rescue those
> things which is much more important than
> destroying a few obstacles along the way.[309]

Progressivism constantly strives for an eternal
improvement, a utopia. This utopia is not real and has
no connection to reality. It is a matter of incomplete
knowledge and incomplete thinking; for example, the
events of the Holodomor in Ukraine, where millions of
people died because of communism and Marxism in the
1930s, are not put into perspective; this is not taught
in schools to the same extent as the Holocaust and
Nazism are taught.[310] The WOKE-generation does not put
their own left-communist ideology in a real world
perspective.

Despite this, left-wing extremists have won the
sympathy and support of the media and the cultural
class. People who otherwise distance themselves from
all forms of violence make an exception when it comes

308 The Absurdity of Socialism, Jordan B Petersen and Dave Rubin
309 Roger Scruton Why Intellectuals are mostly left
310 Why Marxism is so appealing, Jordan Peterson and Thomas Sowell

to left-wing extremists. The fact that there have been explosives and weapons, planned attacks, does not count as terrorism in cultural and academic circles; instead, left-wing violence is looked upon favourably. Left-wing activists who have been violent to the point of imprisonment are heroised by the WOKE-movement.[311] Those who identify themselves as 'extreme left' will stop at nothing to achieve their goals. "The end justifies the means", as Machiavelli put it in the early Middle Ages.

The WOKE-generation develops an identity whose ideology cannot bear to be criticised. All criticism and opposition are considered attacks, as in the Soviet Union's socialist communism or North Korea's communist state or China's communist regime. This quest for an arena in which criticism and open political dialogue are absent means that the debate fails. In this way, the WOKE-generation builds its ideology on weakness – a belief that they are perfect, without the need for a truly diverse debate. It is a generation with an overconfidence in its perception of the world, in its one-sided position. Nor do they contradict each other within the group – opinions are aligned.

In this way, freedom of expression and free speech are increasingly devalued.

> They don't have an argument. They don't say, to me, "your argument is wrong and this is why it's wrong, and here are the following facts which show that you are wrong." They don't have that discussion at all.[312]

The ideas created by the WOKE generation develop into omnipotence that excludes all other opinions. The problem continues when other opinions are considered

311 Uppdrag Gransking, 7 May 2014, episode 15: "The Good Violence". About the autonomous left and the Revolutionary Front. Reporters: Janne Josefsson, Ola Sandstig

312 Melanie Philips (British journalist, broadcaster and author) – Leaving The Left https://www.youtube.com/watch?v=ZkK7lgcLcSo

"wrong" and are not allowed to be part of the public debate. Such a phenomenon can be explained by the underlying reason that contemporary man lives in a discourse where everything is an opinion - instead of there being *objective* truths.

> Yes, you see I believe that we're living in an era, in which truth, the idea of objective truth, has been to a very large extent replaced by ideology.[313]

Why should everyone fit into the prevailing norm? Doesn't that create a dictatorship? A totalitarian environment where new opinions are cancelled and real diversity is suppressed? A dialogue that fails to take place, where concepts become fixed and the conversation is closed? At the same time as revolution becomes a goal - paradoxically, one cannot bear to be contradicted oneself.

> The worst offence in 'brave new world' (Huxley) is to deviate from the norm. This norm has nothing to do with ethics and morality, it has been designed exclusively on the basis of utility[314]

313 Melanie Philips (British journalist, broadcaster and author) - Leaving The Left
314 Roland Huntford, "The New Totalitarians", page 9, 1971

The soft bigotry of low expectations

" ... to boldly go where no man has gone before" - Star
Trek

The contemporary totalitarian state, whose structure
was born in the 1920s, has slowly been transformed into
a totalitarian WOKE-state, where non-left-wing opinions
are belittled and labelled racist - while the elites
can do as they please undisturbed. WOKE uses a post-
colonial narrative where African-Americans and other
minorities, in accordance with Marxist identity politics, are considered oppressed victims, all the way
back to the 17th century when they were enslaved - by
the European, "white" population. But is this really
true in a historical overview? And is it true that
slavery was an invention of the 'right'?

The Maasai and the Manuemas

According to the African-American economist and historian Thomas Sowell, slavery today is described in a
narrative that tells how Africans were captured by
Europeans, but the issue is not nuanced, which means
that the public does not have access to the whole
story. Africans are often described as victims and
"whites" as perpetrators - who, according to science,
also originate from Africa[315].

> We are solely children of Africa-with no
> Neandertals or island-dwelling "hobbits" in
> our family tree ...[316]

---

315 https://www.forskning.se/2012/09/21/ny-dna-studie-visar-manniskans-
komplexa-ursprung-i-afrika/
316 https://www.nationalgeographic.com/history/article/modern-humans-came-out-
of-africa-definitive-study-says

Slavery exists in several other countries in the 21st century, such as North Korea - but does not get the same reaction, because of the Marxist political narrative - that only draws attention to African slavery in order to consolidate the role of African Americans as victims in identity politics. Therefore, much more attention needs to be paid to the issue.

It all starts with etymology - the word 'slave' comes from the term 'Slavs' - the name of the population that came from Slavic countries. This is because many 'white' people from the Slavic population were enslaved in the Middle Ages in large parts of the world. China and India also had a very high level of slavery and more slaves - than the whole of the West. Many famous monuments around the world were built with the help of slave labour. In South Asia, there were even cities where most of the inhabitants were slaves. It is believed, due to the post-colonial Marxist narrative that leaves out parts of history, that Europeans 'invented' slavery when they started bringing African slaves to Europe. However, this is not true. Before the time of Columbus, there were plenty of slaves of European origin in Europe. People were also enslaved in the Middle East and then taken up for military and other service.

> As British historian Dan Jones notes in *Powers and Thrones: A New History of the Middle Ages*,
>
> Slavery was a fact of life throughout the ancient world. Slaves-people defined as property, forced to work, stripped of their rights, and socially 'dead,' could be found in every significant realm of the age. In China, the Qin, Han, and Xin dynasties enforced various forms of slavery; so too did ancient rulers of Egypt, Assyria, Babylonia, and India.

Milton Meltzer's *Slavery: A World History* is both comprehensive and riveting in its presentation. He too recognises the ubiquity of human bondage:

The institution of slavery was universal throughout much of history. It was a tradition everyone grew up with. It seemed essential to the social and economic life of the community, and man's conscience was seldom troubled by it. Both master and slave looked upon it as inevitable...A slave might be of any colour-white, black, brown, yellow. The physical differences did not matter. Warriors, pirates, and slave dealers were not concerned with the colour of a man's skin or the shape of his nose.

Thomas Sowell goes on to say that it is claimed that slavery is an international phenomenon that took place between countries and different peoples, but most slavery actually took place within countries, not least for practical reasons - you could not transport so many people on boats. Those who were enslaved were enslaved because they were fragile and weak within their own societies - not because of theories about different races that can be found in identity politics. Constantly claiming, as we do today, that African Americans were the only victims in the world leads to a belittling view of African culture and to the bigotry of low expectations.

Slaves and people of other races of European origin were enslaved for as long as 600 years before the first African slave arrived in Europe. All over the world, this was a common phenomenon - Africans enslaved Africans, Asians enslaved Asians, and Europeans enslaved other Europeans. In East Africa, the most feared slave traders were the Masai, who, together with Arabs or on their own, enslaved their neighbouring tribes. The

Manuemas, an African warrior people, were also feared slave traders and slave drivers. Africa's relationship with slaves is portrayed in the historical film "House of GA'A"[317]. In 1891, they terrified nearby tribes and destroyed crops. This contributed to the famine that then ravaged the area.

And in fact, it was the British who ended slavery in Tanganika, Africa, according to Sowell, but only in 1922.[318] [319]

A contradiction to the 'white man as perpetrator' narrative is the fact that Europeans travelled to Africa under very difficult circumstances, with disease and hardship everywhere they went. A European was more likely to bring back malaria than slaves during their explorations in Africa. Europeans' life expectancy in Africa was less than a year, because their immune systems were completely different from those of the African population and they were not prepared for all the diseases that hit them. Europeans knew this and therefore only travelled to the ports for trade, where indigenous slave owners traded.

As portrayed in Alex Haley's book on slavery, "Roots"[320], Europeans travelled freely around Africa picking slaves. This is not true. As many whites as Africans died on the ships on the way to Europe. Only when malaria medicine was invented could Africa have been conquered - but by then slavery was already on its way out.

Sowell goes on to say that most African Americans who were slave owners in the Northern United States were nominal slave owners who owned family members and

317 Film: House of GA'A, Netflix, 2024
318 The truth about slavery, Thomas Sowell https://gript.ie/the-truth-about-slavery/
319 Sowell on Slavery, Posted onJun 5, 2024
   https://billmuehlenberg.com/2024/06/05/sowell-on-slavery/
320 Alex Haley "Roots", 1976

others within their circle of acquaintances. Thousands of African-American slave owners were commercial owners - just like their 'white' counterparts in the South. They owned slaves in the same way that 'white' Americans owned slaves and they also fought on the 'white' side in the Civil War. The US then ended slavery faster than other parts of the world.[321]

"I try to give my people a myth to live by".[322] This is how Alex Haley describes the narrative he tries to present in his novel about slavery, in which African and African-American descendants are portrayed as the only victims. On the contrary, the picture of the relationship should be nuanced, not least from an international perspective. This should not lead us to believe that slavery was not that serious. It was, and no one has said otherwise. But there are additional historical facts that need to be presented to make the picture more objective. For example, in the book "White Slaves, Black Masters" it is stated that African slave owners also owned white slaves, former travellers, whom they had captured during their travels.[323]

Professor Henry Louis Gates tells us that some of the black slaves were owned by Native Americans in the American South, who refused to let the slaves go free when the rest of the United States freed the slaves. These people were called Cherokee, Chickasaw, Choctaw, Creek, and Seminole and at that time they were not under the laws of the United States but were separate nations with their own laws. In 1866, however, the US government forced these tribes to free the slaves and make them citizens. The Chickasaw Nation freed their slaves but did not grant them citizenship. The freed

321 The History of Slavery You Probably Weren't Taught in School, Thomas Sowell, https://billmuehlenberg.com/2024/06/05/sowell-on-slavery/
322 Alex Haley, "Roots", 1976
323 Thomas Sowell, "Black Rednecks and White Liberals" p.120, 2006,

slaves were thus neither Chickasaw nor American. Because of the narrative entrenched in the mainstream perspective, these important parts of the history of slavery are not recognised. Another thing that is also not recognised is that most conservatives - or the 'right' - were against slavery. But at the time, the right were the progressives and the left were the conservatives - the Democrats were the ones who actually wanted to keep slavery.

Adam Smith was one of the opponents. He was against slavery, both on humanitarian and ethical grounds. He taught his students with the motto:

> ... we may see what a miserable life the slaves must have led; their life and their property entirely at the mercy of another, and their liberty, if they could be said to have any, at his disposal also. [324]

Adam Smith, who is considered to be one of the founders of capitalism, believed that it was important to look after and care for the inner essence of man.

> It is evident that the state of slavery must be very unhappy to the slave himself. This I need hardly prove, though some writers have called it in question.[325]

The real story

So how is it that racism still counts as 'right-wing extremism'? According to African-American author and professor of political philosophy, Dr Carol Swain[326], it was actually the Democratic Party that voted for

---

324 Slavery, Adam Smith's Economic Vision and the Invisible Hand (1978, p. 178) https://www.adamsmithworks.org/documents/adam-smith-on-slavery
325 Slavery, Adam Smith's Economic Vision and the Invisible Hand (1978, p. 185) https://www.adamsmithworks.org/documents/adam-smith-on-slavery
326 Tenure at Princeton and full professorship at Vanderbilt where she was a professor of political science and a professor of law https://carolmswain.com/about/

slavery. She says they also founded the Ku Klux Klan, opposed the rebuilding of the African-American community, pushed segregation, and committed criminal acts against African-American citizens, such as lynchings. The Democrats also opposed the Civil Rights Act, which established African-American rights in the 1950s and 1960s.

In 1854, the Republicans formed a party with the aim of ending slavery. In 1857, the Supreme Court of the United States tried to block this with the famous case 'Dred Scott v. Sanford' - arguing that freed slaves should not be allowed to carry guns on the grounds that slaves were just property - not people. Democrats opposed several amendments to the Constitution:

> The "13th Amendment", in 1865, which would abolish slavery,

> "14th Amendment", in 1866, establishing citizenship for African Americans and

> The "15th Amendment", in 1869, which would introduce voting rights for African Americans.

Nevertheless, between 1870 and 1935, many African Americans were voted into politics and all of them were Republicans. The Republican side was inclusive in a way that the Democratic side was not. The first woman, the first politician of Hispanic descent, the first politician of Asian descent were all Republicans.[327]

The contemporary left-wing Democrats in the United States portray themselves as inclusive, people-loving and claiming to stand for social justice and anti-racism - for a long time. But is this really true?

Andrew Jackson was the founder of the Democratic

---

327 Carol Swain (former professor of political science & law, Vanderbilt University) https://www.prageru.com/video/the-inconvenient-truth-about-the-democratic-party

Party in 1829, and he did so by taking land from the indigenous people of the Americas to the new European settlers.

> By 1828 - the year Andrew Jackson was elected, the official date for the formation of the democratic party.[328]

As an elected official, Jackson signed a law called "The Indian Removal Act." which meant that Native Americans who were not removed from the country faced a horribly cruel death.

> As president from 1829 to 1837, Jackson is perhaps most famous for his pivotal role in Native Americans' painful and violent history in the United States. He signed the Indian Removal Act in 1830, which forced the relocation of more than 60,000 Native Americans to clear the way for white pioneers. The act helped lead to the "Trail of Tears," in which an estimated 4,000 Cherokee died during the harsh conditions of a long march during a forced relocation in 1838 and 1839. The Cherokees called Jackson "Indian killer"; the Creek called him "Sharp Knife."
>
> A slave owner, Jackson spoke about Native Americans as if they were an inferior group of people. "Established in the midst of a superior race," he said of the Cherokee, "they must disappear."[329]

The historic event was called the 'Trail of Tears' and wiped out a large number of indigenous people. Like most Democrats, Jackson owned hundreds of slaves. Con-

328 Documentary: Dinesh D'Souza, Hillary's America, 2016
329 The Washington Post
    https://www.washingtonpost.com/news/retropolis/wp/2017/11/28/andrew-jackson-was-called-indian-killer-trump-honored-navajos-in-front-of-his-portrait/

ditions were terrible, the punishment for escaping was being flogged to death. Most Democrats argued that slavery was good for both the slave owner and the slave.[330] Afterwards, they tried to deflect and blame the issue of slavery to the Southern part of the United States which was not true - in the Northern United States there were also slaves.

Those who opposed slavery were seen as a threat that sought to strip slave owners of their possessions and wealth - and destroy their economic conditions. Most of the Republican Party opposed slavery but were violently defeated in protest.

Democrats refused to grant citizenship to African-Americans until the 1960s when they finally relented. Republicans had the promise of citizenship written into their constitution and more Republicans than Democrats voted for it.[331]

The Ku Klux Klan was founded in 1865 by Democrat Nathan Bedford Forrest. He served in the government as a Democrat - while also being the first 'Wizard', a higher rank within the 'Klan'. The movement was formed when African-American citizens began to conquer land and capital and the reaction was brutal. They also began to terrorise Republicans and other opponents of slavery. During this period, the Ku Klux Klan killed around 3000 African Americans and 1000 white Republicans.

When we look at the history of KKK it was specifically intended to suppress the African Americans from voting republican specifically.[332]

---

330 Carol Swain (former professor of political science & law, Vanderbilt University) https://www.prageru.com/video/the-inconvenient-truth-about-the-democratic-party

331 Carol Swain (former professor of political science & law, Vanderbilt University) https://www.prageru.com/video/the-inconvenient-truth-about-the-democratic-party

> A lot of black people were voting for democrats because they were being forced to. If you didn't vote for democrats the Ku Klux Klan is going to lynch your eldest son.[333]

An African-American journalist and woman named Ida B Wells, a forerunner of Rosa Parks, refused to surrender her first-class ticket on the train and was thrown out. As a journalist, she attended planned lynchings, authorised by the Democrats, so that they could be publicly reported in the press, which they otherwise were not.

Klanbake

Democratic President and professor Woodrow Wilson, who was in office during the year 1913, supported and re-established the Ku Klux Klan. He showed a terrible propaganda film about African-Americans, created by the 'Klan', thus giving the Ku Klux Klan a new lease of life among Democrats. Despite these historical events, today's Democratic Party says it has always stood up for anti-racism. Like Obama, Wilson won the Nobel Peace Prize in 1919, even though segregation was reintroduced during his time in power.

As a result, in 1924, tens of thousands of KKK members came to the Democratic Convention, later popularly known as 'The Klanbake', marching through the streets of New York City, burning crosses and celebrating the KKK's retention at the Democratic Convention. The event is captured on film.[334]

> The divisions within the party were so profound that fights broke out on the convention floor and across the New York metropolitan

332 Uncle Tom: An Oral History of the American Black Conservative, 2020, Damani B. Felder

333 Uncle Tom: An Oral History of the American Black Conservative, 2020, Chad Jackson

334 40,000 Ku Klux (1925) - British Pathé https://www.youtube.com/watch?v=BnI8SUQPB4k

area. At one point, 20,000 members of the Ku Klux Klan, which backed leading candidate William Gibbs McAdoo, were "battered to a shapeless pulp" an effigy of New York Governor Al Smith, the other front-runner, at a demonstration across the Hudson River in New Jersey. Historian Robert K. Murray wrote in The 103rd Ballot: Democrats and the Disaster in Madison Square Garden.[335]

President Wilson had made a promise to the 'Klan' of protection and the introduction of new lynching laws. At its peak, the Ku Klux Klan had 2-3 million members, as many as Hitler's Brown Shirts.[336]

The Big Switch

So, a large part of the Democratic Party in the United States had supported segregation, slavery and racism, but later started to deny all their wrongdoings - deny it to the end. Now, Democrats are seen as supporting diversity and anti-racism, while the right is accused of racism. This is called "The Big Switch" in the US; the paradigm shift of right and left that took place in the Western countries - and for no apparent reason, the conservatives were displaced as the "bad guys" and the Democrats as the "good guys". This is not taught in schools. An African-American former police officer who has learnt to look for the big picture of historical truth puts it this way:

> I have learned to go beyond just listening to what CNN says or even Fox news (...) and what they are selling - and I'm able to listen and

335 Smithsonian Magazine: June 24, 2024, Why the 1924 Democratic National Convention Was the Longest and Most Chaotic of Its Kind in U.S. History https://www.smithsonianmag.com/history/why-the-1924-democratic-national-convention-was-the-longest-and-most-chaotic-of-its-kind-in-us-history-180984590/

336 Carol Swain (former professor of political science & law, Vanderbilt University) https://www.prageru.com/video/the-inconvenient-truth-about-the-democratic-party

do the research on my own, so I know who I believe in, who I am voting for and why. I used to be a democrat, I used to be a hardcore "Barack-Obama-the-democrats-are-only-here-to-help-the-people" and then I found out that the Democratic party was the party of slavery, Ku Klux Klan, they were opposed to the civil rights movement the 13th, 14th, 15th amendment which freed the slaves and gave black people citizenship and the right to vote; that democrats unanimously voted against all of those rights.[337]

What is not taught today is that more Republicans voted in favour of African-American rights than Democrats. Moreover, the bills were drafted by Republicans. One man in particular who made civil rights and voting rights possible - Everett Dirksen, was then given an award from the NAACP (National Association for the Advancement of the Colored People). What instead took place in the public media debate was that Democratic President Lyndon Johnson eventually signed the bills into law.[338]

President Johnson was able to get the Civil Rights bill passed and it was perceived that it was an effort on the part of the democrats and so that's a perception and a narrative that has been created that caused the community to connect that momentous event to the democratic party and theyve been using that idea to effectively create a perception that the best friend to the black community is the democratic party.[339]

---

337 Uncle Tom: An Oral History of the American Black Conservative, 2020, Brandon Tatum, an African-American former police officer
338 Uncle Tom: An Oral History of the American Black Conservative, 2020
339 Uncle Tom: An Oral History of the American Black Conservative, 2020, Reverend Stephen Broden

After the paradigm shift in 1960, it was rumoured that those Democrats who opposed the rights of African Americans had switched to the Republicans as part of the 'Big Switch'. This helps to perpetuate the narrative that Democrats always have been philanthropic and 'good'.

> When they want to teach you about somebody who was great in Black American history and they happen to be republican - they don't tell you that element; instead they tell you - and this is one of the biggest myths - that the party completely switched.[340]

It is not surprising that the Democratic movement wants to escape responsibility for its political history, given its relationship with African Americans and its association with the Ku Klux Klan.

> They have to say the party switched because they cant acknowledged that they are part of all the worst things that have ever happened to black people in history.[341]

In reality, almost no Democrats switched to the Republican Party. The Democrats did not go from opposing African-American rights to suddenly becoming inclusive, but simply found a new way to capture votes. Several Democrats, led by Al Gore Sr, worked behind the scenes to ensure that "The Civil Rights Act" would never happen, which is called the longest filibuster in the history of the Senate[342] But that's not what they teach in history classes at school.

> Black people have been taught that the democratic party wears the white hat when

340 Uncle Tom: An Oral History of the American Black Conservative, 2020, Candice Owens
341 Uncle Tom: An Oral History of the American Black Conservative, 2020, Brandon Tatum
342 Uncle Tom: An Oral History of the American Black Conservative, 2020

it comes to civil rights and racial justice and republicans have been described as wearing the black hat.[343]

In the 1940s, Margaret Sanger, a Democrat, promoted eugenics and racial biology. Sanger believed, on eugenic grounds, that African-American women should abort their pregnancies rather than give birth. She wanted to eradicate what she called 'bad elements' in society to make way for the 'better elements'. She specifically hired African-American ministers to spread these ideas and set up Planned Parenthood, an abortion clinic located in the poorest areas of the US. She also promoted the use of forced sterilisation, not only on blacks - but also on the weak-minded. The Nazis admired Margaret Sanger, who had a personal correspondence with Hitler.

These historical facts are not part of the public narrative. To stop asking these important questions is to devalue people's origins. Constantly believing that African Americans or other minorities cannot fend for themselves, constantly victimising people is 'the racism of low expectations'. But minorities have not always been victimised. The African-American population was influential after they were freed from slavery. They had been given land, education, careers and lived in nuclear families. The nuclear family has always been an important part of African-American culture - until modern times.

Fatherlessness

In 2023, as many as 71% of African-American children were living without fathers.[344] In the 1960s,

343 Uncle Tom: An Oral History of the American Black Conservative, 2020, Larry Elder
344 Uncle Tom: An Oral History of the American Black Conservative, 2020

fatherlessness was down to 25%[345], while in 2015 as many as 73% were without fathers.[346] According to Walter Williams and census data from 1840-1940, more African-American children lived with both parents than corresponding children in "white" families.[347] Religious beliefs were strong and divorce was not an option. Then something happened that broke up the African-American nuclear family. So what was it that really happened?

The Democratic Party began to win more and more African-American voters. This happened after the New Deal was established in the 1940s, a political programme that left African Americans with little choice. Massunemployment during President Wilson's term made them lose their jobs and the New Deal gave them benefits, which increased the Democratic vote despite the fact that African-American voters reportedly felt they were betraying their political roots.[348] In the 1960s, programmes continued with the Great Society Act, where only women with children received benefits – but only if they were single – causing many marriages to dissolve – just so that the women and children would survive and receive financial assistance. The African-American tradition was slowly crumbling.

With the Great Society Act, families were separated and, in order to support themselves, women 'chose' benefits over the nuclear family. They became "married" to the state. For every child they had, the allowance was multiplied and, thanks to the programme, being divorced became a way of making a living.[349]

345 Larry Elder Pregar U, Black fathers matter
346 National Vital Statistics from the Centers for Disease Control and Prevention
347 Larry Elder Prager U, Larry Elder Prager U, Black Fathers Matter, 2017
348 Carol Swain (former professor of political science & law, Vanderbilt University) https://www.prageru.com/video/the-inconvenient-truth-about-the-democratic-party
349 Larry Elder Prager U https://www.prageru.com/video/black-fathers-matter

When an African-American man or woman manages capital and education in the 21st century and succeeds in a career, they are subjected to racism by their own people, who claim that they are not 'black' but 'white', that they are an 'Uncle Tom' who is betraying the African-American community. Why is this? Where does such an attitude come from? What the public does not know is that the Marxist revolution of the 1960s changed the living conditions and attitudes of African Americans in the United States forever, and that Saul Alinsky helped fuel this political movement. In the context of the African-American Marxist movement of the 1960s, there was talk of the African-American population taking revenge on the 'white' population and of 'whites' being the enemy. As one African-American Democratic speaker put it in a speech in the 1960s:

> We and white people are mortal enemies. They were not made to be our friends they were made to be our enemies and they are that and they cant be nothing but that, they are locked into that. There is no redemption for them[350]

Here too, the Marxist influence led people to see themselves as part of identity politics, as oppressed victims of society. In the 1960s, violent riots broke out. The African-American population turned against American society. Several speakers encouraged African Americans to be angry and rebel.

> There must be a revolution of values in our country because some of the values that presently exist are certainly out of line with the values and the idealistic structure that brought our nation into being.[351]

350 Uncle Tom: An Oral History of the American Black Conservative, 2020, Luis Farakhan
351 Uncle Tom: An Oral History of the American Black Conservative, 2020, Martin Luther King

In the 1960s, there was also a hint of a dream that the African-American population would become independent and develop its potential. In practice, however, they turned away from society and a sense of hopelessness spread. At the same time, institutions, schools and training programmes began to say that the African-American population was subject to racism and that this racism was systematic and pervasive. The postcolonial perspective made its initial appearance. [352]

> I learnt that I was black, I was poor, I was a woman and that I was not supposed to have accomplished the things that I had already accomplished - which was success.[353]

With a stagnant notion that African Americans must be angry, that African Americans are constantly exposed to racism, that African Americans are unemployed - an image of the victim and self-fulfilling prophecy was created. In this way, the population was divided into two groups - 'black and white'. The current US Democratic Party claims that it is the racism of the white population that is the main problem in the African-American community, ignoring the real problems - high rates of fatherlessness and low levels of education.[354]

So today's Democrats claim to be anti-racist. But there is a different picture of their attitude. 2016 Democratic candidate Hillary Clinton said in a speech about eugenicist Margret Sanger:

> I admire Margret Sanger enormously. I am really in aw of her. There are a lot of lessons we can learn from her life and the

352 Uncle Tom: An Oral History of the American Black Conservative, 2020
353 Uncle Tom: An Oral History of the American Black Conservative, 2020, Carol Swain
354 Candace Owens at hearing on Confronting White Supremacy
https://www.youtube.com/watch?v=0cUQqPxw3hc

cause she launched and fought for and sacrificed so greatly for.[355]

The speech, recorded on YouTube[356], supports the work of eugenicist Margret Sanger. Planned Parenthood, the abortion clinic founded by Sanger, is almost exclusively based in the ghettos of the United States. Planned Parenthood has helped abort as many as 20 million African Americans since the 1970s. Here's what Sanger herself has to say about abortion:

> I think the greatest sin in the world is to bring children into the world that have deceased from their parents, that have no chance in the world to be a human being practically. Delinquents, prisoners, all sorts of things just mark when they're born - that to me is the greatest sin.[357]

In 1939, Margaret Sanger, founder of Planned Parenthood outlined her plan to eliminate the Black community:

> The most successful, educational appeal to the Negro is through a religious appeal. We do not want word to go out that we want to exterminate the Negro population, and the minister is the man who can straighten out that idea if it ever occurs to any of their rebellious members.[358]

355 https://2009-2017.state.gov/secretary/20092013clinton/rm/2009a/03/120968.htm
356 Hillary Clinton Honours Margaret Sanger at the 2009 Planned Parenthood Honors Gala https://www.youtube.com/watch?v=r4o4WizW2mQ
357 Documentary: Uncle Tom: An Oral History of the American Black Conservative, 2020, Margret Singer
358 Dr Martin Luther King Jr. And The Civil Rights Of The Unborn https://www.alvedaking.com/mlk-civil-right-of-the-unborn

I used to be a drugdealer

Proffessor Carol Swain says that instead of solving the real problems of the African-American population, slavery is used as an excuse for encouraging violence and criminality - it's interperted as justice and the result of victimisation. It keeps people under control, like a spell. The African Americans who came out of slavery had a better standard of living - with both a career and a nuclear family; than what you have today with shootings, unemployment, demonstrations, bombings and riots.[359]

> The biggest falsehood, the biggest lie that gets repeated, is that the kind of disorganisation and chaos and violence and self-destruction that we are witnessing in the black community is somehow a legacy of slavery and "Jim Crow" laws (the segregation laws).[360]

There are numerous photo albums from before the 1960s with countless photographs of African-American culture, with people dressed up in fancy clothes, attending church and Sunday school. At the time, there were strong Christian values in the African-American community - about work and love for one's neighbours. The religious movement brought hope.[361] An African-American upper class was already thriving, accepted by the rest of society. Many people looked up to them and they were the role models for businessmen and politicians of the time. They even had their own 'Black Wall Street'. As an example of the sophisticated African-American culture that flourished, there were African-American composers who had written operas and symphonies. These are not talked about today. Instead, people only talk about Beyonce and Tupac Shakur. How is that non-racist?

359 Documentary: Uncle Tom II: An American Odyssey, 2022, Carol Swain
360 Documentary: Uncle Tom: An Oral History of the American Black
     Conservative, 2020, Bob Woodson
361 Documentary: Uncle Tom II: An American Odyssey, 2022, Carol Swain

How many of the following African-American cultural figures are known today?

African-American composers:

Joseph Bologna, Knight of St George (1745 - 1799)

George Bridgetower (1778 - 1860), Afro-European virtuoso violinist and composer, 'African Mahler'

Samuel Coleridge-Taylor (1875 - 1912)

Florence Price (1887 - 1953)

African-American opera composers:

H. Lawrence Freeman (1869-1954), *Martyr*, 1891. and 14 more operas composed between 1898 and 1947, including a four-opera cycle called *Zululand* (1941-44).

Scott Joplin's *Treemonisha* (1910)

Freeman's *Voodoo* (1914)

Clarence Cameron White's *Ouanga!* (1928)

Still's *Blue Steel* (1934)

Troubled Island (1939)

Now it's Jay-Z, who openly brags about being a drug dealer, and Cardi B, who are the role models. According to Brandon Tatum, a former African-American police officer, this is not the real African-American culture[362]. Back then, there was religion, culture, duties and rules to live by - in a completely different way. There was no drug use either. Now you rap about sex and drugs and gang crime, to sell records and believe - according to Tatum - that it is African American culture.[363]

362 Documentary: Uncle Tom II: An American Odyssey, 2022, Brandon Tatum
363 Documentary: Uncle Tom II: An American Odyssey, 2022, Brandon Tatum

> What we're seeing today is another religion communicating another meta-narrative and another worldview, and these murals (graffiti on gang criminals who died in gang wars) are the stained glass windows of this new religion.[364]

People shouted "death to America" during Black Lives Matter riots. The protests were huge, beyond anything seen in post-modern times. The destruction was gigantic - shops, streets and old statues are smashed by both African-American and 'white' protesters who seem to want to destroy society to its core.

> You see people try to rewrite history. You see them tear down statues and rename everything. Why is that? Because your history gives you your identity and your identity is the basis of your beliefs.[365]

BLM and the trained Marxist

What many people don't realise is that the leaders of Black Lives Matter are 'trained' Marxists, with the same values as the original Marxists in the East. When the movement was met with concerns about a lack of political ideology, the founders responded:

> We actually do have an ideological frame-[work]. Myself and Alicia [Garza] in particular, we're trained organisers; we are trained Marxists. We are super-versed on, sort of, ideological theories. And I think that what we really tried to do is build a movement that could be utilised by many, many black folks.[366] Patrisse Cullors, 23 July 2015

364 Documentary: Uncle Tom II: An American Odyssey, 2022, Voddie Baucham JR
365 Documentary: Uncle Tom II: An American Odyssey, 2022, Dr Ben Carson
366 "We Are Trained Marxists" - Patrisse Cullors, Co-Founder, Jared Ball of The Real News Network. https://www.youtube.com/watch?v=HgEUbSzOTZ8

The same strategic political ideology that Soviet Communists used when they appealed to people's oppression, their sorrow and pain, instead promising them utopia - is behind the Black Lives Matter movement. Karl Marx wanted to get rid of religion and in its place, icons like Stalin and Lenin were born in the Soviet Union. Instead of what was promised came death, starvation and a more oppressive state than ever. The same basic ideas are enshrined in BLM.

The founders of Black Lives Matter (BLM) are Patrisse Cullors, Alicia Garza and Opal Tometi. These are so-called "trained" Marxists who have been trained in Alinsky's "Community Organising". Their teacher, a former left-wing activist named Eric Mann, has set up the "Trans-formative Organizing Workshop", a centre where students *are trained* to "lead" and organise groups.

Eric Mann organises people who want to become revolutionaries. So he's a 'white' Marxist - the man behind BLM, an African-American movement. It was he who trained BLM's leaders in, among other things, how to criticise the current, traditional society and how to criticise capitalism. Black Lives Matter is a movement of thousands of people who have participated in hundreds of violent riots and destroyed $4 billion worth of cities. Patrisse Cullors became a Marxist at 17 and describes that period in her life as 'when she was angry'.[367]

> When you are angry it's very easy to be deceived, it's very sad to see black people operate in that there's a lot of members in the black community who are operating in a very negative energy.[368]

367 Documentary: Uncle Tom II: An American Odyssey, 2022
368 Uncle Tom: An Oral History of the American Black Conservative, 2020, Michael Ayetrwa

> Black people were always ripe for use by communists, because many of us do come from situations of poverty.[369]

The fact that the African-American population in the United States is the most affluent, liberal, successful "black" population in the world escapes many people. Many of these successful people - well-educated, politicians, academics - own huge amounts of capital. So the idea that African-Americans are not well placed to succeed in the US, is a lie designed to contribute to the self-fulfilling prophecy.[370]

> If you keep yourself in this constant state of "Woe is me, I'm disadvantaged, Ill never accomplish anything", Then you won't accomplish anything.[371]

The man behind the technique of organising revolutionaries is Saul Alinsky. In his book, "Rules for radicals" he teaches both tactics and strategy. It says, among other things, that you can lie and manipulate to achieve your goal - if it's for a good cause. All of his tactics are the same tools that have been used to carry out the BLM revolution. The common perception is that Black Lives Matter is an African-American organisation that has fought for the African-American population. Instead, it is "white" Marxists, such as Alinsky and Eric Mann and their theories that are behind it - theories with the same origins as Gramci's doctrine of the infiltration of a society.[372]

> As early as 1928 the communists declared that the racial differences among our people constituted the weakest and the most vulnerable

369 Documentary: Uncle Tom II: An American Odyssey, 2022, Carol Swain
370 Documentary: Uncle Tom II: An American Odyssey, 2022, Voddie
371 Documentary: Uncle Tom: An Oral History of the American Black Conservative, 2020, Chad Jackson
372 Documentary: Uncle Tom II: An American Odyssey, 2022

point in our social fabric. By constantly probing and staying at this one spot they calculated eventually the cloth could be torn apart and that Americans could be divided, weakened and perhaps even set against each other in open combat.[373]

To divide people in this way, to use their frustration to make them fight with each other, instead of creating common goals; to have their demonstration supported by the media and through protests, threats and the use of martyrs; to make the world believe that the revolution is spread among people and then neutralise all resistance. Name the opponents as fascists, Nazis, anti-Semites, extremists and racists. This way, the techniques of Saul Alinsky and his community organising have been used to make certain groups of people rise up against other groups.

A survey was conducted asking how many unarmed African-American people, out of a population of 334 million, were shot by police in the United States in 2019. 5% said they thought as many as 10,000 had been shot. 50% answered that there were 1000 who had been shot. The correct answer was 12. The difference between what a public opinion *believes* due to media distortion and what is actually true - is gigantic.[374]

> The ideology is implanted in to you subconsciously to believe these things.[375]

373 More Deadly Than War - Lecture by G. Edward Griffin 1969
   https://stateofthenation.co/?p=33996
374 Documentary: Uncle Tom: An Oral History of the American Black
   Conservative, 2020, Larry Elder
375 Documentary: Uncle Tom: An Oral History of the American Black
   Conservative, 2020, Brandon Tatum

White Guilt

It tries to implement that the "whites" are oppressors and the "blacks" are victims. The white oppressors are the holders of a loaded concept called "Whiteness" - a kind of "ownership" of various advantages inherited automatically because of the colour of your skin, which is solely due to the fact that you are "white".[376]

This is one of the pillars of the 'Critical Race Theory', a theory that suggests that a white 'super-structure' is the reason why structural racism exists. Therefore, it seeks to eradicate and minimise 'white-ness'. All other ethnic groups have the right to ethnicity - except the Western one. According to identity politics, the Western ethnic group is permanently indebted to anyone with a different skin colour - automatically.[377]

> When the race problem comes up, they're not driven to fix the problem, they're driven to get that anxiety out of their life; what do I need to do, to get them on my side, to get past this judgment that I live in? and that is what white guilt is, that terror, that automatic judgment that you are a racist.[378]

This is called "White Guilt". They romanticise and ideologise the other cultures - but want to deny their own, Western culture. If you are grateful for your own culture, you are 'racist' against those who, according to identity politics, have a privilege. Shelby Steele is an African-American writer and researcher with a PhD in political science and other fields:

> White guilt is the anxiety white people carry in their everyday life, because they know

376 James Lindsay | WOKE Culture HAS NOT Gone Too Far - 6/8 | Oxford Union
377 Queer Theory is Gender Marxism, James Lindsay, New Discourses
https://www.youtube.com/watch?v=JNW79czfibw&t=122s
378 Shelby Steele - White Guilt and the Identity of Innocence

they're being prejudged on the basic of their race, as whites - and as whites, they are automatically 'reflexively' seen as racists.[379]

According to Steele, this has nothing to do with a real sense of guilt, but rather with an anxiety that is diffuse, and difficult to pinpoint. Instead, there is a sense of guilt and shame that you want to get rid of immediately.

> White guilt has nothing to do with actual guilt, white guilt is the terror of being judged as a racist as a bigot. We talk about universities and political correctness - these are ways to say "I'm innocent!" (...) White guilt causes this drive to prove and establish innocence. White guilt is meant to disarm you of moral authority (...) they're saying you're a racist so you don't have the moral authority to deal with whatever issue we're dealing with.[380]

Steele argues that the phenomenon affects educational institutions by creating a belief in the West that they need to "cleanse" themselves of "White Guilt". Educational institutions, cultural workers and others are guided by the power of the concept.

According to Shelby Steele, it is a weapon used by politicians and the media. One example is the famous quote by Barack Obama, the first African-American president in the West - "Racism is in Americas DNA":

> "Racism, we are not cured of it" ... "What is also true is that the legacy of slavery, Jim Crow, discrimination in almost every institution of our lives - you know, that casts a

379 Shelby Steele: 'White Guilt is Not Real Guilt'
380 Shelby Steele - White Guilt and the Identity of Innocence

long shadow. And that's still part of our DNA that's passed on. We're not cured of it."[381]

The constant search for affirmation of innocence and anti-racism, which the phenomenon of "White Guilt" gives rise to, is in turn transformed into a weakness, which is used - among other things - in election campaigns.

> Hilary Clinton in her deplorable statement now famous as a perfect example of saying: "These people are racist - I am innocent. You vote for me - you prove your innocence. I offer you an identity of innocence" is that susceptibility, that vulnerability in the political arena, people are going to play on it. They're going to exploit this.[382]

80-90% of the US media is owned by a left-wing elite.[383] The same goes for the institutions. This makes it easy to fall into the categories of identity politics. This has not always been the case. The African-American community needs to recognise its own strength, rise up and reclaim its economic and social power and potential; instead of looking down on individuals and communities as victims.

> My parents didn't teach me that I was a victim. But there were other influences that did. Whether were talking about uncles and aunts and the hip-hop industry, the media; it painted a picture of the black man in America as being in a constant state of distress a constant state of disadvantage.[384]

381 WTF with Macron, Episode 613, June 22, 2015
   https://www.wtfpod.com/podcast/episodes/episode_613_-_president_barack_obama
382 Shelby Steele - White Guilt and the Identity of Innocence
383 Documentary: Uncle Tom: An Oral History of the American Black Conservative, 2020, Larry Elder

Leaving already?

The process of moving from the left/progressivism to the 'right', switching sides or becoming 'neutral' is not easy - especially if you belong to the African-American community. Amala Ekpunobi is an African-American and former left-wing activist, who believed that there is a so-called systematic racism that permeates society and prevents African-Americans from advancing in society.

> ...And black America has been programmed to believe that we can't.[385]

Ekpunobi belonged to a left-wing organisation that travelled around schools talking to middle school students to educate them about socialism and Marxism. She lectured so that they, like her, would become more 'WOKE'. She believed she was changing the world. Ekpunobi lived her life through the political feminist and anti-racist perspective. This hierarchical approach felt wrong to Amala Ekpunobi, who went home in the evenings to her 'white' family who had looked after her all her life and ensured she was educated and brought up. Something was simply not right.

She was stopped by police, and because of the media image BLM had spread in the news, she was terrified of being shot. She started crying and tears were flowing. But the policeman just said 'I don't want to hurt you, just slow down' and left.[386] The media and politicians focus on a white police officer shooting an African-American, while 'framing' the fact that it is actually

384 Documentary: Uncle Tom: An Oral History of the American Black Conservative, 2020, Chad Jackson
385 Documentary: Uncle Tom: An Oral History of the American Black Conservative, 2020, Candace Owens
386 Why I Left the Left - Amala Ekpunobi at Washington University in St. Louis, 10 Dec. 2022

African-Americans who shoot most African-Americans in ghettos:

> In Chicago in 2011 - 21 people were shot and killed by cops, in 2015 they were 7, in Chicago which is a third white, a third white and a third Hispanic community, 70% of the homicides are black on black. (...) Where is the Black Lives Matter on that?[387]

> More blacks are killing blacks in one year, then the Klan killed in 70 years.[388]

Why is it that rhetoric is used that contributes to the denial of the real problems that exist in the ghetto? Amala Ekpunobi wondered if the rhetoric that exists is really true. She raised it with the left-wing organisation she was a member of. Their response was 'you just don't know how oppressed you are'. That's when she decided to stop and broaden her perspective. She heard an interview with an African-American police officer who told her a completely different picture of reality, while presenting different statistics. Ekpunobi then felt she was heading 'down the rabbit hole' as she discovered more and more thinkers who contradicted everything she had previously believed.[389]

> The only way I can operate as a human being is via my skin colour, I can't operate via my intelligence, or the things I have accomplished, my resume should be: 'I'm black'.[390]

387 Documentary: Uncle Tom: An Oral History of the American Black Conservative, 2020, Larry Elder
388 Uncle Tom: An Oral History of the American Black Conservative, 2020, Bob Woodson
389 Why I Left the Left - Amala Ekpunobi at Washington University in St. Louis, 10 Dec. 2022
390 Documentary: Uncle Tom: An Oral History of the American Black Conservative, 2020

When Amala Ekpunobi recorded and published a video about her political journey, she received a lot of on-line hate and was called "Uncle Tom" and racist. She had not expected this.

Her experience was that as soon as you were not left-wing, you were completely excluded from the social sphere she had previously belonged to. The organisation did not want to talk about it or listen to her, and this was done quite openly and demonstratively. [391]

> An Uncle Tom is somebody who has sold out by embracing the white man, by becoming a Republican (leaving the left, author's note) by rejecting the idea that you're a victim.[392]

Amala Ekpunobi believes that the education system has a lot of responsibility in this, as they no longer create the conditions for a nuanced education. She believes that the education system has become more left-wing, by publishing biased articles and books that are turned into lectures that are given to students, who after graduation work in companies, schools, education, media and so on.[393]

> I started asking questions like if the white man is holding me back because Im black, why is it that they're not holding Jesse Jackson (democratic African American activist) and his family back, the NAACP[394] and all them - their kids went to the best schools, they had fathers and mothers in their homes and they were doing very well.[395]

391 Why I Left the Left - Amala Ekpunobi at Washington University in St. Louis, 10 Dec. 2022
392 Documentary: Uncle Tom: An Oral History of the American Black Conservative, 2020, Larry Elder
393 Why I Left the Left - Amala Ekpunobi at Washington University in St. Louis, 10 Dec. 2022
394 National Association for the Advancement of Coloured People
395 Uncle Tom: An Oral History of the American Black Conservative, 2020, Jesse Lee Peterson

The African-American role models who were strong and worked their way up in society, such as Professor Thomas Sowell, are absent from mainstream media, school lessons and history books. He uses his research to teach a more comprehensive view of slavery:

> Why wouldn't They teach us about Thomas Sowell in school?[396]

> I know Le Bron James. I know all these rappers. I don't know Thomas Sowell? I don't know about Walter Williams[397]? If there's one person you'd think black America would be celebrating [it would be Thomas Sowell]...[398]

> Its like having a very successful family that you never knew you had until your grandfather dies and you all meet at the funeral. While I was hanging out with my cousin smoking weed, we got people in our family that have gone to Harvard. We have people in our family that own businesses. Highly successful. Why have you hidden this from me?[399]

On her arm, Amala Ekpunobi has a "Black Power" fist tattooed. It is the same fist, which figures in feminism. It is really - the Marxist fist.[400]

---

396 Documentary: Uncle Tom: An Oral History of the American Black Conservative, 2020, Brandon Tatum

397 American economist, commentator, and academic (1936-2020)

398 Documentary: Uncle Tom: An Oral History of the American Black Conservative, 2020, Candace Owens

399 Documentary: Uncle Tom: An Oral History of the American Black Conservative, 2020, Chad Jackson

400 Why I Left the Left - Amala Ekpunobi at Washington University in St. Louis, 10 Dec. 2022

Segregation & domination

- show me the man and Ill find you the crime.

Lavrentiy Beria

Today, feminism represents the largest part of the gender equality movement and a fight for justice. It is a global movement, which can be found in most parts of the world. This movement is much bigger than the men's movement, which many feminists and WOKE people consider unnecessary. Why have a men's movement when it is *only* women who are oppressed and victims of patriarchy? Today, gender theory is taught at many different institutions, universities and colleges. Feminism and the issue of gender equality are taught in schools and - already in pre-schools. The problem is that the women's movement has been hijacked - by Marxism and the Marxist influence means that the feminist movement is infiltrated by identity politics:

> Gynocentric feminism defines women's oppression as the devaluation and repression of women's experience by a masculinist culture that exalts violence and individualism.[401]

Feminism derives its legitimacy from the theory that women have been oppressed throughout history and thus denied access to power, labour and social status. That women have always been victims of patriarchy and the powerful men who denied them life.

However, this interpretation of historical society gives a one-sided picture of the past. A more comprehensive worldview would tell us that many women in history had both good social standing, power and important

401 Christina Hoff Sommers, "Who Stole Feminism" page 73, 1994

246

professions. For example, an upper-class woman had more power and more cultural and economic capital than a working-class man. One powerful woman, Queen Elizabeth I, is reported to have said the following during her reign:

Men fight wars. Women win them.[402]

For example, a large number of educated women philosophers lived and worked from the 12th century until today. These included the world-famous *Hildegard of Bingen*, as well as *Christine de Pizan, Marie de Gournay, Anne Conway, Catherine Trotter Cockburn and Catharine Macaulay Graham,* to name but a few. These women had great power and a good position in most of the top arenas of society.[403] Furthermore, there were educated women who researched, studied and earned doctorates, right from the time when people began to educate themselves. *Julianna Morell* began studying Greek, Latin and Hebrew in 1594 and then obtained a doctorate in law in 1608.[404] Other women not mentioned here held the same position and the reason why people do not know this is because of a lack of interest - not because such women have not existed.

In 1639, there was *L'Ecole des Ursulines de Quebec*, in the United States, an all-female school to which men were not admitted.[405] Not to mention all the ruling women of *the Medici clan*, which in its day was the most powerful family in the world. But even those women who weren't famous or rich had access to status jobs throughout society. For example, women worked as blacksmiths from the 18th century onwards. They had their own smithies because the men - they had to go to war. Throughout history, women have been writers, miners,

402 Queen Elizabeth I
403 Anna-Karin Malmström-Ehrling, "Female philosophers from the Middle Ages to the Enlightenment", 2003
404 Bob Lewis, "The feminist lie" 2017
405 Bob Lewis "The feminist lie" 2017

clerks, factory managers and held other important positions. Not to mention all the noblewomen and land-ladies of higher rank.

My dear, never give up a crown. To anybody.[406]
Cathrine Medici

History is full of women who held powerful roles, good positions and indispensable professions that contribu-ted to the development of society at every conceivable level. If you had asked a powerful woman in the 19th century if she felt oppressed, the answer would not necessarily have been yes.

Voting rights

The same applies to women's right to vote. Women's right to vote in Sweden, as in the USA, came about shortly after universal suffrage for men had been voted in. Before that, only the rich and the upper classes could vote. Before universal suffrage became law, there were also so-called 'suffrage bars'. This meant that you had to do something special to be able to vote, in this case it was, for example, to perform military ser-vice.

> The new electoral system certainly allowed the majority of the productive male popula-tion to fulfil the conditions - but the voting lines and their impact on the electo-rate make it difficult to argue that the right to vote in the 1909 reform was com-pletely independent of class, income and wealth.[407]

> "Salesman Johan Emil Fredlund received a letter ... from the Stockholm magistrate, ...

406 Mrs Cathrine Medici
407 Ebba Åselius, "Den begränsade rösträtten Rösträtt med förhinder. Voting rights in Swedish politics 1900-1920", page 13, 2005

informing him that he was not entitled to vote in the 1911 general election. He had been affected by *the moving line*, ... [he] had recently moved to Stockholm and had previously lived in Spånga. [The same] had also happened to the iron worker Jonas Edvard Andersson ... ." In those days, people paid their own taxes and had to show receipts before moving out of a home.[408]

There were many wealthy right-wing women who entered politics and their membership began to be seen as very positive - in an era where democracy was still a very new form of government. So it wasn't that men had been allowed to vote for thousands of years before women. Democracy and the right to vote did not exist until the end of the 19th century, when it began to gradually replace the old system of power. Many men did not have access to a vote either.

If the right to vote was universal [for men], why were Fredlund Andersson and almost 283,000 Swedish men disqualified?[409]

The First World War made it necessary in the United Kingdom to give the right to vote to men who had fought in the war and who had not previously been allowed to vote. Before that, the vote was a privilege of the upper classes. The same was true for women - in the United Kingdom, upper-class women got the vote first and working-class women ten years later. The vote was a matter of class more than gender.

They couldn't have young men returning from the horrors of the first world war who had served their countries, the ultimate act of

408 Ebba Åselius, "Den begränsade rösträtten Rösträtt med förhinder. Voting rights in Swedish politics 1900-1920", page 11, 2005
409 Ebba Åselius, "Den begränsade rösträtten Rösträtt med förhinder. Voting rights in Swedish politics 1900-1920", page 13, 2005

self-sacrifice and then not have the right to
vote. Up to 40% of men didn't have the right
to vote in 1914 because they didn't own properties and they didn't meet the proper qual-
ifications.[410]

Most politically engaged women voted for the
Conservative Party, which would later be called the
Moderate Party, partly because most of them had a connection to the church at the time. When the right to
vote came into being at the same time as the government
became parliamentary, the democracy that continues to
this day emerged. Parliamentarianism was more opposed
by the right - than women's suffrage, which passed
without major problems.[411] Today, Socialists want to
convince people that they have always been in favour of
gender equality, while the 'right' is supposed to be
against it, which is not true. In the United States,
for example, it was a Republican and Chief Justice
named William Taft who removed the laws that prevented
women from voting.[412]

Who were the heroes?

Many in the movement go back to the origins of feminism
and portray the women who fought for women's rights -
the suffragettes - as heroes. These suffragettes completely ignored all laws and should not be confused
with 'suffragists', who were law-abiding. The suffragettes, who systematically terrorised most of their
surroundings through terrorist violence, have nevertheless been given hero status in today's cultural
establishment in the West. These women, who were upper
or upper-middle class and lived and acted as feminists

410 Channel 4 news Dr Caitriona Beaumont, Associate Professor, London South
    Bank University
411 Ideologies 2019 - Moderate Party ideas, Torbjörn Nilsson
412 Documentary: Uncle Tom: An Oral History of the American Black
    Conservative, 2020, Chad Jackson

in the early 20th century, felt justified in setting arson fires, planning bombings, carrying out acid attacks, threatening and persecuting both men and women who would not obey their slogans. This is not unlike the terror that the Marxists inflicted on their victims in the riots of the Russian Revolution.[413]

> By 1912-1913 you had women ingaging in quite serious violence such as bombing campaigns, timber yards were blown up and homes were attacked, bombs were left on trains and in post offices.[414]

The Women's Social and Political Union 1903-1914, which quickly became a violent organisation, had the motto 'deeds not words'. The deeds referred to were acts of terror of various kinds, such as the bombings and arson attacks that terrorised Britain for a long time and involved hundreds of militant raids. These raids led to the imprisonment of radical suffragettes. These suffragettes and upper-class women thought they could get away with their crimes and they did, as they are now remembered as heroes of the contemporary feminist-Marxist movement.

Most working-class men were not entitled to vote at that time. But Emmeline Pankhurst, the leading suffragist, was not interested in the working class at all. Nor was she interested in working class women, all those women who actually had jobs at the time:

> I may add that there are scores of women in recent years who have taken to men's work and men's clothing, as bricklayers, grooms, navvies, and what not, in order to obtain

---

413 The Suffragette Bombers - Britain's Forgotten Terrorists, Simon Webb, Pen & Sword 2014. & The Incendiary Rage of the Suffragettes - The Fiamengo File 2.0 https://www.youtube.com/watch?v=wVPmoVZCFrA

414 Channel 4 news Dr Caitriona Beaumont, Associate Professor, London South Bank University, Suffragettes vs Suffragists: Did violent protests get women the vote?

their fair wage and that freedom of labour to which they know themselves entitled, though the "women's rights" folk do not seem to know as much.[415]

Because of the wars, there were more women than men at the time, so unmarried women found work faster than married women - who also had to work. As unemployment became more widespread, there was competition for jobs among both men and women. This did not apply to the upper classes. Upper-class feminists of the time were not interested in the fact that working-class women had been active in the labour force for all of history. According to most accounts, there were also many women in the upper classes who worked even though they did not need to.

> If women held, tomorrow, the right of suf-frage, there would not be any more female lawyers, preachers, artists, doctors, than there are today. There is nothing now to hinder a woman from taking charge of a church, if she and the church wish it. Indeed, women, today, hold pastorates, and no one molests them. Probably there is not a village or a city in New England, where a woman would not be listened to respectfully, and given full credit for all her wit and wisdom. Let any woman who is moved to address a public assembly, announce such an inten-tion, and she will have a larger audience then a man of similar ability, and she will have at least an equally appreciative hear-ing. [416]

Just before the First World War, there was a guerrilla war for which the suffragettes were responsible. They attacked churches and shops, causing economic and

415 Michael Hiley, "Victorian working women", page 43, 1979
416 "Gail Hamilton" [Abigail Dodge] "Woman's Wrongs", 1868

252

physical harm to both men and women, mainly from the working class. The suffragettes set fire to letterboxes and poured acid into them, causing the postmen to suffer burns and lung damage.

They burnt down several of their opponents' country homes in Scotland, England and Ireland. A deployed bomb blew out the roofs and windows of buildings. Buildings destroyed included the Bank of England, St Catherine's Church in London, St Mary's in Whitekirk in Scotland, Britannia Pier in Yarmouth in Scotland, St Paul's Cathedral in London and Westminster Abbey, among others. The list is very long. This went on for two years and it went on constantly.[417] For those who were prosecuted and imprisoned, the punishment was lenient. The right-wing suffragettes joked about their imprisonment during a meeting:

> The Daily Telegraph: "(...) Seventy-six of the prisoners are supposed to be serving sentences with hard labour, but none of them are wearing prison clothes, and in only one or two instances have any tasks of any description been given, those generally being a little sewing or knitting." [Again a member of the Women's Freedom League at a meeting on nineteenth of may, 1912, boasted that the suffragettes had wing of their own at Holloway [prison]. "They had nice hot water pipes and all the latest improvements and were able to climb up to the window and exchange sentiments with their friends."[418]

Their atrocities are not now discussed in open debate, nor are they taught in schools. Nor are the many lives of the labour movement and other classes destroyed during the suffragette raids discussed. Some suffragettes

417 The Suffragette Bombers - Britain's Forgotten Terrorists, Simon Webb, Pen & Sword 2014. & The Incendiary Rage of the Suffragettes - The Fiamengo File 2.0 https://www.youtube.com/watch?v=wVPmoVZCFrA
418 E. Belfort **Bax**, "The Fraud of Feminism", page 98, 1913

threw a pickaxe into a hansom cab in which Herbert Asquith, a then politician, was travelling; the pickaxe hit his ear and chin and he miraculously survived. Others poured petrol on carpets and detonated bombs where politicians from opposing parties were due to give speeches. The suffragettes tried to assassinate a judge named Henry Curtis Bennet by sending a letter bomb to his home but also by pushing him off a cliff. Yet they are exalted as heroes, just as other Marxist leaders are exalted by the left. Like other terrorists, they saw their purpose as so good that it justified their actions. Like other terrorists, they saw themselves as martyrs. Emily Davidson attacked a priest and set fire to an opponent's house. Although she was violent, irresponsible and dangerous, there are statues and sculptures all over the world dedicated to her and people look up to her uncritically, which shows that the contemporary feminist movement, like the Marxists, does not want to acknowledge the full truth about the terrible antics that took place.[419]

Because of the violence, the movement eventually split into two parts. *The Suffragists*, not the Suffragettes, were the original creators of the large movement, which had 50,000 members in the UK, led by Milicent Fawsett.[420] The Suffragists carried placards saying "Law-abiding Suffragist" and meant no harm. *The Suffragettes*, which roughly means 'the little Suffragist', were the militant terrorists. Led by Emmeline Pankhurst, the violent Suffragettes had around 5,000 members.

If one were to make a thought experiment out of this and replace the women with men and imagine that it was men who threw bombs and threatened people, destroyed

419 The Suffragette Bombers - Britain's Forgotten Terrorists, Simon Webb, Pen & Sword 2014. & The Incendiary Rage of the Suffragettes - The Fiamengo File 2.0 https://www.youtube.com/watch?v=wVPmoVZCFrA
420 https://www.alistairlexden.org.uk/news/true-heroine-womens-suffrage-campaign https://en.wikipedia.org/wiki/Millicent_Fawcett

property, injured people and put thousands of working class people out of work - then no one would declare them heroes. On the contrary, they would be labelled terrorists and would not accept such behaviour - either in the past or today. Such a divide between the sexes with different conditions exists because of identity politics and the Marxist theory that has infiltrated feminism and the women's movement. These upper-class women are accepted as heroes, while men do not have the same premises. [421]

White Feather

Another example is the White Feather Campaign. In England, the suffragettes were active before and during the First World War. They were involved in the White Feather Campaign, which subjected thousands of men who did not want to fight in the First World War to humiliating behaviour because they were seen as defectors and deserters. Emmeline Pankhurst was more involved with the White Feather Campaign than with her own suffragette organisation.

It all started when "The Four Feathers", a short story written by A. E. W. Mason in 1903, inspired Charles Penrose Fitzgerald to initially enlist the help of 30 women, who would distribute white feathers to the men who for various reasons had not joined the military forces.

The white feather was a symbol of inferior rooster species in cockfighting and in this insulting way they wanted to show that the men who did not want to fight, kill and die - were useless. As illustrated in *Downtown Abbey* and the TV series *Young Indiana Jones*, where it

421 (The Suffragette Bombers - Britain's forgotten terrorists, Simon Webb, Pen & Sword 2014) (The Incendiary Rage of the Suffragettes - The Fiamengo File 2.0
https://www.youtube.com/watch?v=wVPmoVZCFrA)
Janice Anne Fiamengo, born 1964 in Vancouver, is a Canadian literary scholar and Professor Emerita of English Literature at the University of Ottawa

is also shown how the young soldiers did not even have the right to vote.[422] The campaign targeted those men and young boys aged 15 and over who, for various reasons, were unable or unwilling to give their lives in the war.

The campaign quickly spread across the country, with tens of thousands of women handing out feathers to men across England. There are many examples of strong pressure from women. Among other things, it was felt that men should go out and fight to fulfil their 'promises' of protection to women. One example was George Samson, who was harassed by a woman who said he was being persecuted and that he was not fulfilling his patriotic duty. The harassment continued to affect him until he gave in, went to war and lost a hand.

A 17-year-old boy received a white feather, lied about his age and listed himself. He was promised a kiss if he listed himself and returned the feather. Another young man was victimised several times, lied about his age, misrepresented himself and then died in the war.

The example is one of many and involved boys, as young as fifteen, and men who were home from the war for various reasons such as illness. The rest of the men were fighting in the war. The women looked for remaining men on the streets to distribute white feathers and express their message in an oppressive way, using force and psychological violence. Some of the men resisted by showing their mutilated bodies to the women to try to make them realise the gravity of the situation. Women were also outraged by the campaign and many accused these feminists of causing the death of their loved ones.[423]

422 Downton Abbey, season 2 episode 1, The White Feather Campaign scene, original airdate 18 September 2011 https://www.youtube.com/watch?v=gOnMFO21c6Y

423 The White Feather Campaign TFF 2.0. We will not fight: the untold story of World War One´s Conscientious Objectors by Will Ellsworth-Jones. 2008 Aurum Press.

This type of campaign would seem more sinister today if it were instead men who were wreaking havoc in a similar way. Why is this so? Marxist identity politics and conceptual confusion make it more acceptable for some 'roles' or individuals to act in a violent way than others. When Marxism is allowed to influence an issue, e.g. feminism, the issue is filled by Marxist structures with a 'ready-made' set of opinions. This in turn is "hijacked" by the elite. All original ideas are hijacked in this way. The elite themselves have no original ideas because they are not interested in originality. They are interested in maintaining power - by divide and rule. This is how the worthy causes of humanity are hijacked by a hidden agenda.

Feminism and Marxism

> According to the university of Colorado feminist theorist Alison Jadar: "Radical socialist feminists have shown that the old ideals of freedom, equality and democracy are insufficient."[424]

The term "feminism", which actually means the feminine or female, was hijacked by the same Marxist movement as the word "gender", since the word, like "case", is actually a grammatical concept. Marxism and feminism were linked as early as the 19th century by the forefather of Marxism, or "scientific socialism", who wrote one of the greatest Marxist works - Friedrich Engels. In his book "The Origin of the Family, Private property and the state", Engels wrote: "The modern individual family is based on the open or disguised domestic enslavement of the woman." Although the book was not translated into English until 1902, its ideas circulated in the Anglo-Saxon sphere.

424 Christina Hoff Sommers, "Who Stole Feminism" pp 23-24, 1994

Along with other thinkers, it expressed the view that women were enslaved and oppressed victims of patriarchal society, in line with Marxist identity politics. Simone de Beauvoir went even further in her book, writing that it was the triumph of man to assert himself as subject against the role of woman as object.

> Triumph of patriarchy ... [whereby the male's] biological privilege enabled men to affirm themselves alone as sovereign subjects. [425]

De Beauvoir argues that women were not included in history or religion - thus erasing thousands of years of strong women who helped build cities and societies - through work in culture, literature, music, political power and ordinary gainful employment. Ebba Witt-Brattström has written an anthology of famous women, "Nordic Literary History", in which she lists name after name, as evidence of the enormous and indispensable role of women in world history.[426] De Beauvoir is a co-creator of the same victimisation and patriarchy that she claims to be fighting against. Instead of bringing more women into the public eye, she claims the following:

> Women "have no past, no history, no religion of their own; and unlike the proletariat, they have no solidarity of labour or interests [...]. They live dispersed among men, tied by homes, work, economic interests, and social conditions to certain men - fathers or husbands - more closely that to other women.[427]

Marxist feminism affects the idea of gender and the idea of society. If you have a critical opinion, you

---

425 Simone de Beauvoir, "The Second Sex", 1949
426 Ebba Witt-Brattström and Elisabeth Möller Jensen, "Nordisk kvinnolitteraturhistoria", 1993
427 Simone de Beauvoir, "The Second Sex", 1949

are automatically labelled as an opponent or anti-feminist - even women are questioned in this way. It is thus a movement that goes against women themselves - if they hold 'wrong' views, which do not conform to Marxist ideology. Feminism has become embedded in a large part of society; therefore, it is more difficult to pinpoint how it has affected the West. The ideology has had an effect on basic relationships between people, family relationships and relationships between parents and children. As early as 1975, Simone de Beauvoir, one of the great pioneers of feminism, was involved in the following dialogue:

> Betty Friedan once told Simone de Beauvoir that she believed women should have the choice to stay home to raise their children if that is what they wish to do. Beauvoir answered: "No, we don't believe that any woman should have this choice. No woman should be authorised to stay at home to raise her children. Society should be totally different. Women should not have that choice, precisely because if there is such a choice, too many women will make that one".[428]

One example of the shortcomings of identity politics is that the package of opinions includes that mothers should go out to work as soon as they can after pregnancy, so as not to become 'victims' of patriarchy. If a woman wants to stay at home for family reasons and live solely on her husband's salary, she is not considered 'equal' and is criticised.

There is a myth among feminists that if you are not a follower of the Marxist feminist ideology - you oppose all strong women. This is of course not true. Many women who do not want to subscribe to this ideology are strong and well-educated and support women's independence. A confusion of terms has arisen here, where the

428 Christina Hoff Sommers, "Who Stole Feminism" pp 256-7, 1994

word 'feminism' has come to mean 'strong' and 'independent' while its opposite, non-feminist or traditional woman, means 'oppressed' or 'unequal'.

Feminism - thanks to its association with Marxism - has been applied by a slow method of infiltration and has been part of what Marxism calls the cultural . It has infiltrated all state agencies, institutions, the economy, politics, without having carried out a revolution in any real sense or opened up a public debate. Instead of the opponents of Marxism - the rich bourgeois class - it is men who play the role of opponents, alone or in groups through the so-called "patriarchy".

A 'patriarchy' that is part of traditional society has nevertheless built up towns and hospitals, schools, supplies, has made work and education possible. They want to destroy this traditional patriarchy. They believe that men are in power, and when they are in power, despite the positive benefits of the whole society, they use this power only for their own interests. Feminists, through identity politics, are victims, exploited and oppressed by their fathers, husbands, boyfriends, sons and brothers; men as *identity* or *class*, oppressing women as *identity* or *class*.

In many ways, it is a one-sided view of civilisation. If you were to look at the wider worldview, you would see that at the bottom of most societies there are more men. When feminism talks about the male role, it only portrays the men in power to create a better image of the "oppressor". At the same time, no attention is paid to all the men who build houses, fix pipes and work in the forest, who do not have it as easy. Nor do they talk about the fact that it has always been mostly men who have lived as poor and homeless. They forget that, in the past, working-class occupations were not entirely harmless and that women were protected from this - their lives were spared. The example that immediately springs to mind is that of soldiers, but there are other examples such as miners, bricklayers, fishermen and other occupations that took countless and countless lives - men's lives. This is not reflected in the feminist narrative.

The greatest social advances that have been made, such as an increased birth rate due to better medical care, safer workplaces, longer weekends, more lenient sentences, are all overlooked. All the inventions that have facilitated cooking, childcare, communication like the telephone, medicine like penicillin - everything that has also facilitated women and their position, are not counted either. Nor does it mention that these inventions were made in a spirit of humanism and love of mankind, which is best demonstrated by their actual use. People's standard of living has improved considerably over the centuries, and this is forgotten.

To make matters worse, the social injustices that have affected men have been completely ignored. The fact that these men have always gone to war and sacrificed is talked about in neutral terms - suddenly it's about 'people' or numbers. Still, the sacrifice of soldiers is made by men all over the world and still it is not addressed as a purely 'men's issue'.[429] How come it has been completely overlooked? What role does identity politics play in feminism - is a man 'allowed' to be a victim too, or is identity stagnant in women alone?

And how has the role of men changed in post-modern society? In the past, men were seen as potent, strong and independent. Men who lived in families and in society were respected. Men were expected to go to war and perform the most difficult tasks. When feminism took on a Marxist slant, the role of men also changed. Men were given a difficult and complicated role in

---

429 Karen Straughan is a spokesperson for Men's Rights Edmonton. She is a prominent MHRA (Men's Human Rights Advocate) who came to public attention largely through her YouTube channel as GirlWritesWhat.

identity politics; a man has the "oppressor role" *while at the same time* he is supposed to step aside and make room for women. The role thus became unclear, while women retained their former 'female' privileges - men lost them.

This leads to women being able to claim equality - when they need it. There is an inconsistency in this. When equality is an advantage, you argue in favour of equality. Then, when you want to revert to a traditional approach, you do so - without apology, explanation or ideological basis. This arbitrary approach to gender equality leads to gender equality becoming the power tool of feminism, instead of the fight for the true purpose of gender equality - to make society a better place with better living conditions - for all people.

One of the problematic tendencies of the male role is that men have become 'invisible', as male problems are considered less important in a debate; there is less incentive to solve the problems and, above all, to raise awareness of them as a wider social phenomenon. This is a global phenomenon that is happening and has happened in many parts of the world.

One example is that women are still almost always given sole custody when a marriage breaks down, in many countries, as was the case in Sweden before the 21st century. These are modern civilisations like England or Spain. Divorce in these countries creates fatherlessness, while Marxist feminism encourages women to be independent and liberate themselves. In these countries, equality for fathers has not materialised. Fathers who are victimised have to fight, financially and emotionally, for the rest of their lives - for the right to see their children. If they win in court, they are allowed to visit their children on certain weekends. British artist Bob Geldof is one of those who has fought for custody of his children. He publicised his fight and in doing so also drew attention to the struggle of other fathers in the UK. Legal costs are very high and many poor people lack the means to get legal help to assist them in court. In England, this has led to major protests and demonstrations, including a large number of men taking part in a 'Mourning March' across England, organised by the Fathers 4 Justice Fighting for Equality organisation, where fathers and grandmothers and other relatives who were denied access to their children occupied the streets of England. The documentary made by Geldorf shows the agony of fathers and grandparents as they cry out and talk about the pain children and parents experience after the total separation a divorce causes. Because of the anti-male divorce laws, as many as 1/4 children live without fathers in England. [430]

Violence

Another example is the Me-Too campaign, which brought attention to the voices of many women who had been abused - horrific abuse that had been going on for many years. Despite the widespread nature of the campaign, all the men in Hollywood who had experienced the same thing were ignored. In Hollywood, young men who have been abused go through major trauma and mental health problems as a result, but the lid is still on. Sexual violence against men is something that is not talked about. This is true both in homosexual circles and among men who are sexually assaulted by women.

The same applies to women who physically abuse men in non-sexual ways. There is no mention of the physical and psychological violence that women inflict on men and boys - as most female perpetrators are not caught. An underlying misconception is that it is always the

430 Documentary: Geldof On Fathers: "The real love that dear not speak its name", 2004

263

man who is the aggressor - never the woman. The women's movement, which has gained a lot of ground in this area, also seems uninterested in curbing women's violence against children and men. Because society does not talk about the phenomenon, it is more shameful for a man to report a woman who is mentally or physically violent. The consequences are not the same as for a woman who reports, and he does not receive the same support from society - if he dares to report. Violence is not about men beating women, as many people mistakenly believe, but about a phenomenon that spans generations, a generational violence. This generational violence needs to be weakened and stopped. Both men and women suffer violence in childhood. Both men and women initiate intimate partner violence and engage in mental and physical abuse.

Something that is also not talked about, but needs to be recognised as violence against men, is male genital mutilation in infancy. It is an operation, also known as male genital mutilation, which is still performed without authorisation in 2023. Fully healthy tissue is removed and the operation is performed without anaesthesia. The experience is thought to be similar to that of a drowning accident for the infant. Changes occur in the brain as a result; in the worst cases, both direct and indirect injuries occur. In many cases, minor injuries occur, including psychological experiences such as shame, problems with sex life - phenomena that continue into adulthood.

Men's shelters

If women get into difficulties, they almost always have several relatives and friends, a network to fall back on. Managers and colleagues who show compassion in the workplace, if women are late, unmotivated or depressed. Men lack this network. Men are not asked - "how are you?" in the same way. In one experiment, a man and a woman walked into a restaurant under observation and started crying profusely. In the woman's case, both staff and customers try to help her and show full compassion. In the case of the man, they show concern and consider calling the police. The tendency is that the men have been dehumanised.

Women's shelters are supported by specially written scripts that are used when a woman seeks protection and help. It is based on research about women and how they express their feelings. When a woman is going through a divorce or a loss, there is help available. It doesn't work the same way when it comes to a man. If a man goes through a divorce, he finds that his network is not there, or has gone over to the woman's side. The suicide risk for men increases after a divorce.

> In men, the risk of suicide was particularly high in the first two years after separation. ... In men, separation or divorce seems to be a risk factor for suicide even in cases where the person in question had no mental health problems before the separation. This should be taken into account in health care," says Metsä-Simola.[431]

Despite this, it is felt that there is no need for a men's shelter, as the situation in Sweden shows - there is only one men's shelter that operates entirely without government funding, while there are several women's shelters.

Men and women have always participated in different activities to bond with each other, such as hunting. Men could bond with each other. Now there are written and unwritten laws developed by Marxist feminism, which

---

431 New study: Divorces and separations should be taken into account in
   health care
From 2020 https://svenska.yle.fi/a/7-1456429

label men's clubs and men's meetings as "sexist". Men are now not allowed to gather on their own, for example to support each other, such as in a boys' club. This is illegal in most cases and is covered by discrimination laws. However, this does not apply to women in gatherings - where 'feminism' takes precedence.

Men avoid talking about feelings and being seen as victims. Men do not seek help but, on the other hand, they are not offered help to the same extent as women. Research exists, but to a very limited extent because it has not been prioritised or financially supported. The men's shelters that have opened in Sweden have not been funded in the same way that women's shelters have received state support. The Swedish state simply believes that men do not need help. The Social Services Act states that women are specifically entitled to help and financial assistance. Men are completely excluded from the law, which means that the law itself is discriminatory - against men.[432] There is less research on men and men's issues, and no attention is paid to vulnerable groups of men, such as homeless men, who become homeless due to mental illness or other difficult circumstances such as divorce.[433]

Suicide statistics speak for themselves

But yes, there is a need for a men's movement. If you look at the statistics, there are several aspects that indicate that men's rights need to be recognised and, above all, fought for. This is something that does not appear in the gender equality debate or the feminist discourse because all the focus is on women. The struggle of men is invisible, laughed at and minimised. Boys

432 https://jamstalldhetsmyndigheten.se/fakta-om-jamstalldhet/
    socialtjanstlagen/,
    https://www.riksdagen.se/sv/dokument-och-lagar/dokument/kommittedirektiv/
    socialtjanstens-stod-till-valdsutsatta-kvinnor_gtb132/

433 Men's Mental Health: A Silent Crisis, with Karen Straughan. February 27th,
    2018, London Public Library Central Branch Event hosted by Canadian Centre
    for Men and Families (CCMF)

and men are overrepresented in the suicide statistics with a ratio of 1:4, which is not talked about, at least not in a serious way - as a man's problem. How long does it take to raise a human being, how much care does a parent put into their child? How much money, tears, energy, commitment and love it takes to raise an individual human being from infancy to adulthood. But if you have a son, he is 75% more likely to kill himself than if you have a daughter. These are real numbers with a ratio of 1:4.

These statistics are both appalling and uneven. Although mental health is recognised and researched, it is not talked about as a specifically male problem - even though it is recognised that men suffer more.

Not to mention all the men who constantly go to war and have done so throughout history. But isn't that just history, one might argue? Not in most countries around the world. Just look at Ukraine and Russia, and the hundreds of thousands of men who have been induced and sacrificed there. These men are banned from travelling and are required by law to be sacrificed in blood. This is nothing new. Men have been ruthlessly sacrificed throughout history. They have gone to war, served in the army and died from hard labour in the fields.

One of the oldest examples of male discrimination is the treatment of boys and men in ancient Greece and Rome. Throughout Roman times, men had to serve in the army and go out to fight, otherwise they were thrown out of society or executed. Young boys became soldiers at an early age and were used as slaves both in labour and sexually. For a time, there was an even darker era, when all first-born boys would be mercilessly executed - at birth.[434]

434 Tom James, "The History of Custody Law", 2014

Are you offended?

A man can often be offended, but the difference is that men have to swallow and tolerate it 'like a man'. Abusive epithets have been applied to men since ancient times, such as the occupational name 'boy' or 'garçon', which is evidence of how boys used to be forced to work at an early age. In the late modern era, new insults have entered the language. This has had a profound impact on the male role - and continues to do so today. You could say that there are invisible commandments for men - thou shalt not cry, thou shalt not show your feelings, but you also have no right to speak out about the offences you are subjected to. Feminists and Marxist identity politics are making it even more difficult for men to live into the new male role. In the past, they were supposed to be steadfast and manly, taking responsibility for women and children and providing for the home; but when identity politics took this role away from them, only the negative remained; for example, that a man is not allowed to show emotions. "You're damned if you do, you're damned if you don't".[435]

Due to a shift in the male role and masculinity, more buzzwords have emerged that are used to indicate men's underperformance in different areas. It happens everywhere in Western culture, both in private and in public, in the media and in the cultural sector. In non-Western cultures, the role of men is not as oppressed, but when men integrate into Western society, the same ideology is adopted.

The male body is mocked unreservedly and sexist jokes can be made about men. Worst of all, the size of the male genitalia is mocked, which is extremely psy-

---

435 Samuel Snowden (1776-1831), the publisher of the Alexandria Gazette, Commercial and Political (Alexandria, Virginia), published in that newspaper on Thursday 20th February 1817-the phrase occurs in a quotation attributed to an unnamed preacher.

chologically demeaning. This is done without guilt or shame and is not mentioned in any debates. Instead, suicides are on the rise. Men tolerate these jokes, which affect the male role and the psyche of individuals, their self-image and behaviour, young and old, heterosexual and gay men.

Gonadotropin-releasing hormone agonists

> And remember kids, the next time that somebody tells you, "The government wouldn't do that", oh yes they would. [and they've probably already done it] - Wendigoon (Isaiah Mark Nichols (born: 1999-06-02)

Since 2017, the United States and Canada have allowed children as young as six to 12 years old to begin the process of hormonal treatment that will eventually lead to genital surgery. In both the UK and Sweden, the government initially said no to the proposal. However, from 1 July 2025, it will be possible for a Swedish 16-year-old to begin the long process of changing sex. The bill covers both injecting a large amount of strong medication and various sex hormones into the body, as well as operating on the genitals themselves - and living with the side effects that arise, from a very young age, for a very long period of their life.

This very important issue was not put to a referendum in Sweden, nor in those countries where the law is already entrenched. In the United States, the bills that have been passed have gradually gone lower and lower down the age scale. In Canada, it has gone so far that social services have the right to take into custody a child who wants to have a sex change operation - if the parents object. They have also given prison sentences to parents who have opposed hormonal treatment and surgery and instead publicised it in the media, with the justification that the parents are "re-

vealing sensitive information about the child's surgery".[436]

In the US, the process is as follows - children are
asked at an early age if they identify as ''. If the
child answers yes, they are taken to a gender psychologist. [437]

> Trance has become so big in our mainstream
> media that if a toddler says "Im a girl" then
> all of a sudden its time to put this child on
> hormones and to do things to the childs body
> that cannot be reversed.[438]

The gender psychologist conducts an interview with the
child to determine whether the child is eligible for
treatment, surgery and medication. Then, on the gender
psychologist's orders, the doctor is authorised to pump
the child full of hormones and begin the process of
changing sex. This is done without parental consent. If
the parent objects, and perhaps wants the child to wait
until adulthood to have the operation, it is a criminal
offence as the parent is considered to be preventing
the child from acting in their true gender. Parents are
told that there is an underlying suicidal problem among
those who are not allowed to change their gender, which
puts further pressure on parents to agree to the treatment without resistance. The fact that recent research
has shown that suicide rates peak a couple of years
after surgery is not mentioned.

The big problem is that hormone therapy contains the
same sterilising drugs that are given to sexual offenders and prisoners.

> *Gonadotropin-releasing hormone agonists*
> (GnRHa's) are the standard treatment for

---

436 https://bc.ctvnews.ca/b-c-father-who-discussed-trans-child-s-treatment-
against-court-order-successfully-appeals-sentence-1.6514514
437 In Sweden, many of the preschools write a so-called "Gender Plan", which
includes alternative literature on rainbow families and gender.
438 Rob Smith, Prager U

children with central precocious puberty (CPP). We aim to present data on available GnRHa options with an easy-to-review table and discuss factors that influence treatment selection.[439]

Central precocious puberty (CPP) is defined as an early pubertal development that occurs before the age of 9 years in boys and 8 years in girls. It results from premature activation of the hypothalamic-pituitary-gonadal axis. *Gonadotropin-releasing hormone agonists* (GnRHa) have been the gold standard therapy for CPP for more than 30 years.[440]

Gonadotrophin-releasing hormone agonist treatment for sexual offenders: A systematic review. Background: Sexual offending is a significant international issue causing long-term consequences for victims, perpetrators and society.[441]

Androgen deprivation treatment of sexual behaviour Abstract: *Gonadotropin-releasing hormone agonists* are underutilized in patients seeking diminution of problematic sexual drives. This chapter reviews the literature on surgical castration of sex offenders, anti-androgen use and the rationale for providing androgen deprivation therapy, rather than selective serotonin reuptake inhibitors or more conservative interventions, for patients with paraphilias and excessive sexual drive. Discussions of informed

---

439 Gonadotropin-releasing hormone analogue therapies for children with central precocious puberty in the United States
https://www.ncbi.nlm.nih.gov/pmc/articles/PMC9577333/
440 https://pubmed.ncbi.nlm.nih.gov/31580327/
441 https://pubmed.ncbi.nlm.nih.gov/28661259/

consent, side effects, contraindications and case examples are provided.[442]

"In our review, we focused on psychosocial effects, bone health, body composition and metabolism, and therapy persistence in children (<18 years of age) with gender dysphoria undergoing treatment with puberty blockers, *gonadotropin-releasing hormone analogues* (GnRHa)," says lead author Professor Jonas F Ludvigsson, paediatrician at Örebro University Hospital, and Professor at the Department of Medical Epidemiology and Biostatistics, Karolinska Institutet. "I am surprised by the shortage of studies in this field. We found no randomised trials, and only 24 relevant observational studies," he adds.[443]

Other drugs whose side effects have not been fully researched are also used. Doctors who refuse to start such treatment risk losing their licence in the US and Canada. A bigger problem is that because the process starts at such a young age, it is essentially an irreversible treatment. Once you start treatment, you can never have children, breastfeed or completely revert to your normal gender, should you change your mind. Some gender reassignment patients do change their minds. But by then it's too late. Girls lose their breasts and their wombs. According to research and statistics, one in 30,000 have such severe gender dysphoria that they need surgery. But now, with the help of doctors, gender educators and gender psychologists, the number of children and young people undergoing treatment is much higher. If you try to open

442 https://pubmed.ncbi.nlm.nih.gov/22005210/
443 https://news.ki.se/systematic-review-on-outcomes-of-hormonal-treatment-in-youths-with-gender-dysphoria

up a debate on the subject, you are labelled a racist/homophobe/oppressor by the WOKE movement.[444]

How does it work if the child or teenager has second thoughts and realises that it was just a period, a teenage phase they went through? Well, there are several examples of young people who have been through just that. 19-year-old Chloe Cole is one of them. She calls herself a 'detransitioner', which means to go back *from* a sex change operation. She was only 12 when she started a painful programme of hormones and surgery. She considers herself the victim of one of the biggest medical scandals in US history. Chloe Cole is using her difficult experience to fight for other young people and children not to have to go through what she went through. It started when she was diagnosed with gender dysphoria by a gender educator at the age of 12. She later realised that she was just uncomfortable with becoming a teenager and the changes that came with it. So she told her parents that she wanted to be a boy. Her parents, who were immediately concerned, felt they needed help from outside professionals and doctors. Chloe herself tells us:

> It immediately set our entire family down a path for ideologically motivated deceit and coercion. The gender specialist I was taken to, taken to see told my parents that I needed to be put on puberty blocking drugs right away. They asked my parents a simple question - would you rather have a dead daughter or a living transgender son?[445]

After persuasion, the parents agreed to start treatment. The gender specialist said that transgender people become depressed by living in the wrong body. And

444 Why I Left the Left - Amala Ekpunobi at Washington University in St. Louis, 10 Dec. 2022
445 'My Childhood Was RUINED:' Detransitioner Chloe Cole Talks About Trans Procedures https://www.youtube.com/watch?v=DSGgR3W_jjg

that there was a risk that Chloe would engage in self-harming behaviour or even take her own life. Chloe Cole was injected with testosterone and other powerful drugs at the age of 12. She still experiences pain in her body caused by the medication. Her body was changed and the changes are irreversible. When she was 15, she had her breasts removed. Now she has a very hard time with her appearance and seeing herself in the mirror. She can't accept her appearance, or the look that testosterone has given her. Her surgical scars are watery and she will never be able to breastfeed. Chloe Cole says she wasn't suicidal before her operations, she was just a 'different' child - but instead became suicidal after treatment. Her grades got worse and worse. But the doctors said all her problems would disappear once the operations were over. In a speech summarising her struggle, she says:

> We need to stop telling 12 year old's that they were born wrong. That they are right to reject their own bodies and feel uncomfortable with their own skin. We need to stop telling children that puberty is an option. That they can choose what kind of puberty they will go through, just so they can choose what clothes to wear or what music to listen to. Puberty is a rite of passage ti adulthood, not a disease to be mitigated (...) My childhood was ruined along with thousands of detransitioners that I know through our networks. This needs to stop.[446]

She has spoken to the US government's House Subcommittee about her experiences to try to help those who have not yet been through the procedure with her warning.

Scott Newgent is another adult patient who was victimised. Before the surgeries, "she" was an "alpha" fe-

---

446 'My Childhood Was RUINED:' Detransitioner Chloe Cole Talks About Trans Procedures https://www.youtube.com/watch?v=DSGgR3W_jjg

male who was constantly told she was a "he" who was in the wrong body. After persuasion, "she" was transformed into a man through synthetic medicine and as many as seven surgeries. As a result of her treatment, Newgent has been severely damaged - for life. She has suffered a heart attack and accompanying infections that recur every three months. Newgent says that no one told her that this treatment could be very dangerous. According to Mr Newgent, medical transitioning is at an experimental stage; its promoters say there is research showing that medical transitioning helps with mental health problems. But the only long-term study shows that transgender people are at their most suicidal 7-10 years after treatment. And there are no long-term studies looking at hormone therapy - in children. "Lupron" is the common name for the hormone medication given to adults, children and adolescents undergoing treatment - and it is the same medication given to sex offenders during chemical castration. Mr Newgent says that if they managed to talk 'her' into doing this at the age of 42 - the children don't stand a chance. A major problem is that it is considered "transphobic" or "homophobic" to raise the issue for debate and criticise gender reassignment surgery. The lid is put on and it is the individuals who suffer for this.

Are such young individuals really mature enough to decide whether to go through this process - for the rest of their lives? Can a 12-year-old in the United States or a 16-year-old in Sweden really decide whether she or he wants to go through a process that complicates a lifetime and makes the prospect of having children impossible

According to the doctors, "Ryan", who was about to start the process, did not even need to consult a gender psychologist, but was allowed to start taking pills straight away, at the age of 18. Ryan developed a bass voice and his body underwent major changes. A year and a half after the first hormone injection, Ryan had changed his mind and did not want to become a man but wanted to continue his life as a woman. An operation had already been booked and just before the surgery she had a 30-minute consultation with a gender therapist and, despite her change of heart, was approved. However, Ryan cancelled the surgery at the last minute and escaped a life of pain. When she questions and criticises gender reassignment surgery on young people, she is labelled transphobic, Ryan says.[447]

A father in Canada, whose child was subjected to the process of genital surgery without his consent, was arrested after telling his story in the press. The school had not even consulted the parents and changed the girl's name to a boy's name. The father refused to accept the school's approach and the fact that the child would be injected with hormones and prepared for surgery and tried to open up a debate about this in a newspaper. The father considered that the videos shown to the girl by the gender psychologist, who was trying to persuade her to have the operation, were not neutral but propaganda. The father further considered that the operation is an irreversible decision. She can never be a girl again and cannot have children. The father accused the State of child abuse in this way. He was then arrested and sentenced to prison.[448]

The laws on genital surgery on minors have been enforced in an undemocratic, totalitarian way - without a referendum - and are an example of how 21st century society, through manipulation and PR campaigns, has become a totalitarian state.

This is how it happened in Sweden: a new law on genital surgery for young people is supposed to be voted through by the government. The law is crucial for

447 Detransitioning: She Regrets Transitioning From Female to Male
   https://www.youtube.com/watch?v=uOYKIpkueqM
448 CBN news Canadian Father Jailed for Speaking Out Against Biological
   Daughter's Gender Transition https://www.youtube.com/watch?v=DN_WpaAgS6w

the future of many Swedish young people. There is only one mention of the bill in the news - a week before the parties vote. Despite the importance of the law, no information about it reaches the general population. If the newspapers had done their job and written about all the side effects, strong hormones and the terrible fates of families in the US and Canada, people would have had a chance to form an opinion, debate and protest. No one in Sweden wants Swedish 16-year-olds to suffer for the rest of their lives, when they can wait a couple of years until they reach the adult age and really make up their minds. But the Swedish people are not even given a chance. Instead, other articles take up the space on the news feed. One podcast briefly discusses the date and time when the law will be voted through - in government, it's not even a question of 'if'. On the intended date, there are a few reports that the bill - which will affect the lives of thousands of young people - has already been passed. There is also a brief note on which political parties were in favour or against the bill. No information on side effects, heavy medication or hormones for sex offenders.

Voters and civilians - whose children will actually live with the law - are not consulted at all. Nor does anyone know about the change in the law until a week before the vote. For the Western population - the bill is completely impossible to influence. In this way, the people are prevented from democratically influencing their country's affairs, and can thus neither prepare themselves, take part in important information, nor protest.

Every successful conspiracy remains secret after completion

> I am a "conspiracy theorist". I believe men
> and women of wealth and power conspire. If
> you don't think so, then you are what is
> called "an Idiot". If you believe stuff but
> fear the label, you are what is called "a
> coward".[449] - Dave B. Collum, Professor Cornell
> University

This summarising chapter will briefly point out the
reasons why contemporary man finds himself in a political and structural imbalance, with a powerless position
in society, from which he lacks knowledge of what the
political reality really looks like:

1. Overconsumption

The consumerism of the 21st century is the greatest in
human history. The amount of time spent buying and
owning things of wear-and-tear quality - constantly
exchanging goods, old for new - takes up a lot of time
and focus. The average person has less time to pay
attention to and appreciate the world and society for
what it really is. Moving away from this dependency
needs to be done, one step at a time. Trying not to
spend money - first for a month, then for three months,
then six months - frees up a lot of time. Over-consumption also has a negative impact on nature and agricul-
ture by depleting the soil. It also has an isolating
effect, as every man, to the extent of his financial
capital, is left to himself. Status goods lead to unconscious or conscious competition and the strength of
the community is thus weakened. The Western world needs
a comprehensive consumption reform. If everyone decides

449 Dave B. Collum, Professor Cornell University

on a starting date for reform and stops shopping from now on, the greed of big business would be reduced and people would have more time left over - for socialising, family, children and natural way of living.

2. *The hijacked concepts*

Recently, there has been a radical weakening of language. We no longer control the words: the PR companies, media and institutions do, and they have taken over the well-known claim that words are power. The term "revolution" has no meaning and cannot possibly have any connection to contemporary political Sweden, because the word's meaning is now only linked to advertising or film. Other concepts are similarly hijacked - by television, advertisers and politicians. The political concepts, or what is left of them, have been hijacked by the Marxist left. "Equality", "Extreme Right", "Left-wing activism" are a few clear examples, but others can be found. The words or concepts are loaded with positive or negative content that is meant to evoke certain reactions and emotions. It is likely that a reorganisation of the nervous system's connections is needed, by thinking about the correct meaning when pronouncing a word.

3. *Broken minds, broken nervous systems*

Even the nervous system is hijacked by the cognitive illusion created by the top layers of society, together with PR companies and propaganda. Instead of thinking independently, the brain is constantly being forced into reward systems through mobile games and internet shopping. The senses and nervous system are constantly influenced by advertising, information and sensory impressions. In the big shopping malls, you are bombarded by bright lights and an endless perceived variety of goods. People are constantly deprived of their peace of mind and freedom of mind, their time, their participation and self-determination, and their finances. What is needed here is a change, an ecological approach - also on a mental level, combined with the right to decide over one's environment.

3. *The power of action is hijacked*

Real action can nowadays only be observed on film and television. It is said that the great, important and transformative power of real people only happens on film. In real life, people are expected to take a passive approach to the society politicians serve them, and to stay within the bounds of accepted behaviour - which in practice now also means an uncritical approach to the actions of those in power. In theory, it is fine to criticise society, but if you actually do something about it, you are excluded and subjected to character assassination.

> Facing such a danger, with such splendid historical values in your past, at such a high level of realization of freedom and of devotion to freedom, how is it possible to lose to such an extent the will to defend oneself?[450]

People in whom the power of action manages to break through the narrow confines, are nowadays called whistleblowers, or conspiracy theorists; they may be diagnosed with ADHD, labelled childish or naïve, shamed or declared insane. Surely Joan of Arc, Booker T Washington (who wrote the book "Up from Slavery"), Nils Dacke, Socrates and Elisabeth I would all be diagnosed in our time, which would hinder their contributions to

450 Alexander Solzhenitsyn, "A World Split Apart", 8 June 1978, Harvard
   University

world history. Or their efforts would be labelled "left-wing activism" or "feminism" and they would be used as models for left-wing ideology and thus hijacked by Marxism.

If such individualities were to gain access to power in modern times, it would be inconvenient and uncomfortable for the power elite - who, in order to avoid an outbreak of revolution, would prefer, in any case, passive and consuming citizens.

> Maybe the most striking feature which an outside observer notices in the West in our days. The Western world has lost its civil courage, both as a whole and separately, in each country, each government, each political party and of course in the United Nations. Such a decline in courage is particularly noticeable among the ruling group and the intellectual elite, causing an impression of loss of courage by the entire society. Of course there are many courageous individuals, but they have no determining influence on public life.[451]

4. *Do we really have time to think about society?*

If you work from the age of 25 up to the age of 65 and calculate how much of your life you spend in work, you get the following: for 260 of the 365 weekdays in the year, you are in work. 25 of these are holidays. This means that an adult person works about 83,200 hours during their career, not counting work from home, cleaning, household work, overtime and other activities. About 30,000 hours are 'free' hours. How many of these 'free' hours do they really get to decide for themselves? How many of them are spent on social duties

451 Alexander Solzhenitsyn, "A World Split Apart", 8 June 1978, Harvard University

and couples' dinners? When do we have time to reflect on what society is really like? About the power imbalance people live in? About the fact that most people would actually like it to be different from this life's hustle and bustle? And what kind of society do we really want to live in? During the Covid19 outbreak, a large number of people had to try working from home, with reduced working hours. Many companies adapted accordingly and introduced 6-hour working days. It is important to aim for a larger societal reform - 6-hour working day or 4-day working week. After all, people work more efficiently when they are given back the right to their own free time.

5. *Everyone thinks that only they think like they do*

As our thoughts are influenced and controlled by politicians, institutions and the media, it can sometimes be difficult to recognise that other people are in exactly the same position. There are others who think like you and me. But because of the language and the prevailing societal trends, no one speaks openly about it. When they do, a social stigma is created. Freedom of expression needs to be taken back, so that no one feels excluded when they speak freely and openly.

How are you feeling? - No, I'm not feeling well.

Who would dare to answer this?

The mental ill health of the population is probably due to the major shortcomings of society - while at the same time society is considered to be so modern, progressive and technologically developed. Had society been more people-friendly and well-functioning, as it could be in 2025, it could have been adapted to most individuals. In fact, our Western society is backward - because of how it treats its people. Nothing is really impossible in 2025. Unfortunately, during these years, the focus has been more on the economy and profits than on the welfare of citizens. Humanity has come a long way in terms of the economy, technology and the arms industry. But compassion, real support for the weak, and better adaptations have been ignored by the elite powers. Greed has become a fully accepted driving force and the individual has instead been turned into a number in the crowd. Society has not been adapted to individuals - as it could have been with the enormous resources it has acquired.

> The real game isn't between the two teams on the field. It's between the spellbound fans and the sponsor, finding new ways to empty their pockets.[452] - Cliff Jones Jr

6. *Elite media and big business*

People on all continents have made marvellous advanced inventions that could improve and simplify life for the entire world population and reduce both costs and the depletion of the earth's resources. However, all these inventions have been bought by big business, elites and politicians who have let greed take over. What if instead of manipulative PR campaigns and lobbying, we had political leaders who were truly committed to the people? What if all companies gave back to society and invested in good causes instead of French mansions for shareholders? If more people could work on what they wanted, instead of doing meaningless tasks for mega-corporations? If there was a limit to how much big business could earn from factories in India? And real transparency, with the media reporting on everything that was happening?

452 Cliff Jones Jr
https://www.goodreads.com/author/quotes/15600047.Cliff_Jones_Jr_?page=2

What is the alternative?

There is a need in the West to look beyond all current political systems to find new ways for society to develop as it should in the 21st century. Below is a list of proposals that could be included in this new perspective.

Local regulation, real direct democracy with transparent information

Decisions concerning a particular area should be made by the people who live, work and play in the area, similar to a "Town Hall" where people meet and have the opportunity to vote, or vote digitally. People living in Botkyrka should be able to vote on whether or not a forest in Botkyrka should be cleared. Larger decisions are made by a larger population area. If several forests in Stockholm are to be cleared, more people should be allowed to vote on it. If a completely new law is to be implemented, the whole country needs to vote and agree on it. All substantive issues should be voted on - easily via digital button presses or in person. Each vote should be accompanied by an informative text explaining what the issue is about, making it easier for citizens to make their decision. Tools should be provided, depending on the scope of the issue, so that every citizen can absorb the information. On the other hand, all primary school pupils should be taught constitutional law, politics and economics, just as they are taught sport or maths as a general preparation for adult life. At the same time, trust in people is being regained - the same trust that was lost when Freud's theories on the irrationality of the masses took over society 100 years ago. Such trust in people was already observable before Freud's time.

In the 1830s, Alexis de Tocqueville travelled around the United States for research and observation, and one of his observations was that whether he was up in the mountains, in the countryside, in villages or in towns, he was constantly meeting people who were familiar with current political issues.

> The American institutions are democratic, not only in their principle but in all their consequences; and the people elects its representatives directly, and for the most part annually, in order to ensure their dependence. The people is therefore the real directing power; and although the form of government is representative, it is evident that the opinions, the prejudices, the interests, and even the passions of the community are hindered by no durable obstacles from exercising a perpetual influence on society. In the United States the majority governs in the name of the people, as is the case in all the countries in which the people is supreme.[453]

Before complex decisions are taken, a debate can be organised in which experts are invited to debate and give their opinion on the different voting options. The experts should not be decisive, have any additional power or be directly or indirectly linked to any body. The expertise should be neutral and objective.

Constantly making decisions behind the voters' backs is keeping the people out of power and such a system of governance needs to be replaced. Constantly building cities and demolishing old streets without the people's voice being heard is part of such an essentially outdated totalitarian system. The same applies to the transposition of laws. All decisions - even hitherto top-secret military actions - must be transparent and voted on. Individual families and closed societies with large financial capital should not make decisions that

---

453 Alexis de Tocqueville, "Democracy in America", Book 2, Ch I, 1st and 2nd paragraph,

affect the Swedish population; nor should central organisations in Brussels, which should be legally regu-
lated.

*Not getting bogged down in political dogma - cross-
cutting and issue-based policies. Not everything has to
be black and white.*

People need to start living as if they are free and
full of potential, recognising the power and rights
they possess. If you have no power, you take no responsibility. More power and responsibility for the
people. If a large number of people come together and
make themselves known, they have full power and capacity to influence society and prevent decisions from
being carried out. This is the basis of popular government - everything else should be counted as repre-
sentation only.

People need to awaken a curiosity about what they,
through collective action, can achieve - such an ideal
once existed in the leftist spirit, but has now faded.
It was also present in other parts of history. Regardless, in the 21st century, we need to start from the
people, the individual human beings - instead of outdated political ideologies that do not fit in with contemporary society. One motto is "Res Publica" = from
the people. People need to be given access to power
over their local environment and society, and thus over
their own lives, because they are much more ready for
this than they were thought to be in the 19th and 20th
centuries.

How is it that politics today has roots that were created hundreds of years ago, in societies that looked
very different? How is it that the same political
strategies are still used? Is it because politicians
and elites have built in their own rules and systems
that hide behind these outdated policies? Society has

changed radically since the 19th century, where Marxism
and socialism originated. In the 19th century, starving
children sat on the streets, homelessness was a major
problem among the poor in Sweden and other countries.
People were still dying of various diseases - Spanish
flu and pneumonia, tuberculosis and childbirth. Only
the rich had the right to vote. HOW is it that a
political reform created then still has a role to play
in today's modern society? People need each other, to
work on restoring community, trust and reclaiming power
from elites and politicians! It is not we the people
who are each other's enemies through right-wing and
left-wing politics, but the elite and big business, who
are above the right and left scale. What the elites and
the establishment do not realise is that by doing so,
they are suppressing all new and alternative political
impulses that naturally want to emerge and take their
place. Take the place of the outdated political
currents, which have their roots in the 19th century,
written by a man who not only had difficulty keeping
his own finances in order, but who also got his housekeeper pregnant, without in any way recognising the
child or doing the right thing. Well into the 20th century, Karl Marx's illegitimate son had to go in through
the back door to see his mother, who then got a job
with Engels, just so she would keep quiet and not spoil
the image of Marx as an ultra-moral, ultra-communist
leader.

This also applies to the free individual – Marxism
as a basic idea divides people into categories - the
weak against the strong, the victim against the
villain, which divides and rules. Human beings have
come so far in their development that most are now
conscious individuals, with access to information, the
right to vote and to speak out. This also means that
the political playing field needs to change. Modern man
needs a new political starting point, where he can de-

velop his thinking and political stance, without being locked into a political role. They should have the freedom to be both anti-racist AND anti-feminist, i.e. be able to take concepts from both the right and the left and instead relate to the issues. When it comes to the question of how long babies should stay at home with their parents, you might want a more traditional, "anti-feminist" approach, while when it comes to labour, you might want to be more equal on the issue. Either way, this freedom should exist for each individual.

Moreover, since the issues differ from area to area; there is a difference between political issues in Degerfors and Malmö, for example, a centralised, omnipotent party cannot possibly support the voters' needs in all aspects, even if they wanted to. Sticking to the issues makes it easier to achieve both self-determination and real democracy. If, for example, the entire population of an area gets to vote on the merits of whether to build a motorway, then the conditions for democracy in its truest sense are met.

A non-partisan government means that people no longer define politics as part of their own identity or role. The right-left, black-and-white divide also disappears to make way for a new, more vibrant, more human community. You begin to see real nuances, beyond identity politics and thus also see the whole of the actual person sitting in front of you. You start to think for yourself and dare to let new political ideas and solutions emerge. You detach yourself from the old and can thus appropriate reality as it really is. This helps people to create and mould better solutions to the political problems that require our involvement in the present.

In recent decades, new or different political ideas and visions have been dismissed and neglected in favour of those who remain in power. The new is labelled as the dissenting, the alternative - the consequence is that those who speak out are silenced. By donning a kind of normative garb, they seek to marginalise any new thinking, any 'threat' they perceive to today's elite society and political establishment. Large mega-corporations, which themselves have no real interest in political theory, do as they please, based on their own financial interests. One example is when SEB, after strong criticism, went out in the media and announced that, as an investment power, it would withdraw from after the Ukrainian war broke out, as a sanction measure. Six months later, this had still not happened.[454]

One example of a political innovator is Dominic Barter, a lifelong charity worker in South America. He argues that we need new political structures and systems where people are part of the solution process and dialogue is a way to reduce problems and conflicts. He says that every organisation - every school, community, town - needs to ask itself anew - what works here? Instead of running the same centralised system everywhere, adapt to the community in question. The capabilities that are then found have enough expertise to solve the problems that exist. Most states, when they find problems, study the problem remotely, and then throw the solution at people, like school politicians do with teachers. A better way is to ask the question - how have people coped so far? To have survived, they must have possessed qualities of great value - how do we use this in a positive way? According to Mr Barter, instead of teaching and giving answers, we should learn and ask questions.

To resolve conflicts and differences, we need to engage in dialogue, instead of saying "they are racist" or

---

454 https://www.svd.se/a/k6Ovz6/seb-avslutar-verksamheten-i-ryssland, https://www.finansliv.se/artikel/seb-kvar-i-ryssland-minimal-verksamhet/

"they are upper class" or "they are communists". We need to find new ways to co-exist and according to Dominic Barter, this already exists within human contexts, we just need to ask the questions more locally. When you celebrate together, you strengthen bonds and even when you face difficulties together.

He also proposes a new justice system that reduces harsh punishments and works restoratively. According to him, crime can be reduced if we stop excluding and punishing people and instead work together, through dialogue - the more you alienate people, the more they need to act to have their voice heard and their needs met. [455]

Party monopoly

What is happening instead in political West can be characterised as a party monopoly. The parties in power have been there for many years, without any substitution. It is about a few political parties with great power, which means that innovative parties and ideologies, which dare to stand up against corruption, have, due to the current system, more difficulty in getting into the public eye and being discovered by a larger number of the population. The current political party monopoly does not support new emerging parties, either financially or politically. They are left to fend for themselves in terms of the means they use to get into parliament. They also face opposition in the form of the media labelling them as "conspiratorial", "alternative" or "racist" and find it difficult to compete with the large financial capital backing the major parties. This makes it harder to be seen in the media, to run PR campaigns and to make the party's ideas more visible. Voters then believe that they can only vote for the Social Democrats and a couple of

455 Dominic Barter, researcher and author, Restorative Circles, European forum for Restorative Justice

other parties, when in reality there is the possibility of greater political breadth. Voters are limited in this way - even in their ability to choose political parties.

As a result of the party monopoly, the already established parties offer their staff the promise of a career and a high salary, which attracts certain personality types, who are interested in large financial capital and power. When a party is formed, it is different. In the early stages of party building, certain attributes are required, such as fighting spirit and love of humanity - qualities that should be among the most important attributes and character traits of any politician - instead of greed. In the party monopoly, it is different and few have these attributes in their CV - for real. Therefore, the profession of politician needs to be reorganised to take on a more administrative role, instead of the position of power they are attributed today. Politicians should work for their people and be adequately paid. This will increase the chances of attracting the 'right' people to the profession.

Less work, more time

If you reduce consumption, you do not have to work as much either. People can work on meaningful tasks rather than bureaucratic tasks that are not enjoyable or meaningful. In this way, people would free up time, which in itself would mean that they could contribute more, by being involved in social issues and in shaping the local community.

Less consumption, contributes to better production

People's lives are structured so that they become addicted to spending money. If people stopped spending for several months, they could instead focus on reclaiming the nerve fibres, emotions and thoughts that have been hijacked by advertising and the mass media, and free themselves from the consumer role Bernays created over a hundred years ago. During the Covid-19 crisis, there was a break from consumption and labour and many people found their way to a new kind of community, a natural community. The space created by the lack of consumption is instead filled with culture and community, as we watch big business fall like a stone - one by one.

> It is not possible that assessment of the President's performance be reduced to the question how much money one makes or of un-limited availability of gasoline. Only voluntary, inspired self-restraint can raise man above the world stream of materialism.[456]

When big business has less power, it can stop exploiting countries like India and China and instead resume domestic production, which would increase creativity while restoring the natural sustainability and good quality of products.

Government stops hijacking culture, action returns
We live in a totalitarian society where many of our opportunities for action and heroism have been hijacked and displaced - from being part of a natural expression of the will of all people, as a natural part of culture; to fantasies, images and stories for film and television. Acting on heroism is considered out of bounds - instead, it's the superheroes on TV who are responsible for this. This is part of the outdated totalitarian system that leads to the passivity of the population. The average person has fewer opportunities to act "concretely" and make things happen, get things

---

456 Alexander Solzhenitsyn, "A World Split Apart", 8 June 1978, Harvard University

done. All impulses to action and heroism have been banished in human consciousness to the world of film, but this needs to change. We need to defend our culture from being hijacked by the state and the oligarchs, defend our language from being hijacked by big business, and defend our agency so that it can return to its natural place.

First they came for the Jews

and I did not speak out --

because I was not a Jew

Then they came for the sick and uncurables

and I did not speak out

because I was not sick

Then they came for the Catholics

and I did not speak out --

because I was not a Protestant

Then they came for the trade unionists

and I did not speak out

because I was not a trade unionist

Then they came for me

and there was no one left to speak for me[457]

Transparent media and journalism

News will cover the events that actually happen and the decisions that are taken. A new neutral media body offering oversight should be set up. All corrupt media

457 Pastor Niemoeller victim of the Nazis in Germany

companies will be shut down, one by one. The new administrative politicians will inform readers about their activities and the political situation. All co-operation between the government and media outlets, other than informative co-operation, will be curbed by new anti-corruption laws.

Education and training

Universities and schools are really the most important institutions for the establishment of real human freedom. Schools should educate students from an appropriate age in political science. In the 17th and 18th centuries, all the heirs to the throne were trained in statesmanship - as young as 7. Why should today's 19-year-old not be able to do it? At the same time, educational institutions need to create an unconditional arena for open critical debate and discussion. At the same time, cultural heritage must be preserved, and ideologically coloured and uniform phenomena must be kept out of education.

> The continuous supremacy of the Church from the Middle Ages until 1860 gave it an unchallenged hold on the people. Its monopoly on all education maintained cultural isolation and the uniform structure of intellectual life.[458]

All education should be critically scrutinised to ensure that it is - neutral. If you want to read about identity politics, Critical Theory and Community Organising, you can do so in individual courses, but all general education should not be infiltrated by this thinking. A neutral group of experts consisting of researchers and professors should be able to teach without the interference of politically coloured actors.

458 Roland Huntford, "Blind Sweden" (The New Totalitarians), 1971

Culture, religion, and education, are conspiracies to standardise worldviews
- Mokokoma Mokhonoana

Transparent politics with politicians as
administrators, never elites

"Goverment is the one thing we all belong
to"[459].

Contrary to what Obama claims in the quote above, it is
the government that should work for, and thus belong
to, the people. To think that only a few are talented
enough that they alone can make decisions about all
human development in all parts of the world is wrong.

Major decisions will be shaped and communicated by
politicians to the voters only, and the new role of
politicians will be that of administrators and secre-
taries of the people - no longer handing over power
over an entire country to a few. Bills are drafted by
neutral political administrators whose job is to serve
the people - and not the other way round, as in the old
feudal system.

One does see the same stones in the
foundations of a despiritualised humanism and
of any type of socialism: endless materialism; (...) concentration on social structures with a seemingly scientific approach.
This is typical of the Enlightenment in the
18th Century and of Marxism.[460]

Politicians who are not on the ground themselves, who
have no personal experience or understanding of the
issues behind a proposal, should not take decisions either. For example, Sweden has always had school

---

459 DNC Video: "The Government Is The Only Thing We All Belong To"
   https://www.youtube.com/watch?v=6gLa9Te8Blw
460 Alexander Solzhenitsyn, "A World Split Apart", 8 June 1978, Harvard
   University

ministers - who have never set foot on school premises as teachers. No wonder they are met by frustrated teachers and preschool staff, as proposal after proposal is pushed through - with no grounding in reality. Civil servants are making large sums of money for themselves without being able to meet the needs of teachers, who need to be able to do a good job. The teaching profession is important, but it is not prioritised over pupils' education. And children and young people, the future generations, are not being prioritised - at a time when technology and amenities are at their most advanced.

The time of the old politicians is over; those who amass capital and rule behind closed doors. The new politician will instead serve the people, who will have greater access to power, not from a sham democracy created by PR consultants, but for real. Government actually has a big and important role. It is when the elite, big business, the military and politicians go beyond this role and get in over their heads that a government becomes harmful to society. Unless the current political system is changed to allow more people-friendly policies to take over, people around the world may start to resist. For example, people around the world may stop voting for a period of five years. A political movement, a 'No-vote November', would contribute to a much-needed political reform - politicians would be forced to listen to people.

> A patriot must always be ready to defend his country against his government[461] - Edward Abbey

461 Fire on the Mountain, Edward Abbey

*Free capitalist market, bans and limits on greed, no
state-owned monopolies*

In some countries outside the West, privatisation and
private ownership do not exist. If everything you do
can be taken away by a totalitarian state, you don't
want to be innovative. In the West, there is the possibility to be creative and to innovate, through small
businesses and associations.[462] If you take away all
popular capitalism and all private small businesses,
Western society goes back to the time when people
didn't own anything and the elite gets even less competition and more capital. Instead, you should invest
in individual entrepreneurship and thus give people
meaningful work, which increases the individual's
choice. People are constantly building, creating and
innovating. They have great potential, even though we
don't talk about it. In innovation lies, among other
things, their power. [463]

> Sing your marvellous song, little bird! Sing
> it louder than the thunder, for a storm is
> coming to Green Valleys![464] - Elaine Santos

Instead, all monopolies need to be curbed. The state
does not fulfil a good function in a role where it
decides too much. Instead, the free market helps to
make people economically independent. Small businesses
exercise autonomy. More small businesses mean that
monopolies and oligarchs disappear and the quality of
products increases.

Because most big business owners are driven by
greed, the impact of a product on consumers is often
not recognised. Any research in this area is short-term
and receives less funding than other research. Instead,

---

462 Restriction of speech, Konstantin Kissin
463 Jeffrey Tucker anarcho-capitalist, https://www.youtube.com/watch?
   v=8OZGhHpWTSg
464 Elaine Santos, The Children of Allura

products are produced and sold in a frenzy, which modern society calls progressivism. This is why information on the negative impact of products is only published after the fact. After a long period of time, big companies have time to escape and no longer have to take responsibility. Instead, consumers pay for the bad products in various ways. If industry had been guided by compassion and love for people, it would have tested its products thoroughly first.[465]

In order for rich big business owners to earn more than they need, production has been shifted to India and China, where factory workers make the products that are then consumed in the West. If there were small businesses instead, each would be directly responsible for quality and factory workers abroad would have a chance to develop a better working environment and get out of the industrialism rich oligarchs keep them in.

Furthermore, private individuals around the world have invented countless good things that are free and good for nature, such as various new ways of purifying water. But these are bought up by oligarchs and instead of using simplifying and good inventions, they impose their own systems on the consumer and make money from them. Or they buy the product and then charge for it - even though it is free. There should be a worldwide council that recognises such philanthropic inventions and protects them with the help of a patent, so that the inventions can benefit humanity. Imagine how different the world would be with inventions that provide access to free water, electricity and food?

Moreover, schools do not teach personal finance, so that many pupils who leave upper secondary school incur debts and end up in a debt trap - where the interest goes to the profits of big business. Several big banks are owned by large corporate groups through shares or

465 Jeffrey Tucker anarcho-capitalist, https://www.youtube.com/watch?v=8OZGhHpWTSg

otherwise, and the same applies in the rest of the world.

Healthy nationalism, less globalism, vigour

There is a need to invest in national, inspiring projects that are inclusive and contribute to genuine wider community. Unless governments and states can take responsibility for such community-building measures, crises such as Covid19, or resistance and revolution will naturally bring people together.

Central government, as the outdated power it is, needs to be broken up so that people have a chance to build their own lives. Central government means that powerful corporate actors, hiding behind politicians and central organisations, control our lives. This kind of totalitarian 'neo-imperialism' or 'neo-feudalism' is actually outdated - imperialism was already criticised when it happened in the open, during the reign of Queen Victoria of England. Now people are even deprived of the opportunity to criticise this system, because imperialism is being pursued - through ingenious PR campaigns - within the hidden corridors of power.

If anyone is going to save humanity, it must be the people themselves. We have to save ourselves, stand up and speak the truth and stand up for our lives. Every human being has a great potential that is currently being abused by the powers that be in a society that is not being managed and handled as it should be, and above all as it could have been.

> We must learn to accept individual responsibility for the worlds problems or be willing to live by the terms of those who do.[466] - William Cooper

---

466 William Cooper, "Behold a Pale Horse", 1990

Liberty, Fraternity and Equality

Were told to remmber the idea and not the man. He can be cought. He can be killed and forgotten. But 400 years later, an idea can still change the world. [467]

Evey (V for Vendetta)

The opposite of globalism, whose goal is a large centralised power apparatus, is nationalism, but not the nationalism that was "displaced" to the "white power" movement. The term nationalism needs to be washed away from the label undeservedly given to it during the "Big Switch" or paradigm shift, which implies that "nationalism" would automatically mean hostility to other nations. This is not true. Instead, one needs to bring out the good qualities of the concept. The term nationalism actually means local, national power and community. All you have to do is go back to the origins of the term, which was coined in the 16th century. In the beginning, the idea of greater national unity contributed to greater equality - *within* a country's ranks and birth; more power to the people, less power to kings and emperors. The original nationalism was about a class struggle, as was the later class struggle. In the 16th century, as now, there was a central government in the form of feudal lords, and through rebellion and national unity, equality between people was increased.

It began with various orders, nobility and warriors who were called blue blooded, and clergy, mediation, workers and peasants who

467 Evey (V for Vendetta)

300

were red blooded and served the upper order. (The red blooded and blue blooded were considered to be different types of people, which could not be mixed.) It was believed that there was a big difference in their bloodtype and it was not possible to be born a peasant and then become a nobility.

The first among nobles - the King, was sovereign, the sovereignty was god-given. Nationalism replaced this religious consciousness, with values of individual freedom and equality, and emerged in England because of the *War of the Roses* (the war between two clans within the Plantagenet family). It began in the 15th century. A conflict arose and lasted over several decades. The nobility, feudal aristocracy of England that ruled the country prior to that, including the royal family of Plantagenet (to which Richard the Lionheart belonged) was physically destroyed. The new dynasty - the Tudors needed an aristocracy which started a nobility from the red blooded people, thus changing the view on class.

The word "people" meant, in that time, plebs, scum and lower class. The word "nation" meant a very tiny elite of representative of cultural and political authorities. The two concepts mixed, and someone from the new nobility tried to rationalise it and concluded that the English people is a nation and thus nationalism was born. The redefinition of the common people and elevation of those who decide the cultural and political values of the community started to take its place. This is how the idea of the nation as a sovereign community of fundamentally equal members was born.

Nationalism is consciousness, a way in which we imagine reality, and how we construct reality, a cultural framework. It replaced religious type of consciousness. The latter had focus out of the world and the former moved it to the world. The world is divided into sovereign communities of equal members that are called nations. It is the basics of democratic values and institutions that started in the 16th century.

The word *nation* was first defined in the first so called renaissance English-Latin dictionary, the dictionary of Thomas Elyot in 1538. The word nation from that time on was the collective noun referring to thinking, feeling and behaviour related to this new concept of the nation. England was the only country for 200 years to experience this at first and then the rest of the Europe followed and also Asia (and now also Oceania).

Nationalism implies dignity of individual identity; if a member of the community is equal to all other members of the community including the most powerful one, it is a very dignified identity and distinguishes this identity from every other form of identity. The English then became highly competitive and as a result very powerful.

Everybody started to imitate England. And nationalism started to spread, to France - they understood that the English success was connected to nationalism. It was the French who invented the term nationalism. They explosively told themselves - we also have to have nationalism. Nationalism also spread to Russia at the same time. Those countries were second nations in the world after England. The English then colonised North America and

302

went there with their consciousness and values. And so the United States of America was also one of the second nations in the world. And this is the only nation that is purely "nationalistic", it didn't have any pre-national existence prior to that (hence "the american dream", the ability to be able to make class journeys).

Because of the English colonialism, nationalism spread to countries such as India, the Indians then became nationalist and felt that it became undignified for them not to be sovereign. While the Muslims ruled over them for a thousand years they did not feel that need, it started only when the Englishmen exposed them to it. With this, the idea of democracy spread around the world. When the French became nationalists they started to spread the message of nationalism: "liberty, equality, fraternity".[468] *

*

James Sharpe, Professor Emeritus of History, called Guy Fawkes -

...the last man to enter Parliament with honest intentions.[469]

468 Extract from a lecture by Liah Greenfeld, Professor of Sociology and Political Science at Boston University.
https://www.bu.edu/anthrop/profile/liah-greenfeld/
469 Sharpe, James (2005), Remember, Remember: A Cultural History of Guy Fawkes Day (illustrated ed.), Harvard University Press, ISBN 0-674-01935-0

Bibliography

Alinsky, Saul, "Rules For Radicals", 1971

Almqvist, Kurt "The importance of capitalism for the development of Swedish society and prosperity" 1850-2016, 2017

Bax, E. Balford, "The Fraud of Feminism", London, 1913

de Beauvoir, Simone, "The Second Sex", 1949

Beck, Glenn, "The Overton Window" 2010

Boëthius, Maria-Pia, "Heder och samvete", p 151, 1991

Berling Åselius, Ebba, "Rösträtt med förhinder. Voting Rights in Swedish Politics 1900-1920", Stockholm University Stockholm, 2005

Bernays, Edward L, "Propaganda", 1928

Butler, Sir William Francis, "Charles George Gordon", 1892

Chomsky, Noam "The common good", 1996

Cooper, William "Behold a Pale Horse",1990

Dahlberg, Hans, "Sweden during the Second World War", p 88, 1983

"Gail Hamilton" [Abigail Dodge] "Woman's Wrongs", 1868

D´Souza, Dinesh, "Death of a Nation. Plantation politics and the making of the Democratic Party", St Martins Press, 2018

D´Souza, Dinesh, "Stealing America", 2015: what my experience with criminal gangs taught me about Obama, Hillary, and the Democratic party"

Freud, Sigmund, "Civilisation and Its Discontents", 1929

Ganser, Daniele "Illegal wars", 2016*

Geduld, H. M. "Bernard Shaw and Adolf Hitler," 1961 pp. 11-20. Published by: Penn State University Press

Gillette,King C, "The Human Drift" 1894

Goldberg, Jonah, "Liberal fascism: the secret history of the American left, from Mussolini to the politics of change", 2009

Haley, Alex "Roots", 1976

Hawthorne, Rachel "Dark of the Moon" novel - August 25, 2009

Hiley, Michael, "Victorian working women", page 43, 1979

Hoff Sommers, Christina, "Who Stole Feminism: Women Who Betrayed Women", Touchstone, 1995

Howe, Frederic C, "The Confessions of a monopolist", 2022

Huntford, Roland, "Blind Sweden", Roland Huntford, 1971, *The New Totalitarians*, 1972

Höglund, Zeth "Hjalmar Branting and his life's work", *d.2, p.130-131*

James, Tom, "The History of Custody Law, Tom James", 2014

Janney, Peter, "Mary's mosaic: the CIA conspiracy to murder John F. Kennedy, Mary Pinchot Meyer, and their vision for world peace", 2016

Jaurés, Jean, "A Socialist History of the French Revolution", Pluto Press, 2022

Jonsson, Bibi, "Brown pens. Nazi motifs in Swedish women's literature", 2012

Lindberg, Hans, "Swedish refugee policy under international pressure 1936-41" p 118

Lidforss, Bengt, "Drafts and Silhouettes", 1922

"Fragment och miniatyrer - uppsatser i skilda ämnen af Bengt lidforss", Stockholm, Albert Bonniers förlag, 1904

Lewis, Bob, "The Feminist Lie", Bob Lewis, 2017

Lundborg, Herman, "Svensk Raskunskap" 1927

Nordin, Svante, "The History of Philosophy. The Adventures of Western Reason from Thales to Postmodernism", 2017

Malmström-Ehrling, Anna-Karin, "Female philosophers from the Middle Ages to the Enlightenment", 2003

McNamara, Robert S, VanDeMark, Brian, "In Retrospect The tragedy and losses of Vietnam", 1996

Mills,Charles Wright Professor of Sociology "The sociological imagination", 1959

Mills,Charles Wright Professor of Sociology, "White Collar: The American Middle Classes", 1951

Myrdal, Gunnar & Alva "Crisis in the population issue", p 260, 1934

Orwell, George "1984", 1948

Scruton, Roger "How to be a concervative", 2014

Sennerteg, Niclas and Berglund, Tobias, "Swedish concentration camps in the shadow of the Third Reich", Natur & Kultur, 2008

Sharpe, James, "Remember Remember, A cultural history of Guy Fawkes", Harvard University Press, Massachusetts, 2005

Smith, Adam "Lectures on Jurisprudence" p208, 1978.

Sowell, Thomas, "Black Rednecks and White Liberals", Encounter Books, 2005, 2006

Sutton, Antony C, British-American writer, researcher, economist, and professor, "Wall Street & The Bolshevik Revolution" 2001

Sutton, Antony C, "Wall Street and the Rise of Hitler" 1976

Sutton, Antony C, "Triology Of Western Technology And Soviet Economic Development 1917 To 1930, 1930 To 1945, 1945 To 1965, 1968"

Sutton, Antony C, "Wall Street and FDR: The true story how Franklin D. Roosevelt colluded with Corporate America" 1975

Sutton, Antony C, "America's Secret Establishment: An Introduction to the Order of Skull & Bones" 1986

Talbot, Davis "Devils Chessboard", 2015

Tocqueville, Alexis de, "Democracy in America", Book 2, 1831

Thurén, Torsten, "Theory of Science for Beginners" Torsten Thurén & Liber AB, 2007

Witt-Brattström, Ebba and Möller Jensen, Elisabeth "Nordisk kvinnolitteraturhistoria", 1993

Wright Mills, Charles, White Collar: The American Middle Classes, 1951

Byrd wrote to Senator Theodore Bilbo of Mississippi in 1944: When affirmative action was White by Ira Katznelson (New York City: W.W. Norton & Company. p. 80/81.

* Dr phil. Daniele Ganser is a Swiss historian who specilises in contemporary history since 1945 and international politics. His research topics are peace reaserch, geo-strategy, covert warfare, resource wars and economic policy. He teaches at the University of St Gallen course on the history and future of energy systems. At Basel University he tought in the post-graduate course on conflict and analysis with a focus on the global fight on pertolium. Daniele Ganser is founder and director of the SWISS institute for peace and energy research (SIPER) in Basel. SIPER reasearches the possibility of a transition to 100% renewable energy supplies and how conflicts might be solved peacefully.

Lectures:

Alexander Solzhenitsyn, "A World Split Apart", 8 June 1978, Harvard University

Dr Daniele Ganser: Can we trust the media?
https://www.youtube.com/watch?v=4bF-3rulJz0&t=931s

Dr Daniele Ganser, Illegal Wars
https://www.youtube.com/watch?v=vOuGpnORiwk

Dr Daniele Ganser: Kennedy assassination in Dallas 1963 (Dresden 25.10.2020)

Annie Jacobsen, Operation Paperclip
https://www.youtube.com/watch?v=DdoIKaCLOIo&pp=ygUjQW5uaWUgSmFjb2JzZW4sIE9wZXJhdGlvbiBQYXBlcmNsaXA%3D

"Ideologies 2019 - The Moderates' ideas". Torbjörn Nilsson, Professor, research on ideology and politics, voting rights. Often with a Nordic perspective. Teaching on ideologies and academic writing - Department of History and Contemporary Studies

Ideologies 15 February 2019 - Left-wing ideas part 1 of 4: The roots of the Left, Engelsberg Mill, Ängelsberg - Svante Nordin, Professor of the History of Ideas and Learning, Lund University

Ideologies 2019 - Ideas of the Left, Part 3 of 4: A New Left? - Anna Hallberg Phd Södertörn University

Ideologies 2019 - Ideas of the Left part 4 of 4: A new left? - Björn Östbring

"Historical Axess 2019 – Democracy 100 years" (2019). Leif Lewin, professor emeritus (professor skytteanus) at Uppsala University 1972-2008 & Torbjörn Nilsson, Professor, research on ideology and politics, voting rights. Often with a Nordic perspective. Teaching on ideologies and academic writing - Department of History and Contemporary Studies

Anna Hallberg Phd Södertörn University, Axess TV
https://www.axess.se/tv/en-ny-bok/vansterns-ideer-med-anna-victoria-hallberg/

Shelby Steele - White Guilt and the Identity of Innocence
https://www.youtube.com/watch?v=JLkJpCj42iQ

Rupert Sheldrake Ted talk The Science Delusion
https://www.youtube.com/watch?v=1TerTgDEgUE&t=79s

The Best Enemies Money Can Buy: An Interview with Prof Antony C. Sutton
https://www.youtube.com/watch?v=zTDvLmEBESY

Wall Street and the Bolshevik Revolution - Antony Sutton
https://www.youtube.com/watch?v=kEVOIO4TbZs

Did Wall Street fund FDR, Hitler and the Bolsheviks? Looking at Prof Antony C Sutton's theory https://www.youtube.com/watch?v=SnbFpR1m0zA&t=1602s

Antony C. Sutton - The Bolshevik Revolution Speech (1976)
https://www.youtube.com/watch?v=yKvfdvOB5Sk&t=1502s

KASB Webinar on Investing in emerging markets - lessons from Russia with Hasan Malik

"Bankers & Bolsheviks": an interview with Hassan Malik

Discussion by Roger Moorhouse and Norman Davies on the 75th anniversary of the Soviet attack on Poland, accompanying "The Devils' Alliance" book launch.

17 Sep 2014 at the Embassy of the Republic of Poland in London. 17 Sep 2014 at the Embassy of the Republic of Poland in London.

Roger Moorhouse - Hitler and Stalin: the Forgotten Relationship Between the Two Superpowers of WWII, 2 January 2020. Muzeum II Wojny Światowej w Gdańsku (Museum of the Second World War in Gdansk)

Interview with Yuri Bezmenov, https://www.youtube.com/watch?v=9apDnRRSOCk

David Talbot Who killed JFK, https://www.youtube.com/watch?v=KEEsddcHBmE

The Absurdity of Socialism, Jordan B Petersen and Dave Rubin
https://www.youtube.com/watch?v=QpjCca9Beww

How the left took over everything, James Lindsay
https://www.youtube.com/watch?v=g_NTXZymro8&t=1070s

Why I Left the Left - Amala Ekpunobi at Washington University in St. Louis, 10 Dec. 2022
https://www.youtube.com/watch?v=WA4RDoTjwLk&t=3249s

More Deadly Than War - Lecture by G. Edward Griffin 1969
https://stateofthenation.co/?p=33996

Konstantin Kisin: WOKE Culture HAS Gone Too Far - 7/8 | Oxford Union
https://www.youtube.com/watch?v=zJdqJu-6ZPo

James Lindsay | WOKE Culture HAS NOT Gone Too Far - 6/8 | Oxford Union
https://www.youtube.com/watch?v=3Zut8akB4h8

Origins and History of Woke | HISPBC Ch.1, Victor Davies Hanson
https://www.youtube.com/watch?v=FX5Jv2Yldmw

"I'd Organize Hell" - Saul Alinsky TV interview 1966
https://www.youtube.com/watch?v=OfAyNrEsgic

Critical Race Theory, Queer Theory & Maoist Education, James Lindsay, New Discourses
https://www.youtube.com/watch?v=EHWDmg4rfhM

The Ideological Roots of WOKEness, with Helen Pluckrose and Helen Joyce
https://www.youtube.com/watch?v=nTcKHegvMCQ

Melanie Philips (British journalist, broadcaster and author) - Leaving The Left https://www.youtube.com/watch?v=ZkK7lgcLcSo

Roger Scruton, How to be a conservative
https://www.youtube.com/watch?v=1eD9RDT16tM

Jeffrey Tucker anarcho-capitalist
https://www.youtube.com/watch?v=8OZGhHpWTSg

Yeonmi Park, What I Learned about Freedom After Escaping North Korea,
https://www.youtube.com/watch?v=fZGYbTgRpr8&t=873s

Research etc:

Feminist Media Studies. Publication details, including instructions for authors and subscription information: "It's up to the women" by Jane Marcellus

"Eugenics and the Nazis -- the California Connection" - A Study of the United States Influence on German Eugenics, Cameron Williams, East Tennessee State University, Edwin Black

Newspapers in Sweden during World War II from "On Resistance and Collaboration - Sweden in the 1930s and 1940s" - Part of the Past to Present project (www.pasttopresent.org)

A History of the Institute of Racial Biology (Gunnar Broberg Ugglan 4, Second edition, Lund Studies in the History of Science and Ideas) "Reform eugenics and medical genetics: activities after 1937

The transit of German soldiers through Sweden from "On Resistance and Collaboration - Sweden in the 1930s and 1940s" - Part of the Past to Present project (www.pasttopresent.org)

ENGL 308 A: Marxism and Literary Theory, Alys Eve Weinbaum
https://english.washington.edu/courses/2021/winter/engl/308/a

"MARX, KARL" - Michael Rosen
https://scholar.harvard.edu/files/michaelrosen/files/karl_marx.pdf

Bernays and Goebbels: "The strange case of Dr Jekyll and Mr Hyde, Kerrie Milburn 2023

"Bernard Shaw and Adolf Hitler," H. M. Geduld, The Shaw Review, Vol. 4, No. 1 (January, 1961), pp. 11-20. Published by: Penn State University Press

Smith, Adam. Lectures on Jurisprudence. Pg.208 Ed. R.R. Meek, D.D. Raphael, and P.G. Stein. Oxford: Oxford University Press, 1978.

Unleashing the Power of Knowledge: Transforming Lives and Shaping the Future, Richard Mark Wood https://www.interesjournals.org/articles/unleashing-the-power-of-knowledge-transforming-lives-and-shaping-the-future.pdf

Dominic Barter, researcher and author, Restorative Circles, European forum for Restorative Justice

Articles:

Smithsonian Magazine: June 24, 2024, Why the 1924 Democratic National Convention Was the Longest and Most Chaotic of Its Kind in U.S. History https://www.smithsonianmag.com/history/why-the-1924-democratic-national-convention-was-the-longest-and-most-chaotic-of-its-kind-in-us-history-180984590/

The History of Slavery You Probably Weren't Taught in School, Thomas Sowell https://billmuehlenberg.com/2024/06/05/sowell-on-slavery/

Gramci, Antonio ,"Audacia d Fide' in Avanti! Reprint In Sotto la Mole, 1916-1920, p. 148.

Labour (1904: 14/4) The Galician danger, p. 2 https://lup.lub.lu.se/luur/download?func=downloadFile&recordOId=1528967&fileOId=1528968

"The War Years and the Birth of the People's Home" - Aftonbladet's editor-in-chief Rolf Alsing describes the Swedish 1940s - which began in the shadow of war and ended in the joy of peace and the emergence of welfare Sweden - Material reproduced with special permission from Aftonbladet and the author

Friedrich Engels, "The Magyar Struggle," first published in Neue Rheinische Zeitung No. 194, January 13, 1849

Friedrich Engels, The Hungarian Question (Neue Rheinische Zeitung) 1848/49

Karl Marx, "The Victory of the Counter-Revolution in Vienna," Neue Rheinische Zeitung No. 136, November 1848

Chinese Society under Mao: Classifications, Social Hierarchies and Distribution. Published online by Cambridge University Press: 21 March

2019 "Class Status" (A Social History of Maoist China, Conflict and Change, 1949-1976) by Felix Wemheuer (https://www.cambridge.org/core/books/social-history-of-maoist-china/chinese-society-under-mao-classifications-social-hierarchies-and-distribution/4836D7D43D69906AC7A618C671186B82)

Ben Carson Said Saul Alinsky Was Hillary Clinton's Hero. Who Was He? By Mahita GajananJuly 20, 2016 4:18 PM EDT https://time.com/4415300/ben-carson-saul-alinsky-hillary-clinton/

How the Clintons robbed and destroyed Haiti By Takudzwa Hillary Chiwanza, African Exponent, Feb. 18, 2020 https://canada-haiti.ca/content/how-clintons-robbed-and-destroyed-haiti - Canada-Haiti information Project

Dr Martin Luther King Jr. And The Civil Rights Of The Unborn https://www.alvedaking.com/mlk-civil-right-of-the-unborn

Slavery, Adam Smith's Economic Vision and the Invisible Hand https://www.adamsmithworks.org/documents/adam-smith-on-slavery

Wikileaks: Moroccan King Donated $12 Million to Hillary Clinton - Fredrick Ngugi, October 21, 2016 https://face2faceafrica.com/article/wikileaks-moroccan-king-donated-12-million-to-hillary-clinton

Bernard Shaw, The Listener 7 Feb 1934

Swedish concentration camps in the shadow of the Third Reich / denial / invisibility is hereby brought to an end! https://sussstensson.wordpress.com/2008/09/01/svenska-koncentrationslager-i-tredje-rikets-skugga-fornekandet-osynliggorandet-far-harmed-ett-slut/

Borås Tidning, https://www.bt.se/boras/bt-journalist-avslojar-svenska-koncentrationslager-i-ny-bok/Niclas Sennerteg

Tiden / Third year. 1911 no 345 (1908-1940) https://runeberg.org/tiden/1911/0351.html

Documentary:

Alain de Botton Philosophy: A Guide To Happiness - Epicurus on Happiness, Channel Four, 2000

Swedish Events - BT Kemi (2012)

Death of a Nation. Dinesh D´Souza, 2018

Hillary's America, Dinesh D'Souza, 2016

"The Soviet Story", 2008

Secret story: The Gulag Archipelago, 2008

Uncle Tom: An Oral History of the American Black Conservative, 2020

Uncle Tom II: An American Odyssey,2022

Their Secret World War: Stephen Kinzer on The Brothers, John Foster Dulles and
    Allan Dulles. Massachusetts School of Law at Andover

The Century of the Self 2002 British television documentary series by
    filmmaker Adam Curtis

House of GA'A, Netflix, 2024

The Real Adam Smith: Morality and Markets

Swedish Radio:

"Tage Erlander responsible for Swedish concentration camps" Swedish Radio,
    Published Sunday 31 August 2008 at 08.38
    https://sverigesradio.se/artikel/2283366

"Bofors deal in Indian court again" https://sverigesradio.se/artikel/147010

Parliament:

Motion 1922:38 First Chamber No 38 https://www.riksdagen.se/sv/dokument-och-
    lagar/dokument/motion/motioner-i-forsta-hammaren-nr-38_dj2c38/

Minutes 2015/16:96 Thursday 21 April § 1 Notification of subsidiarity tests 42
    Prime Minister STEFAN LÖFVEN (S) https://www.riksdagen.se/sv/dokument-och-
    lagar/dokument/protokoll/protokoll-20151696-torsdagen-den-21-
    april_H30996/html/

https://www.riksdagen.se/sv/dokument-och-lagar/dokument/kommittedirektiv/socialtjanstens-stod-till-valdsutsatta-kvinnor_gtb132/

PragerU clip:

Larry Elder Prager U, Black Fathers Matter, 2017
https://www.prageru.com/video/black-fathers-matter

The Inconvenient Truth about the Democratic Party, Carol Swain, May 22, 2017
https://www.prageru.com/video/the-inconvenient-truth-about-the-democratic-party

YouTube clip:

40,000 Ku Klux (1925) - British Pathé
https://www.youtube.com/watch?v=BnI8SUQPB4k

James Lindsay sounds the alarm on the 'national danger' of Marxism in schools | Liz Collin Reports, Alpha News

James Lindsay sounds the alarm on the 'national danger' of Marxism in schools | Liz Collin Reports, Alpha News https://www.youtube.com/watch?v=1AFRtSWOHPghttps://www.youtube.com/watch?v=1AFRtSWOHPg

Queer Theory is Gender Marxism, James Lindsay - New Discourses
https://www.youtube.com/watch?v=JNW79czfibw&t=122s

Nellie Bowles, Ex-NYT Reporter: The world went crazy!
https://www.youtube.com/watch?v=wKHSE9eISRg&t=884s

DNC Video: "The Government Is The Only Thing We All Belong To"
https://www.youtube.com/watch?v=6gLa9Te8B1w

CBN news Canadian Father Jailed for Speaking Out Against Biological Daughter's Gender Transition
https://www.youtube.com/watch?v=DN_WpaAgS6w

Detransitioning: She Regrets Transitioning From Female to Male https://www.youtube.com/watch?v=uOYKIpkueqM

'My Childhood Was RUINED:' Detransitioner Chloe Cole Talks About Trans
    Procedures
https://www.youtube.com/watch?v=DSGgR3W_jjg

"We Are Trained Marxists" - Patrisse Cullors, Co-Founder, Jared Ball of The
    Real News Network
https://www.youtube.com/watch?v=HgEUbSzOTZ8

Why Marxism is so appealing, Jordan Peterson and Thomas Sowell
https://www.youtube.com/watch?v=4yowxcqdM7E

Sen. Hilary Clinton, 2004 in New York
https://www.youtube.com/watch?v=1sGwGB71KE0

Hillary Clinton Honours Margaret Sanger at the 2009 Planned Parenthood Honors
    Gala
https://www.youtube.com/watch?v=r4o4WizW2mQ

Hillary Clinton: A 13 Minute Montage of Lies
https://www.youtube.com/watch?v=7syNUYAXHwo

Clinton statement on the passing of Senator Robert C. Byrd
https://2009-2017.state.gov/secretary/20092013clinton/rm/2010/06/143705.htm

The events of the summer night: Jan Guillou, Peter Bratt and Håkan Isacson
https://www.youtube.com/watch?v=5YsOshACvAs

Documents from the inside: IB agent Olof Wahlund
https://www.youtube.com/watch?v=gT3uzpLtEik

Film:

Harry Potter and the Order of the Phoenix, 2007

The 2023 sugar experiment

Terminator 2, 1991

House of GA'A, Netflix, 2024

Lord of the Rings 2001